BRAVE TALK

Building Resilient Relationships in the Face of Conflict

MELODY STANFORD MARTIN

Broadleaf Books

BRAVE TALK
Building Resiliant Relationships in the Face of Conflict

Cover illustration: Melody Stanford Martin
Cover design: James Kegley

Print ISBN: 978-1-5064-6244-8
eBook ISBN: 978-1-5064-6245-5

For Amy, my mother.
Though we may always disagree,
you never cease to
sharpen and inspire me.

CONTENTS

ACKNOWLEDGMENTS   VII

INTRODUCTION   XI

PART I: UNDERSTANDING IMPASSE   **2**

1. **THREE SECRETS OF IMPASSE**
   ENGAGING THE ELEPHANT IN THE ROOM   3

2. **UNRAVELING FEAR**
   TRIMMING THE TAPROOT OF CONFLICT   27

3. **CONFLICT AND POWER**
   GOLIATH AND THE HARE   47

PART II: ENGAGING IMPASSE   **76**

4. **WHY WE NEED DISAGREEMENT**
   LEAPING FROM THE TRAPEZE   77

5. **A GUIDE TO GREAT QUESTIONS**
   COMMON CURES FOR LOUD-THOUGHT SYNDROME   107

6. **DEALING WITH FEELINGS**
   TOO MANY *%$@! BLUE CARS   121

PART III: TRANSFORMING IMPASSE   152

7. **ASSUMPTIONS AND THE AWESOME IF**
    SINGING TO WORMS   153

8. **BUILD A BETTER HOUSE**
    RHETORIC AND ARGUMENTATION FOR THE REST OF US   175

9. **CREATING RESILIENT RELATIONSHIPS**
    HOW DO WE LIVE THE DREAM?   211

EPILOGUE: EPIC IMPASSE PEP TALK   242

APPENDICES: TOOLS FOR THE REAL WORLD   244

Appendix A: **Brave Talk Base Camp**
A Group Exercise for Practicing Courageous Dialogue   246

Appendix B: **Top Ten Conversation Hazards**   247

Appendix C: **Difficult Conversations
on Social Media**   250

Appendix D: **All Aboard the Talking Train**
Deciding What to Share, When   252

Appendix E: **Glossary of Awesome Words**   255

RECOMMENDED READING   265

BIBLIOGRAPHY   265

ENDNOTES   270

Acknowledgments

I am filled with gratitude for so many people who have been instrumental in the journey of this book.

I owe a huge debt of gratitude to Tom Porter, Founder of the Religion and Conflict Transformation program at Boston University. This is the space where I first was able to explore academic and personal conflict transformation with transparency and rigor. Thank you, thank you, thank you, Tom, for your incredible work. This book would not exist without you.

Profound thanks to my publisher, Broadleaf Books, especially my editor, Lisa Kloskin, and former editor, Silas Morgan, for seeing enough potential in this book to give it a whirl. I am tremendously grateful for the faith you have shown and the doors you have opened. Thank you to everyone at Broadleaf who made this book what it is.

Thank you to my parents, Revs. Joe and Amy Hunt; my sisters, Marissa, Maddy, and Megan; and my brothers-in-law Fr. Scott and Evan. You have shown great patience, vulnerability, and grace in our long family struggle with religious and political impasse. Though it's been rocky at times, I am deeply grateful that you continue to put love first. Thank you for your leadership and courage in our times of conflict. I am inspired by you all. A special note to thanks to my mother, Amy, for her insight and perspective in helping to develop this work. Mom, for all our conversations, your encouragement, your countless hours of editing, and for all the time you've made to artfully disagree with me: I am in awe of your mind and heart.

Thank you to Patricia Heinicke, astute managing editor, friend, and co-founding editor of IndigiPress. Your amazing work and wisest feedback helped get this book into pitch-ready shape.

Many authors and thinkers have inspired and challenged my imagination as I was writing this book. Notable among them are John Paul Lederach for tremendous pioneering work in conflict transformation; the framework Donna Hicks so elegantly outlines in *Dignity*; Rupert Ross's on-the-ground demonstration of restorative justice in *Return to the Teachings*; the work of Emily Townes on intersectionality and her work on "fantastic hegemonic imagination" in *Womanist Ethics and the Cultural Production of Evil*; the pioneering work of Paulo Freire's *Pedagogy of the Oppressed*; the theme of seeing in Amanda Palmer's *The Art of Asking*; the work of allegory in Hannah Hurnard's *Hinds' Feet on High Places*, which made such an impression on me as a child; Nietzsche's *Thus Spoke Zarathustra*, which expanded my capacity as an adult; and the essays of Anne Lamott and Donald Miller. In addition, countless storytellers and poets have taught me the power of narrative in teaching ethics and social wholeness.

I have been blessed with phenomenal educators and role models who taught me to love literature, writing, and critical thought: Jennifer Musselwhite, Jonathan Trumbull, Jeff Montiero, Dr. Scott Sullender, Dr. Buyoung Lee, Dr. Pamela Lightsey, Dr. Kwok Pui Lan, Dr. Elisabeth Schüssler Fiorenza, Dr. Nimi Wariboko, Dr. Michelle Sanchez, Dr. Steven Sandage, and Dr. Mary E. Hunt. All of these thinkers and many more have inspired me to teach as I have so carefully and patiently been taught. Special thanks to Dr. Pamela Lightsey for modeling transformative intersectional pedagogy. And finally, I want to thank Elisabeth Parsons, instructor at BUSTH, who first encouraged me to look outside of academic writing and bring my ideas to a general audience. I was annoyed at the time, but today I stand humbled and grateful that you saw this potential in me.

I thank Dr. Debbie Blades, my friend and mentor, who saw early potential in me as a thinker and theologian. She who tells it like it is, who laughs from her gut, and who taught me the strength of my woman power, I dance with you.

Thank you to Rev. Bentley Stewart, conversation partner, spiritual space maker, and dear friend: you have been with me through the ugliest and happiest of times. I salute the many ways you have taught me about chaplaining discomfort. Thank you for being one of the first people I could lean on for shaping the framework of this book.

Thank you to Rev. Allen O'Brien, Jeff Manildi, and all the folks at Irenicast, for helping me find my public voice in over a hundred podcast episodes working as my sassy alter ego, Mona. Thank you for your tireless diligence and questing minds.

Thanks to my legendary writers group. Joe "Wolfpack" Downey, Johnny "Burrfly" Gall, and Corey "Surrogate" Martin, thank you for your help in workshopping and strengthening this book.

Thank you to the wonderful Steve Dry, my dearest friend Christy Wright, and the Harvard-Epworth Entrepreneurs' League. I am grateful for all the discussions of this work over so many lovely meals. You were keen sounding boards in helping me file down the sharp edges of my ideas.

Finally, thank you to my brilliant Corey—love of my life, partner in goofydom—who puts up with the brunt of my clumsiness and challenges me in every way. He who instead of laughing when I said I wanted to write a book, replied without hesitation or guile, "Go, baby, go!" You renew my faith in love every day.

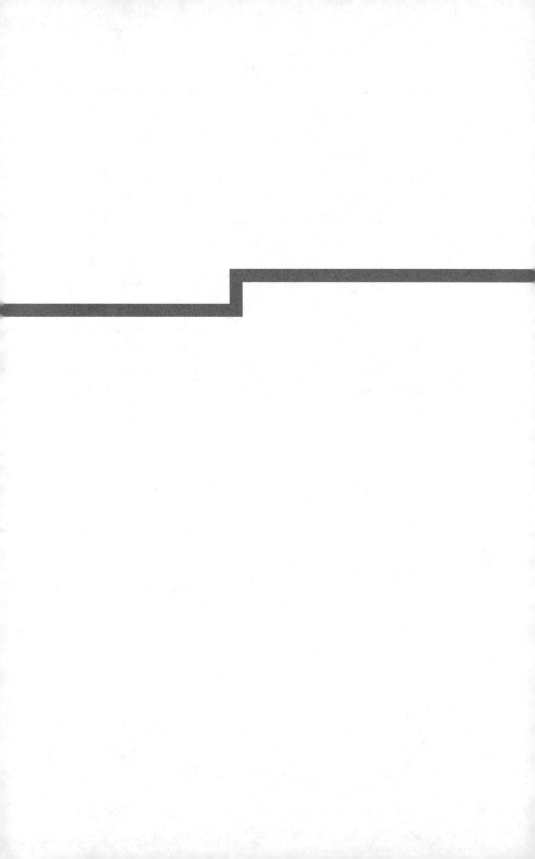

Introduction

I was sitting around a campfire in the backwoods of Maine with my siblings and our respective partners. We were tired, it was late, we hadn't seen each other for a year, and for some god-awful reason, we started talking about religion and politics.

The conversation became explosive so fast, it was as if we had been plopped into a *Die Hard* movie. We were open and honest with each other in ways that only family can be: step one, obtain fire poker; step two, heat with lava; step three, aim for the heart. The repercussions lasted months.

How could we have prevented this? *Should* we have prevented this? Did anything valuable happen in the rugged truth-telling of that night? Would we be able to bounce back in the wake? Would we ever be able to engage hard topics again?

Many of us struggle with these kinds of tensions in our close relationships. Conversations like this are the inspiration for *Brave Talk*. This book takes a real look at the impact of interpersonal conflict in our lives and teaches better ways we can deal with it.

Conflict is central to our human experience—central to our myths, histories, and even the testing grounds of our entertainment. It saturates our familial and national landscapes, seeping into our neighborhoods, and even creeping into our silent personal visions of the future.

Humans are basically guaranteed to experience conflict. We may even encounter conflict that seems to have no beginning and no end.

Despite conflict's ubiquity, many of us have never been trained in dealing with it. We stumble along in the dark, trying to find our way, often bashing into each other.

Plenty of resources on the market aim to teach peacebuilding and conflict resolution, and these resources help a lot of communities. But they can be highly theoretical, academic, or written for highly trained practitioners. Some of these books even suggest that if we work hard enough, we can overcome conflict entirely.

For many of us, such a hope feels hollow.

The hardest conflict is the kind that won't go away. It's the kind that *can't* be resolved.

What happens when we humans meet each other in a state of impasse— when neither party is willing to budge on strongly held opinions and beliefs, yet we possess a deeper, primal desire to live in community?

We struggle. We struggle painfully.

My History with Impasse

Impasse has been a significant part of my life. For the last decade, I have experienced conflict—religious, political, ideological, relational—seemingly inescapable conflict.

I grew up in a sleepy farming town on the central coast of California. Most people think of California as Rodeo Drive, surfing, and red convertibles gliding blithely up Highway 1. My experience was more like broccoli fields, strip malls, rodeo queens, and hanging out at church. Mostly it was hanging out at church, because Dad was a Pentecostal minister.

Up through my early adulthood, I found my faith tremendously life-giving. As I got older, this began to change, despite my best efforts to hang on. I began to take a very different path than the one I'd inherited. I chose to pursue left-leaning graduate education and began exploring more progressive identities and ethics. During this personal evolution, I was faced with a difficult choice: tell the truth, which would cause pain to close friends and family, or not tell the truth in order to keep the peace.

I chose to be honest about the ways I was beginning to see the world. This honesty was heartbreaking and scary for people I love. While I maintain a deep respect for my roots and treasure many aspects of the way I was brought up, my journey has taken an immense toll on some of my closest and most important relationships. After ten years, my family still grapples with the aftershock of a beloved child "leaving the fold." And I grapple with the paradox of loving while disagreeing.

*　*　*

I was married at twenty-three, but four years later, my spouse and I came to terms with the fact that we were not compatible. With a pain-filled sense of responsibility, we concluded that the right thing to do was to end our marriage, especially before bringing children into the world.

As much as my choice to divorce before the age of thirty was a deep personal tragedy, it created ripple effects of grief through my community. Though they acknowledged that the death of the marriage was the only choice that made sense to me, many friends and family members were shocked and baffled. Many thought I was in the wrong. People I held dear told me they would not recognize my divorce and would still consider me married.

Impasse. Heartbreaking impasse. Difficult, *frustrating* impasse.

*　*　*

In 2012, I decided to pursue the big questions of life, and seminary seemed to be a good place to go searching. I found my way to Boston University, into a branch of studies called conflict transformation.

Even in conflict classes, I felt like a rebel. Once, I asked a professor why all the case studies we were reading seemed to have tidy ways of resolving the conflict. They had "answers" that a person could find if they looked hard enough. This wasn't my experience with conflict. "What happens when there *is* no answer, because neither side is willing to change or compromise? What then?" I asked. He chuckled and thanked me for being in the class.

Another time, a sweet elderly bishop came to lecture on the subject of forgiveness. I raised my hand and asked if we could "talk about rage instead." I didn't mean to make a joke, but as you can imagine, this garnered a few laughs from the rest of the class. The bishop graciously answered, "Yes, there is a time to talk about rage. But let me get through my material." Some of my colleagues piped up and said, "With all due respect, Bishop, we would love to talk about rage too. We've all heard a million sermons on forgiveness. What do we do with our anger in times of conflict and powerlessness?"

So you see, even highly trained people struggle with these issues. I have yet to meet someone who has impasse completely figured out.

My studies, though important for my development as a thinker, have only helped me navigate the complexities of impasse in an indirect way. I never found a magic formula. I only found increasingly difficult questions and painful conversations with loved ones. Looking back on all these years, I wish I'd had some better tools at my disposal.

I began writing *Brave Talk* in order to create such a tool kit: a set of skills that can help everyday people engage conflict and impasse more effectively and build stronger ties with others across hard differences.

If, at the very least, this book helps readers improve their relationship with conflict—if it awakens imaginations to seek new and creative ways to transform conflicted situations, if it restores even an ounce of hope for mending fractured relationships—then I will consider it a success.

* * *

Those of us living now, in the early twenty-first century in the United States, are experiencing a constant, toxic gridlock. The labeling, the sound-bite takedowns, and the demonizing on all sides of the aisle are tragic to my patriotic heart.

If right now our society were illustrated like a comic book, perhaps we could see the cracks that have formed in our relationships—the cracks that run through our democracy, gouging their way through families, splitting through even our concepts of human dignity. We'd see a world broken, with whole people swallowed. Such images would exist in that strange emotional space where cartoons drop their neon glow of comedy and start feeling too familiar.

In a stratified world, where global populations are increasingly polarized and segmented, we need people who can build bridges across those invisible cracks. Though my personal journey with impasse has not been easy, something significant has happened. Because of my background, I've become something of an ideological polyglot—someone who is able to speak multiple religious and political "languages." While it is true that my voice today comes from a more leftist political and religious standpoint, and my convictions are indeed fierce, I am a liberal who remembers what it was like to be a conservative. My desire to be a well-meaning and loving person in the world has never changed, despite my shift in views. Because of this, I believe it's vitally important to empathize with the "other"—in my case, the other I used to be.

But as many of us know firsthand, empathy can be a challenge. It can even be a social liability, a riptide of folly in a shaming and shut-down culture. More than once, I've feared that if I publicly express too much empathy for the other, I will be pelted with rotten vegetation.

How did we become so stratified, so entrenched in animosity? It strikes me that screaming past each other is counterproductive; it is far from our collective best interest. In our zeal to be right, and in exercising our right to scream, many of us destroy relationships, relinquish credibility, and become completely ineffective to the people we most want to influence. Yes, we live in a noisy world, and it takes a lot to be heard, but this is nonsense.

Who is to blame for the state we find ourselves in? The credit for this turmoil can't possibly be the sole victory of a handful of government pundits or news-hawking media giants. No, this broken landscape can only come about by many, many people *choosing* to participate in broken ways of relating.

How do we turn it around?

The answer is not a magic formula. The answer is changing our relationship with conflict itself. It means learning skills of *healthy* disagreement. It means that we can hold fast to our convictions while allowing others to sharpen us and our ideas. And it means engaging impasse in ways that help us truly *see* each other and let ourselves be seen.

This is how we reclaim our society: we build resilient relationships that can handle the weight of conflict.

* * *

I have bad news for anyone reading this book: conflict will probably always be with us. Impasse, or unresolvable conflict, will probably still be impasse. It will remain that uncomfortable place of trying to have a relationship by "agreeing to disagree."

Blech.

Some conflict never goes away, and it's unrealistic to expect that it will. Humans have different needs. Beliefs are at odds. Values misalign. We hold different visions of how the world should operate.

But here's the good news: we can learn not only to deal with conflict and impasse better, but also to see its value and appreciate its vital role in our lives.

I can speak from personal experience. My family has taken a long time to be able to have conversations about "real" things that don't escalate into tear-filled festivals of agony. Yes, we still have our arguments, and it's likely we will never agree on really important issues—issues close to the heart of who we are. We are definitely still a work in progress. However, over time, we have gotten better at dealing with being at odds. We have gotten healthier in the ways we interact, healthier in our boundaries. We have learned to let ourselves be uncomfortable, for the sake of each other. We have learned to bounce back and show love, despite the existence of hard truths. Each time we come together, we get a little stronger in our skills; we can talk about tough things a little longer than the last time without wanting to run away.

It didn't happen overnight; it still takes work and patience and practice, and we still have work to do. But now that we have developed stronger skills, talking about hard things is almost productive. It brings us closer. It makes us deeper and more loving people.

The point is, it is *possible* to get better at conflict.

Though it's hard, working through these things is worth every ounce of effort. Why? Because we are not the type of family that is content to be just talking about the weather. While disagreeing on important things feels unacceptable, being distant from each other is more unacceptable. That primal drive to be in community, that desire to share utter and unconditional love, is irreplaceable.

I wouldn't trade it for even the quietest corners of conformity.

About This Book

Brave Talk explores a paradoxical set of questions:

- How do we care for each other while we navigate impasse?

- How do we honor the complexities of difference while keeping a firm grasp on the values we do share?

- How do we transform the animosity of impasse into resilient relationships that are the bedrock of community?

This is first and foremost a book of stories. Our brains don't hold lists of values or rules very well. We are most at home in stories. Stories are what connect our brains to our hearts. Stories get under our skin and expand our capacity to imagine and act.

I created *Brave Talk* around the belief that true wisdom leans into curiosity, humility, and a small amount of foolishness. This book is a hybrid of sorts: It draws from rigorous contemporary scholarship in critical theory, rhetoric, ethics, and restorative justice while being unapologetically quirky and embracing the fullness of humanity.

My goal in writing this book was to create a resource that truly is for everyone, not just academics or community organizers. Why? Because everyone deserves the chance to build healthy skills of conflict transformation. Many people don't have access to this kind of training. Since we all deal with conflict and impasse, we all deserve chances to get good at dealing with it.

Using This Book

Brave Talk can be read by individuals, but it shines best in community. The book is designed to be used in a book club or a workshop format, so groups can learn together. In addition to *Brave Talk*, which is full of ideas and concepts to fuel group conversation, I've created an interactive tool called Brave Talk Base Camp. Base Camp is a unique, repeatable exercise that helps groups practice difficult conversations in a structured, co-creative environment (see appendix A for a sneak peek).

Consider gathering a diverse group of people together and meeting weekly. Each week, the group can read a chapter of the book to learn skills and ideas and then stage a Base Camp to practice what they learn. You can find out more at bravetalkproject.com.

> **NOTE:** If at any time conversations around this book become dangerous or abusive, put down the book and seek professional help from a helping professional, such as a psychologist, mediator, crisis counselor, chaplain, or clergyperson.

What This World Needs

I hope *Brave Talk* sparks a movement of bridge builders: imaginative, full-throttle, fluid thinkers and speakers who bring the expansiveness of their energy and creativity into the challenging and difficult places of impasse.

I welcome the vision questers and the second-guessers, the cynics and the jokers, the logical thinkers, the wishful thinkers, and even those who take themselves way too seriously.

Your light is desperately needed in a fractured world.

Part I

UNDERSTANDING IMPASSE

- Engaging the secrets of impasse
- Exploring how fear works at the center of conflict and impasse
- Addressing the ways power shapes impasse

CHAPTER 1

Three Secrets of Impasse

Engaging the Elephant in the Room

It's a sunny afternoon in May. The whole family is gathered around a table under a shady tree to celebrate Timmy's birthday. Mom appears with a candlelit cake, Grandma is crying and holding her camera, and children squirm in their chairs, jealously gazing at the birthday kid. Excitement ripples through the crowd, waiting for Mom's signal.

"Happy birthday to you / Happy birthday to you / Happy birthday, little Timmy / Happy birthday to—"

But no one sings the last note. They leave it hanging.

* * *

As you read that story, did you subconsciously fill in the last note with "you?" Maybe you even sang it out loud?

Most people will experience a strong sense of annoyance if they hear the song without that last note. There's actually an explanation for this. In music theory, the "tonic" is the base note that pulls all the other notes toward it. Ending the song on the tonic gives a sense of completion. The "supertonic" sits just above the tonic, pulling listeners like a magnet back to the tonic. In "Happy Birthday to You," the supertonic is the "to" that comes before the final "you." Without the tonic—the last note, "you"—that supertonic "to" has a heavy sense of gravity but nowhere to land.

For those of us who have listened to popular music our whole lives, we are conditioned to search for and even expect the tonic's resolution. When the resolution should come but doesn't, we can feel lost and even disoriented. In other words, we crave resolution.

It's the same in conflict. When conflict is clean and resolves—when the "good guy" wins and the "bad guy" gets what he deserves—that feels like redemption. It feels as if the world is restored to the way it ought to be. When two people vocalize a problem, fight cleanly, fix the issue or misunderstanding, and hug it out as if they're in a scene from a nineties sitcom, that feels right to us. Something inside of us sighs with relief.

Resolution feels deeply gratifying.

However, a lot of real conflict simply doesn't play out that way. In the real world, there's no team of writers engineering a story line. There's no season finale, when all the loose ends magically come together.

Reality commonly looks like two stags, antlers locked, unable to disentangle and unwilling to back down. Too often, there isn't a clear good guy or bad guy. We find ourselves colliding with warring, overlapping needs and interests.

Just like the stags, we usually don't fight to be cruel. We fight for legitimacy and survival. This can create an extreme and unresolvable form of conflict: impasse.

Impasse Affects Us Deeply

"Please see me. I am trying to see you."

"Neither of us will move. Neither of us can move the other."

"How do we make sense of this? Where do we go from here?"

This is the language of impasse. Impasse is when each party holds an internally consistent understanding of reality and meaning, but those understandings are utterly at odds. It's is an extreme type of conflict that can put us in a perpetual state of upendedness with people we're supposed to be close to. It's the supertonic note with nowhere to land—a state of unresolvable difference.

Impasse often takes us to a weird in-between emotional space where we don't know how to act. Anthropologists and cultural experts have a word for being socially in-between: *liminal*.[1] Liminal space is where suspension and transition happen; it's a space where something old has passed away, but the new thing hasn't come yet. A classic example is a rite of passage ceremony where a young person is no longer to be considered a child but will be recognized as an adult. For a brief moment in that ceremony, there is a liminal space where childhood is suspended to make way for adulthood. That point of transition or border, where the old is no longer but the new is not yet, is the liminal.

Sometimes liminal spaces last a lot longer than a moment. They are meant to be temporary, yet we can get stuck in them. Impasse can cause us to get stuck in the liminal. We can't live in peace as we once had, because we are at odds, but we can't move forward, because we can't resolve things, so we find ourselves in this place that feels ambiguous, structureless, and even difficult to talk about.

When there is nothing anyone can do, when neither side is willing to budge, our inability to resolve things or move forward can short-circuit our brains and inspire strange actions.

Sometimes impasse simply gets ignored as we try to live "normal" lives. Impasse is the elephant in the room that everyone silently agrees to avoid. It's that holiday meal where everyone is loudly *not* talking about the issue; instead, with smiles plastered, they pretend nothing is wrong. Over time, this avoidance causes relational damage. Discussions and connections stay at surface level, and we drift apart without realizing it. We lose our ability to be close to each other.

Other times, impasse goes nuclear. It sparks terrible fights and wounds. We lash out because the unspoken issue is so important to us and we have no idea how to navigate the tension that won't go away. It can end up looking like a battle of the bands with every band angrily blasting its own kind of music at the same time. Harmony, respect, and sense often feel impossible. When this happens, relationships can be damaged beyond repair.

No matter the outcome, impasse generally feels awful. It can seem highly risky to address or unpack. It's tempting to cut the journey short with a terse "let's just agree to disagree."

However, let's explore a significant, important thing that happens when we say the words "we are at an impasse." When we name this reality, we are recognizing that we can't change the situation, and we can't convince anyone else to change it. We are in the liminal space, but we are at least both here together. Naming an impasse means we have decided not to use force to get our way. We are, for the sake of love or justice, trying to accept the unacceptable while knowing that, by definition, "accepting the unacceptable" is impossible.

When we accept our inability to control each other, we open a door to a set of opportunities.

We may never like conflict or be comfortable with it, but we can learn to transform it. We can learn to turn away from antagonism and instead turn toward possibility. Whether the conflict we experience is resolvable or unresolvable, we have a lot of choice in how we engage.

Three Secrets of Impasse

To be in true community with our family and neighbors who see the world differently than we do, and to have meaningful relationships and a healthy society across hard differences, we must learn to meet each other in impasse and harness its power for the better, before it gets the better of us. There are three secrets that can help us do this. These secrets of engaging impasse are not magic formulas, but practicing them can change our relationship with conflict and make it more productive.

1. Approach Every Conflict as if It's an Impasse

This first secret is the central idea of this book: focus on relationships, not on resolution. Yes, you read that right. I'm suggesting that the best approach to conflict is to put off trying to resolve it. Pretend the situation is unresolvable, at least temporarily, until both parties feel they've had enough time to mend the relationship and feel heard. Even if you think there's an answer or there should be an answer, try sitting in the awkward middle space of impasse.

Why?

When we focus on finding a resolution, we often skip the important steps of actually understanding each other. When we make it our priority to really *see* one another, when we focus on trying honestly and openly to "get" where each other is coming from, resolutions will often present themselves almost as if by accident. Deepening our understanding and building relationships over and above trying to resolve issues may seem strange, but it is often more effective than trying to resolve issues directly. It helps us see the bigger picture in new and important ways.

On paper, this might seem easy, but in practice, it is incredibly challenging. We might have to work against our own instincts to make this kind of space for each other.

I grew up near the beach, and sometimes my family would drive out to the water only to encounter a metal sign bearing a riptide warning, letting us know that swimming was not allowed that day. A riptide is a phenomenon that happens when the top of the ocean water seems calm, but below the surface, there is a powerful undertow that carries swimmers away from the shore. Getting caught in one can be a terrifying experience. Usually, when someone is caught in a riptide, instinct kicks in to struggle against the tide and get to land as quickly as possible. The problem is, a riptide is too powerful. Even experienced swimmers will dangerously expend all their energy before they make it to land. To survive, some ocean experts advise, the swimmer should lie back and float; others advise swimming parallel to the shoreline. Either way, the hope is that the tide will circle back and land the swimmer on the beach. It might take a long time, and the swimmer might get washed up far away from their starting point, but working with the tide instead of fighting it can help the swimmer live to tell the tale.

Impasse can feel like getting caught in a riptide; it's larger and more powerful than we are. Like a swimmer who encounters a riptide, when we find ourselves out to sea in a difficult conversation, we will often find that it's ineffective to try to force resolution or fight against it. Doing so will only distract us and wear us out. Once we stop kicking and screaming to control the situation, we can slow down, study our surroundings, and access better information. We can see the bigger picture. Importantly, when we suspend the desire to resolve, we might not end up in the place we originally wanted to be, but we will have a healthier experience.

The frustrating yet *amazing* thing about impasse is that when we recognize that we can't change other people—when we put aside the need for control—we create opportunities to connect on a very human level. Saying the words "I can't change you; you can't change me" might come with a deep sense of sorrow, but it's also an incredible way to recognize the basic rights and dignity of our conversation partner. This doesn't mean we forget we have strong opinions; it means we recognize that we don't know everything and that we are open to learning new information. Taking this posture goes a long way in building trust.

When we approach every conflict as if it's an impasse, instead of rushing to resolve it, we free ourselves. We free ourselves from the tension and resentment that result from people trying to control each other. We free ourselves for incredible curiosity, discovery, empathy, and relationship building. Setting aside the drive to resolve, control, or win creates a space of lower pressure, a space that helps us stop reacting and start reasoning, together. It drives a spirit of collaboration instead of antagonism. It starts to restore and heal the relationship by helping us look at the bigger, longer-term picture. If any resolution can take place later on, the things we learn from these processes will be vitally important.

Bottom line: this process is important, so take your time. It might be counterintuitive, but approaching every conflict as if it's an impasse is the tool that helps us begin to unpack the root causes of the conflict. By holding off on resolving conflict and focusing on the more important task of building relationships, we ultimately make things easier on ourselves.

2. Be Open to Discomfort

Being a little uncomfortable for the sake of building relationships is an incredibly useful skill to develop. When we are willing to embrace a little discomfort for each other, we make space for healthy conflict and disagreement.

Perhaps this idea elicits feelings of revulsion. You might think, "Gross! Why in the world would I choose to be uncomfortable? Why not just hunker down and only talk to people who agree with me?"

Yes, you can certainly hunker down. You are totally free to surround yourself with only your crew. But since you are reading this, my hunch is that deep down you don't believe that's enough. You might recognize that you have things you'd like to teach, but you will only be able to teach those things if you establish strong, trusting, even difficult relationships. By the same token, you might recognize that you don't know everything, and that people from different walks of life can be your teachers. You might recognize that societies are better when they protect freedom of thought, press, and expression. You might recognize that developing our skills of discourse makes us better thinkers and more well-rounded people. You might recognize that, once upon a time, you changed your mind not because someone screamed at you, but because someone took the time to engage your imagination. You might recognize that loving your neighbor may be one of the most powerful and revolutionary ideas in the history of the world.

Or perhaps you are just curious.

The point is, some of the most incredible things happen in conversations when we let ourselves be a little uncomfortable—when we sit in that weird, suspended, structureless liminal space of impasse and see what we can learn from it.

A wise professor at my alma mater Dr. Jerry Root used to say, "If you're not awkward, you're not growing." Discomfort can be a sign that we are doing something right. Discomfort can be a sign of cognitive dissonance, meaning that we gain information that messes with our structure of meaning and creates tension within us. This tension might not feel great, but it is often the sign of an expanding heart and mind.

If we are willing to be a little uncomfortable, we get to practice new and better skills of listening and speaking. We get to learn and stretch. Of course, this doesn't mean we put ourselves in unsafe situations or give up our voice. Boundaries are still important. While no one should advocate emotional danger, consider that conversations can become much more fruitful when we are willing to let ourselves stretch. It might feel awkward, but stretching is good for our ideas and relationships.

3. Learn to See and Be Seen

So many miscommunications arise when people talk past each other. It's all too easy to walk into a tumultuous situation with guns blazing. It's much more difficult to see and be seen. It's much more difficult to sidestep antagonism by trying, first, to understand.

What does it mean to see and be seen?

- *Seeing* someone means making an honest, open, curiosity-driven inquiry into the center of who they are and what makes them tick. Seeing means pausing judgment and trying instead to explore the ideas, values, and beliefs of our conversation partner and how those things connect for them. Seeing means that while we hold tight our own strong convictions or opinions, to the best of our ability we seek to empathize and understand those with whom we disagree.

- *Being seen* is the other side of the coin. It is gently letting someone into our world and what makes us tick. This means passionately, ethically, and effectively articulating our stance while honoring and sharing power with our conversation partner. Being seen is an act of trust; it is letting someone pick up our opinions and test them, hopefully for mutual benefit. As we do the work of seeing someone, we in turn invite them to see us.

Conflict is an unparalleled opportunity for deeper understanding. It allows us to practice remarkable skills of communication and emotional regulation while making our relationships stronger.

Making space for seeing and being seen is what it means to have "courageous dialogue."

To picture courageous dialogue, consider a huge influence on *Brave Talk*: a book called *Dignity*, by Donna Hicks.[2] Dr. Hicks, an international conflict mediation expert, has helped many people, including international leaders, navigate situations of turmoil. By mediating between rivals and even enemies, her highly effective method rests on a single goal— restoring basic human dignity. In *Dignity*, Dr. Hicks writes that many conflicts arise from the violation of dignity itself. By fixing broken relationships and focusing on the ways people treat each other before doing any work to resolve conflict, we can access deeper causes of conflict and therefore strategize more lasting solutions.

When we engage in courageous dialogue, we effectively stand up and proclaim, "I refuse to live my life in a state of fragile relationships, separation, or avoidance. I refuse to reject or demonize people who disagree with me." This is an utterly brave act. It is brave to embrace the paradox that we can stand strong in our convictions while holding an open heart and hand to those with whom we disagree. Showing this kind of leadership can bring us closer to our neighbors; it is the kind of act that keeps society functioning.

Our world doesn't need more sanctimonious debates or more gotcha moments. Our world needs courageous dialogue. Imagine what this place could be if everyone could truly learn to see and be seen.

Real vs. False Impasse

"Impasse" suggests that two parties stand on relatively equal footing, but what happens if there is a power imbalance or coercion? What happens if one party simply has a lot more say-so than the other? Surely, not all impasse is created equal, nor can all gridlocked conflicts be called impasse.

Imagine you are hanging out at home on a lazy Saturday afternoon, drinking your favorite beverage and binge-watching your favorite show, when you hear a knock on your door. It's a lady you've never seen before. She introduces herself as Cheryl. After making small talk, she says, "Okay, here's the deal. You want this house. I want this house. We are at an impasse."

No, Cheryl, that's not an impasse. That is Cheryl trying to take your property.

Now, if you were squatting in that house, and you didn't own or rent it, but Cheryl did, it would be very generous of her to call that situation an "impasse," because she would be well within her legal rights to have you evicted. Context is everything.

Now imagine you own your house, but Cheryl pulls governmental strings and "legally" purchases the land beneath it. She shows up to the land with a piece of paper that is the deed and tells you to leave. When you refuse to leave, she says, "It seems we have an impasse." That is still not impasse. It's hegemony pretending to be impasse. Context and power structures are everything.

Abuse of power cannot claim to be impasse. Using legal systems to undermine rights or oppress others is not impasse. The response to "Your actions are hurting me" should not be "It seems we are at an impasse."

Human rights and basic human freedoms are not up for negotiation. If one person says, "I believe all people should be free and equal," and another says, "I think we should kick all the tall people out of the country," it would be false to claim that those two ideologies are at an impasse. There is no valid argument for denying someone's basic human rights.[3] The central narratives of these people are not on equal footing.

True impasse lies in *valid* oppositional realities. Valid oppositional realities tend to be religious differences, political differences, and differences of beliefs about the nature of morality, governance, ethics, and ways we should live. Saying a view of reality is valid doesn't mean we are saying its true; in fact, we can say something is valid while completely disagreeing with it. Valid means we can see how the view could be reasonable and defensible and doesn't trample anyone's human rights in a free and equal society.

But all of this raises an important question: who gets to judge what are and aren't valid realities? If I am talking to a stranger at the grocery store and they start saying horrible things, how do I decide what to do?

The Potluck of Ideas: Who and What Do We Engage?

Ideally, the world of ideas is like a giant potluck. Everyone brings their dish to the table, and we all share and learn from each other. Hip hip hooray for diversity.

But what happens when someone brings a plate of dog poo to the potluck? In other words, someone brings a set of ideas that are indigestible, harmful, and destructive to the very concept of human dignity. Do we keep that dish on the table? No, obviously we remove it before it hurts someone.

Okay, but what if the dish is actually *not* dog poo, but meatloaf, and we just thought it was dog poo?

Here's the problem. Mislabeling someone's homemade meatloaf as dog poo has horrible repercussions. This often happens in online or anonymous arguments, where one party aggressively mocks, shames, or silences another for sharing their beliefs and ideas.

Sure, there are poo-bearing trolls in the world who will bring poo to the table just to get a rise out of people. There's always a chance one person at the party is actively bending truth to suit their own purposes.

Other times, Billy is bringing his grandma's meatloaf and genuinely wants to be part of the conversation. But Billy is treated as if he brought poo, and he is banished from the table.

What does this do to Billy? What does he now feel toward the people who shamed him? It's highly unlikely Billy will feel comfortable spending time with these folks after having his beloved dish tossed into the garbage. It's highly unlikely the vision of the trash can will make him magically change his belief structure to agree with the people who shamed him. Most likely, in a flurry of anger and embarrassment, he will fall deeper into his meatloaf loyalties.

While some ideas may be truly unacceptable and unfit for the table, and while some people may truly have malicious motives, perhaps "poo at the potluck" is not quite as common as we might think. If we get it wrong, our community table might become a sacrificial altar.

Holding a commitment to freedom of speech and freedom of ideas means we should value keeping our table open, even to people who make us uncomfortable. In fact, those values should encourage us to sit next to people who are eating food we don't care for. Why? Because the guest is more important than the dish.

Yes, it's hard, even painful, to stretch our table to include people like Billy. But it's the only way to have healthy relationships and healthy communities.

Here are five questions you can use to determine whether a dish (idea) is worthy of being left on the table—in other words, how to determine whether an idea is valid and worth engaging:

1. Can this idea be supported (even if we don't agree with its conclusions)?

2. Is this idea relevant (even if we don't want to engage it)?

3. Is this idea well-meaning, and does it resist harm (even if we think it has a shadow side)?

4. Does this idea share power (even if we think it might be unbalanced)?

5. Is the person who brought the idea trustworthy (even if it's hard to relate to them)?

Shaming and shutting down people we don't agree with is a completely ineffective strategy, because it destroys relationships and any future hope of influence. This should not be an option except in extreme cases of self-protection where there is definitive malicious action. If someone is earnestly trying to be in conversation and community with us, even if we really don't like what they bring to the potluck, it's vital to remember that the person is more important than their ideas.

As for the poo bringers of the world, perhaps we might find bounded yet creative ways to engage, hear stories, and find out why they are tending toward

What to Do When Someone Brings a Questionable Idea
TO THE POTLUCK OF IDEAS

CAN IT BE SUPPORTED?

NO If it is wildly false, it is poo.

YES It's food, not poo. Maybe it is made with low-quality ingredients, but it's still valid.

NOT SURE Explore its truth claims.

IS IT RELEVANT?

NO If the idea is intentionally distracting or misleading, it's sure looking like poo.

YES It's food, not poo. Maybe it doesn't fit the party theme, but it's still edible.

NOT SURE Be generous. Not everyone is an expert conversationalist.

IS IT WELL-MEANING / DOES IT RESIST HARM?

NO If it calls for dehumanization or harm, it's poo.

YES It's food, not poo. Maybe it's food you hate, but it deserves a place at the table for the sake of freedom.

NOT SURE Explore its supporting values.

DOES IT SHARE POWER?

NO If it justifies inequality, denies human rights, or props up domination, it's poo.

YES It's food, not poo. Don't eat if it upsets your stomach, but the person who brought it should never be shamed or rejected for participating.

NOT SURE Explore its consequences.

IS THE PERSON WHO BROUGHT IT TRUSTWORTHY?

NO High chances of poo. Proceed with caution.

YES It's food, not poo. The person who brought it wants to be at the table and contribute. Honor that!

NOT SURE Get to know them.

If it's poo, gently remove the dish and set healthy boundries with the guest. If it's food, you don't have to eat it, but leave it on the table and appreciate the guest for showing up.

ideas and actions that isolate themselves from Community. While we might not trust poo bringers with leadership or a public microphone, their experiences and pain are likely to be valid. They are still worthy of kindness, even if that kindness has strong boundaries. We always have the choice to wrap up some of our non-poo food and offer it to them to take home. In other words, we can always choose to show courage, respect, and love, even if they won't (or can't) show it in return because that's the world we want to create.

Cheap Peace

When people talk about things like "expanding our table," sometimes it comes with a tone of "We should all just get along. Don't rock the boat. Just keep the peace."

That word *peace* comes up a lot in conversations around conflict and impasse. Every time I hear it, forgive me, but I cringe a little.

Don't get me wrong, peace is something I long for. I long for it so deeply that I hold all claims with a high degree of skepticism. Too many times, peace is cheap. It can be downright cowardly, a Band-Aid fix, a state we arrive at too quickly because we don't know how to cope with discord and ambiguity.

Peace can also be coded language for death: a state of ultimate and changeless resolution. "Peace" sometimes represents an ominous point of no return.

Let me give some context. When I was in high school, I was the president of a student club. One of my fellow club officers developed strong feelings about the way I was running the group but didn't talk to me about it. Instead, the student sent a letter to our entire two-hundred-person email list, outlining all the ways I was incompetent. The letter actually used the word *incompetent*. As you can imagine, I felt blindsided and totally humiliated.

I approached a couple of adults whom I respected, and I asked for advice on what to do. Both adults told me to let it blow over, to just "take the hit." I followed their advice. The weekly attendance of the club shrank from over one hundred kids to eleven.

To this day, when someone asks me to be in charge of something, my heart skips a beat in panic.

When I think about that memory, the most painful part is not the kid who sent the email. Kids do inconsiderate things, and maybe I wasn't the best leader. What still hurts is how those adults failed to counsel me in a meaningful way. They basically said, "It's totally healthy to pretend everything is fine." I was taught to embrace cheap peace in a way that hurt my confidence and my concept of leadership. I was taught that avoiding conflict was okay. Maybe the adults were trying to teach me that leaders should not let themselves react to criticism, but something about being that passive felt wrong.

Cheap peace often represents missed opportunities to engage some of the best, most complicated questions. In avoiding that conflict in high school (and many others afterward, as avoidance became my working model), I missed an opportunity to grow from understanding why the other student characterized my leadership negatively or why they had larger issues with me. The other student missed the chance to properly register a grievance face-to-face.

Demanding peace too quickly can lead us to gloss over a number of significant emotions, expressions, and questions. Cheap peace robs us of chances to become better thinkers, better neighbors, and better leaders. It ultimately robs us of opportunities to strengthen relationships and leaves us in a state of constant fragility with no real closure.

It's possible I can never be fully at peace with someone with whom I strongly I disagree. The relationship may never be 100 percent comfortable and free of tension. I may never be fully in unity with them; I may never reach a place of full comfort. Therefore, it's not realistic to anticipate or expect peace when it comes to impasse.

This might seem bleak, but let's not lose hope. Once we get beyond idealizing peace and start to practice the secrets of impasse, we can start to transform conflict and make it work on our behalf.

Transforming Impasse: From Antagonism to Collaboration

Whether we recognize it or not, most of us already have a set of unspoken boundaries for how and how not to try to change people's minds.

Let's say Harry is wearing a Denver Broncos shirt. I walk up to Harry, slap him on the back, and say, "Hey there, partner, I intend to convince you that the Broncos blow. Only spineless, worthless jerks like the Broncos. It's just a fact. You should root for the Pats. Period."

Harry is now immediately on the defensive. He probably wants to sucker punch me. My words were not those of friends talking smack; they were a full-blown agenda. I just told Harry that I do not accept his current state of being. My friendship is conditional. How can we have any kind of real conversation after that exchange? How can we truly grow to understand each other's deep love for our teams if Harry knows I am hell-bent on changing him?

Maybe it would be ridiculous to approach a conversation about sports this way, but this is often how we approach differences on larger issues.

To restate it bluntly: when we approach a disagreement or conflict with the primary intent to resolve it or change the other person, we are already careening toward failure.

It might sound strange to say, "We are going to engage impasse, but we are going to try not to resolve it. We are going to suspend the drive to change each other." But in most cases, this is the only way to proceed. Suspending the desire to resolve conflict creatively disarms strong emotions, lets people be where they are, creates space for everyone to share with mutuality and respect, and upends fear of retribution. Surprisingly, *not* resolving conflict but instead trying to see each other is one of the best ways to jump-start a stuck situation and begin to move forward, out of destructive cycles.

What we're ultimately talking about here is conflict transformation. Conflict transformation is the art of turning animosity, hatred, and domination into a spirit of collaboration, creativity, and Community.

This isn't a new idea. Conflict transformation is a growing field of study, and is a relatively new term, but it is not a new idea. It is inspired by people's movements around the world such as:

- The Indian Satyagraha non-violent resistance movement and the work of Mahatma Gandhi

- African American Christian theological traditions, U.S. Civil Rights, and the legacy of Rev. Dr. Martin Luther King Jr.

- South American liberation theology and the work of scholars and activists like Fr. Gustavo Gutierrez

- The South African anti-apartheid movement and the work of Nelson Mandela, as well as the establishment of the Truth and Reconciliation Commission

- Mennonite Christian pacifist tradition, especially the work of Dr. John Paul Lederach at Notre Dame University

- Native peacemaking and indigenous justice systems.

Instead of rushing to resolve or simply try to contain violence, conflict transformation practitioners focus on restoring broken relationships. Conflict transformation is often paired with the idea of restorative justice, which draws from indigenous wisdom traditions around the world that seek to restore someone who has committed an offense to right relationships instead of punishing them.[4]

Though it might seem counterintuitive, mending relationships has incredible power to heal wounds that lie beneath conflict and impasse. In other words, oftentimes conflict is a symptom, not a cause. Causes are often much bigger. A focus on resolving conflict often leads to shortsighted, Band-Aid fixes. Healing relationships is much harder but produces more long-term solutions. Conflict transformation not only seeks to address the root causes of why conflict happens here and now, but also seeks to prevent cycles of destruction and violence in the future.

"But what about all those books I've read on conflict resolution?" you may ask.

It is true that in some situations, seeking resolution is ultimately practical. But let's consider for a moment that the term *conflict resolution* seems to presume that conflict itself is a problem—something bad, something we need to fix or get rid of. This approach often misses the value of conflict and disagreement in our lives. When engaged meaningfully, conflict and disagreement can make our ideas and relationships stronger. Conflict is not inherently a problem; it's a natural part of life. What makes the difference is how we choose to act within conflict.

The table (below) provides a breakdown of the differences between a conflict resolution approach and conflict transformation approach.

TWO APPROACHES TO CONFLICT

CONFLICT RESOLUTION	CONFLICT TRANSFORMATION
Conflict is bad.	Conflict provides important opportunities to learn and grow.
The other side is my opponent or enemy.	The other side is my conversation partner and fellow human.
We should agree and get along.	We should collaborate and create healthier ways of interacting.
The highest priority is finding a solution that can solve the conflict.	The highest priority is understanding each other and building stronger relationships, so we can create trust.
We should end conflict.	We should identify and disarm the destructive underlying cause of conflict and build something better.
Conflict is making me uncomfortable and anxious. End these bad feelings now.	I am uncomfortable and anxious, but I won't let these feelings rule my contributions. In the long term, working through hard feelings will be worth it.
Ambiguity is a sign of failure; one voice deserves to win.	Ambiguity is a sign of paradox; many voices deserve to be heard.
Success means moving on despite long-term consequences.	Success means seeing with new eyes and creating a positive, collaborative plan of action, so we don't repeat the mistakes of the past.

Adapted from *The Little Book of Conflict Transformation* by John Paul Lederach

When we seek to transform conflict in order to keep relationships healthy, it doesn't mean we stifle passionate argumentation, paint ourselves with flowers, or sing "Kumbaya" (no offense if that's your jam). Engaging impasse through a conflict transformation approach is not flimsy work. Conflict transformation is intense, requiring immense strength, intentionality, and patience. In many cases, it means we have to completely relearn how to communicate. Some of us, including myself, have to learn new ways of thinking and relating.

Individual Relationships: The Basis for Community

We've been talking quite a bit about Community, so let's pause to define it and explain why I've capitalized it. This word is capitalized when it's meant to emphasize an ideal. Being in Community (with a capital C) means being in each other's lives, showing up when it matters, and protecting and advocating for each other. It means taking the time to understand and care for each other, so that when we experience conflict and impasse, our relationships remain resilient—strong enough to take the pressure and bounce back. Real Community nurtures strong relationships, including the presence of difference.

In some shape or form, people need other people to experience happiness and purpose. We need to be connected to each other in meaningful and productive ways. Without Community, we fail to thrive.

How do we measure the health of Community? Community is only as strong as its smallest interactions.

Let's flesh this out with an example. Picture a vineyard on a crisp, blue morning. Rows of tethered vines roll up a jade hillside lined by old houses and cypress trees. A breeze rustles through the leaves and kicks up a refreshing smell of wet earth. You walk toward the vines and notice they look a little strange. Instead of finding bursting, dew-covered grapes, you see that half of the fruit is small and withered, and the other half has fallen to the ground.

A vineyard is only as healthy as its vines, and each vine is only as healthy as its grapes. Therefore, the health of the whole vineyard comes down to the grapes. If the grapes go sour or fall off the vine, the whole vineyard suffers.

We can use this metaphor to help us think of Community on three levels: the grape, the vine, and the vineyard:

1. **One-on-one relationships are the grape level of Community.** Our one-to-one relationships are the building blocks of what it means to be in each other's lives. Without the tight bunch of strong interpersonal relationships, our sense of significance can become hollow and insecure. When our grape-level ties are healthy, we know that we matter. We know we are accepted.

2. **Our small groups are the grapevine level of Community.** The small groups in which we participate may include our families, schools, faith centers, businesses, clubs, and local government. When we function together for a common purpose, we are like a healthy network of grapes working alongside each other. In contrast, without strong group ties to the vine, our sense of purpose can become stagnant, and our groundedness begins to fade. When our grapevine-level relationships are healthy, we know that we are rooted. We have a place.

3. **Our big groups form the vineyard level of Community.** The big groups we participate in generally include institutions, systems of exchange, state and national governments, and the world order. If we lack strong systems that help us live alongside each other in the grand scheme of things, our ability to function in the world is compromised, and we become unsafe. When the inner workings of large-scale relationships and systems are healthy, we know we are secure. We know we have stability.

This book specifically focuses on the grape level—the area of interpersonal relationships—because without strong interpersonal ties, larger forms of Community can't be healthy. When interpersonal relationships are fragile—when grapes fall out of the bunch too easily—every level of Community suffers.

As you read this, you might be wondering, "Wait a minute, is it a grape's fault if it falls off the vine? What about the weather, soil, pests, and caretaking of the vineyard?" You're right. Grapes don't get to decide. And just like grapes, people have to deal with a lot of factors beyond our control: our social location (class and economic status, gender, nationality, ethnicity, race, and historical context); our family systems; our past traumas; our education, experiences, motivations, and beliefs; our bodies and the ways we are wired; and even our future stories and dreams. There are many, many factors. But unlike grapes, we humans do have power over how we act. To a significant degree, we can work to be healthy and connected grapes, or we can choose to be sour and alienated. The sum of the small, individual choices within our control make up the health or illness of our world.

SUMMARY: Becoming Seers Is the First Step toward Transformation

Transforming impasse from antagonism to opportunity starts with a true desire to understand.

This is the first and foremost question. How do we truly see each other? How do we learn to understand the complexity, nuance, structures of meaning, and humanity of those we are taught to disregard or even war against?

Taking the time to understand a fellow human being is one of the most fundamental, difficult, amazing honors of being human. Practicing equality and empathy are what make us human. Especially when we extend these gifts across lines of harsh difference, our communities continue to exist. We interact with each other. We cooperate, despite disagreement. We get stronger.

In ancient times, a "seer" was someone with special abilities to predict the future. Likely, seers were people of great wisdom who could peer into the present circumstances of a situation or a person's life and make intelligent guesses about what was to come.

What is a seer today? Mystical interpretations aside, we can understand a seer to be someone who predicts—and even creates—the future through careful understanding, analysis, and strategic action. A seer says, "I see you. I hear you. I want to understand deeply. I want to know the nuances of what you're about. I want to know your intentions and motivations. I want to grapple with you and be utterly challenged by you. I want you to move me. I want to believe the best of you. I want to co-create a future with you."

How wonderful to enter a conversation where you know you will be seen—where you don't have to worry about being yelled at, ignored, or converted. If I knew I was walking into a room where, despite disagreement, someone was going to sit down with me, look into my eyes, and really try to understand me, I would walk into that room differently.

In fact, I would be so moved by that experience, I would want to return the favor.

This brings us back to the central idea of this book. Something powerful happens when we treat every disagreement and every conflict as if it is an impasse—when our approach is to deeply understand, to deeply relate, instead of trying to change someone's mind. When we take the time to first, before anything else, see others, we will learn some vitally important things about their world. Even if we can't find resolution, we will gain chances to truly connect and dispel myths and fear. We will build trust, empathy, and collaboration.

Engaging impasse takes courage: The courage to ask deeply, listen deeply, and share deeply. It is talking with, not talking at. It is learning from each other, sometimes learning hard truths that are difficult to grapple with. It is sharing with mind and heart together, setting aside antagonism, and being uncomfortable for the sake of building resilient relationships and a healthier world.

You can do this. I believe in you.

1. What did you think of the idea that we should treat every disagreement and conflict as if it's an impasse?

2. On a scale of 1 to 10, how strong is your need for resolution? How does this affect your life? Share a time when you experienced impasse or conflict that was difficult to resolve.

3. When it comes to addressing difficult situations, are you more familiar with a conflict resolution approach or a conflict transformation approach?

4. Share or name a situation of false impasse. What were the long-term consequences?

5. Have you ever kicked someone out or been kicked out of the potluck of ideas? What was that like? Do you wish things would have been different?

6. Share or name a situation where you saw cheap peace resisted.

7. What's your experience with the three levels of Community (grape, grapevine, vineyard)? Is there one level you feel more comfortable engaging than others? Is there one level in which you feel things are healthier for you than in others?

8. When is the last time you were really seen by someone? What did they do or not do to make you feel seen?

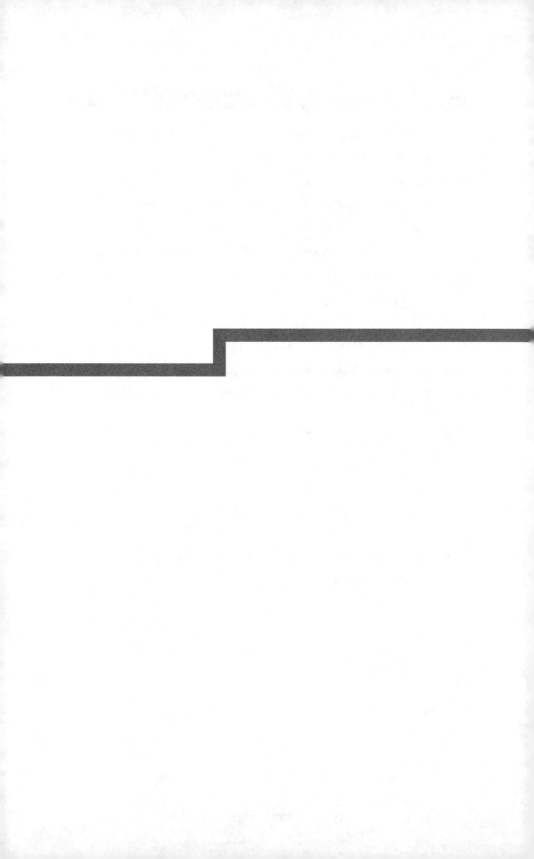

CHAPTER 2
Unraveling Fear
Trimming the Taproot of Conflict

Conflict is what happens when our wounds and fears come into contact with another's.

It can arise from any of a variety of sources: oppression, misunderstanding, competition for survival, history and tradition, differences in culture or religion, differences in language interpretation, violations of dignity, or even different fundamental ideas about the way the world ought to be. Sometimes we may find that a single form of conflict is present. And just as a body can experience multiple forms of physical illness at the same time, we often find ourselves in situations of social and emotional unease where many kinds of conflict are happening all at once.

Likewise, the impact of conflict varies. Some conflict is easy to deal with; it involves a five-minute conversation to clear the air. Other conflict, like impasse, is complex and may be impossible to solve. Conflict leads to fighting, warfare, and smashed relationships. At the most, it can turn neighbors into enemies; at the very least, it can cause people to avoid each other and grow apart.

In this chapter, we explore the inner causes of conflict and its impact on our lives.

Concentric Circles of Conflict

For the last decade, my family has struggled to navigate what it means to hold oppositional religious and political views. Half of us are pro-life Moral Majority Evangelicals, and half of us are liberal rainbow train agnostics. It has come to feel as if we live in different universes; we speak different languages, practice different cultures, and pursue different visions of how the world ought to work. Especially because we love each other, and especially because we respect each other despite warring ideologies, impasse has been emotionally and mentally hard for all of us.

How do we speak our truth while honoring the *other*? How do we protect freedom of conscience when we feel our loved ones have lost their marbles for believing as they do?

To make matters worse, my family feels like a microcosm of what's happening in our larger society.

The United States has always been a conflicted place. Our democracy is built on the fundamental power of protest. Think of the Boston Tea Party, federalism versus states' rights, abolition, suffrage, and the civil rights movement. Protest—a type of confrontation that seeks to transform conflict—is written into our national identity. The three branches of the US government were created with the intention of balancing and bridling power; effectively, tension is baked into the very crust. This tension facilitates conflict that produces long-term change and, hopefully, justice. To a large degree, it's no accident that we have legally enforced rights like voting, free education, nondiscrimination, and reasonable work hours. These rights are the direct result of everyday people choosing to engage conflict and choosing to engage it effectively.

Despite this rich democratic legacy, our national landscape has become conflicted to an intense and explosive degree in recent years. As I write this in 2020 the United States of America feels like the Divided States of America. We are an utterly polarized nation, the Left and Right nearly diverging as different species. We're at an impasse.

For many, it's overwhelming to continue to face the news every day and still continue to care. People on every point of the political spectrum are expressing feelings of powerlessness, frustration, and fatigue. And there are simply no easy answers.

Zooming out from a national context, the planet Earth by many accounts seems to be heating up as resource scarcity, environmental factors, globalist economic privatization, and political unrest are causing increasingly widespread refugee crises, destabilizing poverty, and war.

Many of us feel the pressure of concentric circles of conflict closing in on us. It may be no coincidence that people living in the modern age are plagued by stress-related diseases like hypertension, anxiety, obesity, and heart disease despite unprecedented access to health technologies and health knowledge. In the United States alone, the American Psychological Association estimates, we spend $300 billion every year in order to mitigate stress-related issues.[5]

A significant contributing factor to our stress may simply be the burden of knowledge.[6] It seems our minds and bodies are just not evolutionarily suited to be aware of all the bad things and all the conflicts that happen around the world all the time. We are not biologically suited to be such consumers of information, yet many of us feel responsible to stay informed and feel guilty if we do not.

This vicious cycle can take a toll, and it can have a deep impact on our lived experiences with conflict. While forces like unbridled media consumption, infotainment, politicking, smoke-and-mirrors tactics, identity politics, and cyberwarfare may be fully at work in the ways we see reality and treat each other, many of us deal with these circles of conflict by digging ideological trenches and launching verbal grenades. We have become a perpetually panicked people, enacting furious and destructive behaviors toward anyone who disagrees with us.

Why?

I believe it's because most of us feel powerless. We are terrified of an uncertain future. While most of us want to see the greater good realized in the world, we seem to have different definitions of what's at stake and how to fix it.

Fear Is the Taproot of Conflict

There are many, many sources of conflict, but most conflict is fed by one central element: fear. Fear is not just a root, but the taproot—the root that is biggest and lies right in the center of the root structure.

What is the function of a taproot? Consider the seemingly magical art of bonsai—the ancient practice of growing teeny-tiny yet fully alive trees. I used to believe that these trees (also called bonsai) were special tiny plants grown from tiny seeds, but the reality is much more amazing. Bonsai trees are completely normal trees that have had their taproot trimmed. A tree's taproot is its biggest root, which stretches down the farthest and stabilizes the tree against the elements. Thousands of years ago and without the help of modern biology, ancient Chinese and Japanese horticulturalists discovered that the size of the tree will adjust to the length of the taproot. Removing the taproot doesn't affect the health of the tree. It just changes the tree's proportions and asks nature to create a new perspective.

Many people believe—understandably so—that the taproot of conflict is anger. Strong emotions, especially "righteous" or justifiable anger, are common companions to conflict and are usually responses to injustice, which is when our ability to thrive or have basic rights is taken from us. Anger is often an important tool of self-protection, but it is a tool that our bodies employ after we are already afraid of what may come. Therefore, anger is, in fact, a symptom, not a root cause.

The taproot of conflict is fear.[7] Fear determines the scale and intensity of the conflict. In other words, conflict is always proportionate to the fear the drives it.

This is not to say that fear is trivial or can be easily dealt with. In fact, fear plays an important role in how we navigate the world. Our deepest fears are shaped by the ways we experience and interpret reality. Here we are not talking about irrational fears, like fear of the dentist or fear of squirrels, but extremely rational fears cultivated by our values, our beliefs, and our good and basic human instinct to survive.

Our deepest fears are real, in the sense that they arise from the ways we have experienced the world. Real fears spring from what we personally know and believe to be true.

Once we know what to look for, we can begin to see all the real fears working in the center of things. For example:

- Real fear of having your rights stripped away—if you have felt powerless

- Real fear for a loved one's eternal soul—if you believe in damnation

- Real fear of the chaos of ignorance—if you believe history repeats itself

- Real fear of not having enough—if you've known what it's like to be hungry

- Real fear of being controlled—if you believe institutions tend to be controlling

- Real fear of not being loved—if you have been rejected in the past

- Real fear of national failure—if you understand that even an empire like Rome can fall

- Real fear of being wounded—if you grasp the utter frailty of your human being

Real fears are contextual. Different people, living different lives, will have different real fears. If my lived experience hasn't included hunger, it's hard to understand my neighbor's real fear of food scarcity. Without working to relate empathetically to her, it's impossible to honor the impact the real fear of hunger has on her life and the role it plays in her decision making.

In other words, real fears are expressions of intelligence. They hedge the boundaries of our values and beliefs, protect our structures of meaning, and guide our actions.

For all of us who care about our families, our communities, and the wider world, we share one common, ultimate set of real fears that can be summed up in the idea of avoiding chaos. We work hard to protect ourselves against fundamental uncertainty.

In other words, most of us don't want the world to fall apart. Chaos is such a scary prospect that it's hard for many of us to even consider it as a possibility. We spend a lot of our time on earth doing everything we can to resist it. Sociologists have a word for this ultimate, existential kind of chaos: *anomie* (pronounced like *canopy*, with emphasis on the first syllable). Anomie is the collapse of structures—the breaking of any kind of order that gives meaning to the ways we interact with each other and the world around us. Anomie is rejecting the rules of society in a way that causes ultimate nothingness, or void.[8]

In other words, anomie goes beyond zombie apocalypse, where a faithful band of people stand together and rebuild society against monsters. It is the kind of chaos that demolishes even the concept of society. Anomie is the disintegration of our very ideas of social order—the ideas of having neighbors, freedoms, common languages, law, belief systems, education, work, governments, transportation systems, food distribution, sharing and exchange, symbols. These are all human inventions. We take these systems for granted, ascribe them meaning, and rely on them for survival. We have constructed these technologies over the long course of human history, but they are human-made. They are not necessarily Eternal Truths.

They can break.

Fear of anomie is ancient. It is linked to our natural human desire to survive. We are hardwired to fight against perceived threats to life and order. Since we are human and therefore limited, we know in our deepest core that we cannot prevent anomie completely. In a finite world, we can only keep chaos at bay.

Importantly, we can't fight chaos alone. Any structure we develop to protect meaning and to make society function must be done with other people in mutual agreement.

ANOMIE AND CORE BELIEFS

Have you ever wondered why, in the modern era, people in many parts of the world seem to be getting less religious? In demographic studies of religious affiliation, unaffiliated people are now the world's third-largest category.[17]

The question of why modern people are less prone to be religious has fascinated scholars and practitioners alike. Anomie may have something to do with the explanation.

Imagine wandering in a desert with your family but without any modern technology, science, or medicine. Imagine not having modern methods of food and shelter, not having an internet browser or smart phone to find information or news whenever you like. You have no GPS, no telephone, no motors, no modern weapons, no passport, no international human rights law, and no government to protect your person and property. Imagine wandering through hostile land with nothing, feeling anomie in your very bones—the utter fragility of life bearing down on you, like the hot sun overhead.

Your life, by all accounts, walks a razor's edge between survival and void.

Now imagine that someone comes along and proclaims, with great conviction, that if you pray every morning by rubbing sand between your fingers, the gods will keep you alive and safe. Wouldn't you be prone to participate?

If that were me, I would pray the sand prayer. I absolutely would. I would probably even rail against anyone who didn't do the sand prayer, for fear that the gods would become angry and stop protecting my people.

Of course, the study of religion is much more complex than the fear of anomie. To suggest anomie is the only reason for religion would be damaging. I use this example to suggest that the closer our lives get to the edges of anomie, the more that real fears play a direct and significant role in the ways we act in the world and the things we believe and hope for at our core.

For example, we collectively agree to use a certain kind of paper, to call it money, and to trade it for things. For monetary systems to exist, many people have to believe money has value and keep using money. In the same way, we vote to keep governments existing. We send our children to school to keep education existing. We talk to each other to keep language existing. We seek basic agreement on what symbols mean. We develop basic standards for the way humans should treat each other. These activities happen on huge, global levels, like the United Nations, and on small, interpersonal levels, like two neighbors interacting.

Keeping anomie at bay doesn't always mean complete agreement. But it always requires some kind of cooperation between people.

If we stop cooperating with our fellow humans, the structures we know, love, and rely upon start to fall apart.

The closer we are to the edges of society, to the edges of chaos, the less stable our lives feel, and the more real fears affect the things we embrace, believe in, and hold dear.

If we are someone for whom life is highly predictable, controllable, and technologically privileged, we might fail to comprehend the plight of people who live on the razor's edge because we've never been there. Importantly, just because we don't experience the same fears as someone else, it doesn't mean their fears aren't real and valid. In fact, their fears might be more real and present and driving than ours.

If a real and nearly universal fear of anomie drives each of us to create structures of order to survive, then we have arrived at an ancient paradox: there is, at the very least, a kernel of truth on *all* sides of *all* conflicts.

With this understanding, we can conclude that it is healthy and right to honor the reality of real fears, even real fears we struggle to understand.

The Problem with Fear

While real fears may be primal and natural and may help us self-protect, we should also learn to hold fear with a level of suspicion.

Why?

As much as fear hedges, guides, and even protects us, fear is a powerful motivator. Sometimes great big conflicts are being propped up by a huge taproot of fear and have grown way out of proportion. Fear goes haywire quickly, making normally kind people do and say unkind and even nonsensical things. It can make us hurt each other for the "greater good." It can make us hunker down into our trenches and launch grenades. It can make us regard people we can't seem to relate to as bad or inhuman. It can make us misunderstand and misinterpret reality.

The way fear operates within us on a primal level can make us vulnerable to people with bad intentions who seek to take advantage of us by turning our fears against us.

If fear can destroy our concepts of basic human dignity and break our channels of communication, if it can make us more vulnerable and less prone to cooperate with each other, then ultimately the fear of chaos has a strange ability to bring about the chaos we are all trying to prevent.

Giving in to fear is not in our best interest.

We can appreciate the role of fear in our lives, but often we don't *need* fear as much as we think we do. When the taproot of fear doesn't serve us—when it gets in the way, skews our perspective, and makes things become overwhelming and out of control—it might be time to trim it back.

Ultimately, it is impossible to deal with conflict in healthy ways unless we choose to believe on a deep level that the vast majority of people in this whole wide world are small, scared, and doing their best. Even if we don't agree on a single thing, humans have to stick together, or chaos wins.

Conflict Within

We've discussed how conflict and fear can affect us on a societal level, but let's turn and look at the impact on our individual, day-to-day lives.

My mother and I are normally very close, but we haven't always been good at boundaries.

Several years ago, after a particularly bad run-in, I was too afraid to confront her and have a brave talk. I felt my boundaries had been ignored one too many times (and I failed, of course, to look at the ways I was complicit).

I decided to send her an email (famous last words) outlining all the ways she had hurt me. I listed the things I felt I needed from her, and I proclaimed that if she couldn't change, we simply were not going to have a relationship anymore.

A couple of days later, she sent a curt reply, something brief to the effect of, "Sorry. That makes sense."

I interpreted this as "she's not taking this seriously." I was deeply hurt. For the next four months, we didn't speak. For *four months*, I didn't speak to the woman who gave me life.

Three months into this time period, I found myself in physical therapy, in so much pain I was barely able to walk. I shuffled around like a ninety-year-old in a twenty-nine-year-old's body. I couldn't point to a cause; it made no sense. The therapist couldn't diagnose me. She worked with me several times and finally said, "Honestly, I can't figure out what's wrong. I'm not a psychologist, but sometimes I see patients develop chronic pain when they are dealing with emotional issues in their personal life. Do you think that could be what's going on?"

Lying on the exam table, I felt tears prickle down my face. Something inside me knew that was exactly what was happening.

I still didn't speak to my mom. It was only after one of my sisters leaked the news that "Mom is really not doing well" that I broke down and called her.

I found out she had also been miserable, to the point of falling into dark depression and illness. And her email—the short, delayed one? She said the email was short because she was stunned and challenged by what I had said. It was late because she had taken days to digest my words. She told me she initially composed a lengthy email answering my concerns point by point but then discarded it, fearing it sounded defensive and unaccepting. She didn't want to cloud our conflict by making a bunch of excuses or using flowery language. She opted for brevity and acceptance. Words that she thought conveyed simplicity and depth I regarded as negligence.

Once we reconciled and started working through our issues, we both started to recover physically.

Through this bizarre and troubling experience, I learned firsthand that when humans don't deal with conflict, it doesn't just go away. It goes somewhere. It might spill out into other relationships, contribute to addictions, or foster other destructive behavior. In my case, the pain of my conflict went into my body and physically affected my ability to function.

Medical professionals talk about relational stress having horrible effects on our organs and brain chemistry.[9] Conflict affects our ability to sleep, learn, make decisions, and cope with daily life.[10] It can foster unhealthy habits and self-destructive behaviors.

Even with all of this emerging research, most of us still pretend we can handle conflict impassively, because we don't want to look weak. We act like everything is fine.

Fear of weakness is a common real fear, because all of us are actually weak. We are frail, mortal, limited human beings. Why do we pretend we aren't?

Usually, it's because we've been hurt, and we fear being hurt again.

The Fear Bunker

Some people can't or won't participate in difficult conversations because they feel safer in what I like to call the fear bunker.

The fear bunker is the place we go when we feel threatened. It's not shameful to have a fear bunker; sometimes we go there for good reason. The more we have been hurt by conflict in the past, the more conflict can feel hazardous, and the more likely we are to jump into our fear bunker.

FEAR BUNKER

—WHERE WE GO WHEN WE FEEL THREATENED—

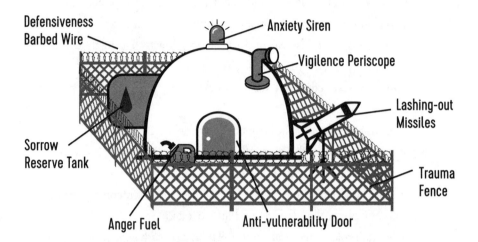

Defensiveness Barbed Wire

Anxiety Siren

Vigilence Periscope

Lashing-out Missiles

Sorrow Reserve Tank

Trauma Fence

Anger Fuel

Anti-vulnerability Door

Every part of our fear bunker holds information about what is safe and unsafe. It helps us make decisions about what we can handle and what we can't. If you are well-acquainted with your fear bunker, you are definitely not alone.

Fear bunkers usually come with anger fuel, a red panic siren, a reservoir of sorrow, and an anti-vulnerability door. Some might have lashing-out missiles or a periscope of vigilance. If someone forces their way through that door, the bunker will be compromised, and that person may self-destruct.

Wrapped around many fear bunkers is what I call a trauma fence. A trauma fence is a collection of our significant wounds that are interconnected. Tug on one link in this chain-link fence, and all the links down the line will often move, which can be disorienting and troubling.

Trauma is what happens when we are so deeply wounded that the body stays in a state of permanent alertness and stress.[11] If someone gets triggered during a conversation ("trigger" has become a buzzword, but here I mean triggered in the sense of medically informed trauma theory), all of the experiences remotely related to that trigger will get brought up in that person's mind and body. In a highly sensory way, the person relives those experiences as if they are happening all over again. Here is a more formal description of a trigger from the University of Alberta's Sexual Assault Centre:

> A trigger is something that sets off a memory tape or flashback transporting the person back to the event of [their] original trauma. Triggers are very personal; different things trigger different people. The survivor may begin to avoid situations and stimuli that [they] think triggered the flashback. [They] will react to this flashback, trigger with an emotional intensity similar to that at the time of the trauma. A person's triggers are activated through one or more of the five senses: sight, sound, touch, smell, and taste.[12]

When someone is triggered, it's like a jolt of electricity runs through that trauma fence, sending a big red-alert signal: "Get away! Not safe!" Sometimes even a small touch of the trauma fence can cause a strong and even overwhelming reaction, depending on how strongly that fence has been constructed by the body.[13]

This might sound like a harsh system, but our bodies build trauma fences to protect us from further harm. For example, if someone was mauled by a dog and their brain developed lasting symptoms of trauma, hearing the sound of a dog barking may trigger a trauma response (also known as a fight-or-flight response). The person may sweat, try to physically escape, hyperventilate, or look for a weapon. If recurrent, non-rational trauma responses happen, psychologists might diagnose this as post-traumatic stress.[14] Trauma fence responses can be so strong that the person has little control over them. Panic attacks are a prime example of the trauma fence at work (for further discussion of trauma, see chapter 6).[15]

Why are we talking about bunkers and fences? Because fear and trauma play such a huge role in the ways we interact during conflict. When someone has a fear or trauma response, especially if they or the people around them don't understand what's going on, situations can escalate quickly.

Our fear bunkers and the trauma fences are not bad. They are a kind of body intelligence, protecting us from harm, sending us information when things are dicey. And while some physical responses are largely out of our control, we do have options in how we choose to respond to these sensations. The choices we make can have a significant effect on our ability to navigate conflict.

Fear Bunkers Isolate Us

Fear bunkers work to protect us, but they are built for only one person. When we are inside them, we are isolated from other people.

My friend Jordan is a great guy who has been a part of a local dance community for many years. At a dance several months ago, the dance organizers took him aside and told him he had done something inappropriate and offended one of the women dancers. He asked who it was, so he could speak with her, and they said they couldn't tell him. He said he understood and perhaps they could tell him what he did wrong, so he could know what not to do in the future. They said they couldn't tell him that either. He asked if they would arrange some kind of mediation between him and the woman, so he could apologize and clear the air, and they said that wouldn't be possible. He asked if he could send a message of apology to her through them. They declined.

Since Jordan was unable to address the problem, had no idea what he had done wrong, and had no idea whether he would cause further offense without meaning to, he no longer felt welcome. He stopped going to the dance night completely, and as a result, he effectively lost a community that meant a lot to him.

My hunch is that the unnamed woman in this story had a trauma fence response. Many people have a level of trauma that can be extremely difficult and even debilitating to live with. With immense compassion and validation for this woman's pain, and with awareness of the difficult job of the dance organizers to keep everyone safe, I believe this situation could have been different. Given that the woman sought protection but avoided any attempt to transform the conflict, it sounds like she dove into her fear bunker. And given that the dance organizers attended to one dancer's need to be protected but glossed over the other dancer's need to make things right, it sounds like they also dove into their fear bunker. This caused Jordan to dive into his fear bunker. With everyone isolated and afraid, Community shut down.

We humans are pack animals—tribal creatures. We have socially adapted as a species to warn each other of danger, even on subconscious levels. We learn about what is safe and not safe by watching each other carefully.[16] Basically, we are like a big herd of zebras sitting by the water. When one zebra thinks it has spotted a crocodile nearby, suddenly all the zebras are galloping away frantically.

When we sense one person diving into their fear bunker, our primal instinct is to dive into ours.

Since we are all wounded, many of us wounded deeply, how do we navigate conflict and impasse without making things worse? It can take an intense amount of work to stay out of our own fear bunker when we don't need to be in there, figure out what to do when other people are in their fear bunkers, and navigate trauma fences without doing further damage.

For us to move forward in changing our relationship with conflict, it's highly important to use a clinically informed understanding of fear and trauma. With this knowledge, we can learn how to interpret fear and conflict as we experience it in ourselves and witness it in others.

Responding to Fear: Interpreting and Acting

Before we can interpret and navigate fear, we need to learn to identify it. In this section, we will explore four levels of identifying fear and three ways to address it.

Identifying Fear: Four Levels of Interpretation

Often, we project a hard exterior that shows people we aren't affected by conflict, while on the inside, we are holed up in our fear bunker. The door is locked,

the panic alarm is wailing, and the trauma fence is electrified. Sometimes, on the outside, we are screaming at someone, but on the inside, we are in the fetal position, crying for the conflict to stop.

It's common that the ways we act on the outside are different from what's happening inside. This makes it hard to read a situation.

We can interpret situations more effectively by realizing that when we engage conflict and impasse, we are interacting with four realities: (1) my inside feelings, (2) my outside actions, (3) my conversation partner's outside actions, and (4) my conversation partner's inside feelings. Interpreting fear on four levels therefore means asking ourselves the following questions:

1. What are my inside feelings? Am I okay, or am I locked in my fear bunker?

2. What are my outside actions? What signals and energy am I putting out?

3. What are my conversation partner's outside actions? What signals and energy are they putting out?

4. What can I guess about my conversation partner's inside feelings? Is there anything they say or do that can clue me in? Are they in their fear bunker? Maybe I can find a way to ask how they are doing.

Becoming well versed at interpreting these four levels can be a game changer when dealing with difficult conversations around impasse. Recognizing there is a lot under the surface we can't see and learning to read situations better will help us prepare for action.

Dealing with Fear Bunkers: Smoke, Coax, or Flow

When it comes to dealing with fear bunkers—either our own or someone else's—we have three options: smoke, coax, or flow.

1. **Smoke.** We try to smoke someone out of the fear bunker by attacking them, showing strong emotions like anger or frustration, or threatening punishment if they don't come out. This represents a form of control that is rarely effective.

"Stop being afraid, Nina. You're so ridiculous! Why can't you just get over it?"

"Hey, self, you're so stupid. Just quit acting like this. Turn off your feelings."

2. **Coax.** We can try to coax out the person with patience and gentleness. This approach is hit or miss. In its worst form, a coaxing approach represents manipulation or not truly caring about someone's needs. However, when this approach is done well, it is attentive, protective, and kind, and it speaks to the person and the relationship between you.

> **Less effective:** "Hey, self, do you think you can get it together? You aren't really under threat; it just seems like it. Can you please just stop being scared now?"

> **More effective:** "Hey, Nina, I want you to feel safe with me. Are you okay? You seem a little freaked out. What can I do to help? Talk to me."

3. **Flow.** We can go with the flow and respect the fact that sometimes people just need to be in their fear bunkers. In this approach, we trust that they will come out when ready, and we make sure they know we are there to support and encourage them whenever that time is to be.

> "Nina, I'm getting the sense that you are having a strong reaction to this conversation. I want to be a safe person for you to be around, and I will never force you to open up if you don't want to. I'm here whether you

want to talk or not, and I won't leave unless you want me to. Take all the time you need. Know that I really care about you."

"Self, you're doing your best. It's okay to be scared. Everyone gets scared. Your pain is valid. Feel that? That's the ground under your feet. Breathe.

Take your time. It's going to be okay."

SUMMARY: If Fear Isn't Serving Us, Hold It at Arm's Length

Fear might work to protect us, but it also isolates us and can drive us to unhealthy behaviors. To experience Community with each other, we have to venture out and be a little vulnerable. Because fear bunkers have space for only one person, strong relationships and connection can happen only outside the fear bunker.

Since humans are pack animals and we learn from watching each other, it's a powerful and loving thing to lead the way and be the first person to step out of our fear bunker. Instead of waiting for someone to come along and love us out of our fear bunker, we each have a unique ability to be the first to step out. Each of us can choose to show leadership by modeling safe and healthy ways to step outside cycles of fear.

How do we do it?

We raise a hand and ask, "Is this fear serving us, or is it getting in the way?"

1. Have you ever felt as if you have concentric circles of conflict in your life? What impact has this had on you?

2. Do you agree that fear is the taproot of conflict, something we have the power to examine and trim back when necessary? Why or why not?

3. What are some of your real fears—the fears that guide your actions and thoughts? (Share if you are comfortable.)

4. How do you keep anomie at bay? What kinds of things do you do to uphold order and stability in your world? When do those things come under fire?

5. When is a time you held your fears with suspicion? What was the result?

6. Have you ever experienced a symptom of conflict in a way you didn't expect? For example, has conflict ever affected you physically, mentally, or emotionally in a surprising way?

7. What is your fear bunker like? When do you most often find yourself spending time in it? What helps bring you out of it? If you feel comfortable sharing, do you have a trauma fence? If so, do you know why it exists? Having this experience, what is your best advice for people living with trauma?

8. When is a time you have shown leadership in stepping out of your fear bunker or helped someone to get out of theirs? Did anything meaningful happen as a result?

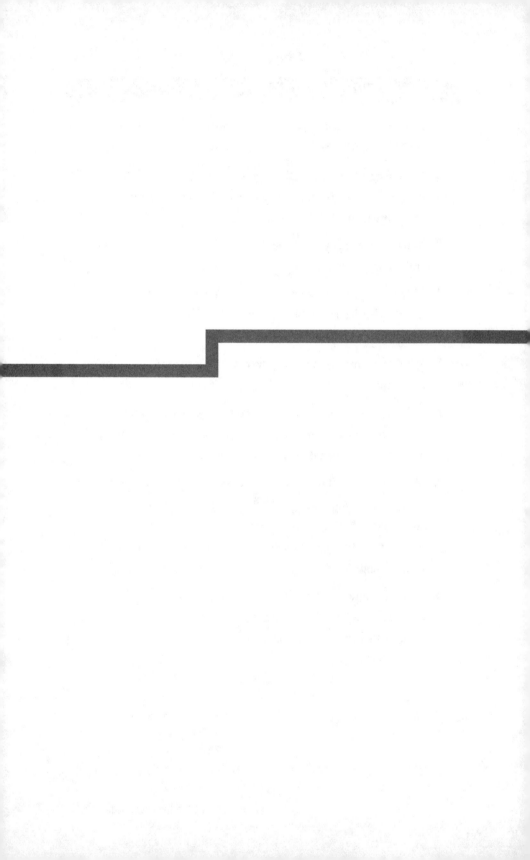

CHAPTER 3
Conflict and Power
Goliath and the Hare

What does power have to do with conflict and impasse? Everything. The ways we use power will determine whether conflict is transformed or escalated.

Power has an impact on the entire outcome of difficult conversations and conflicted situations. It is the single most important factor in determining whether conflict is real or false impasse. To meet each other in impasse, to really see one another, we need to approach each other as equals. We need to share instead of dominate.

If power is directly related to equality, understanding power helps us understand justice. It helps us understand the consequences and conflicts that arise when justice is not enacted, when equality is withheld. Conflict—even conflict that seems irrational—is a logical and right outcome in situations where power is unbalanced and human flourishing is obstructed.

If we want to be conflict transformers, it's vitally important to explore how each of us can use power in healthier ways.

It's forty-five minutes after work, and you're late meeting a friend. As you head toward your car, you catch sight of something awful. With all the courage and politeness you can muster, you walk up to the scene and say, "Excuse me, sir, you just hit my car."

"No, I didn't," he replies.

"But I literally saw you drive your car into my car and then park across the way. I watched you do it. I don't want any trouble. Please just do the right thing and give me your insurance info."

"It wasn't me."

You start to get frustrated. "But I can see scratch marks on your car with the same color paint as my car, and my car has a dent in it. All evidence points to you hitting my car. Now please, make it right, or I will be forced to press charges."

"You must have me confused with someone else."

Because this person refuses to acknowledge what he did, and because you don't want to have to pay for the damage out of pocket, you feel you have no other option but to call the police. Surely they will fix this.

When the police arrive, they smile at the guy who hit you and say, "Hey, it's Bob! How's it going, Bob?" Before you can get a word in, Bob tells the officers that *you* were being aggressive toward *him*. You try to explain what happened, but one of the officers interrupts, "Listen, Bob is a good guy. Go back to your car, and drive away." The officer turns sideways, casually showing you the gun on his hip, and gives you a look that seems to say, "If you're smart, you'll obey."

At this point, you are feeling disoriented and incredibly angry. You just spoke to the people who are supposed to protect you from the Bobs of the world, but they failed you. Though you may be in the right, you feel that leaving is your only option.

A week later, you are driving around town, and you see that guy Bob walking down the street. You decide to pull over and confront him.

"Why did you tell those officers I was being aggressive? That was completely unfair! I can't believe you would do that!"

And he replies, "You should be thankful. I could have told them *you* hit *me*."

* * *

This entire situation played out the way it did because Bob was wielding his power in a destructive way. The conflict that resulted seems to have been "resolved," but, of course, that depends on who you ask.

What Is Power, Anyway?

For many years, I believed that power always equates with pride. I struggled with confidence, thinking I was supposed to be meek and apologetic, not powerful. I thought that holding strong opinions and speaking loudly with conviction were a dangerous game. Despite my parent's encouragement that I was a born "leader," I struggled to see this as a good thing. To me, power was a liability.

As an adult, I have learned a helpful definition of the word *power* that has completely changed the way I think. My working definition comes from the world of community organizing.

> Power, in a social-political sense, is the ability to effect any kind of change.[18]

If we see it this way, everyone uses power all the time, every day. The change we effect can be as big as setting up a new government or as small as forming a new opinion, choosing to love someone, giving to someone in need, or brushing our teeth. We are using power if we get up and go to work in the morning. We are using power if we argue an opinion. We are using power when we buy local apples versus imported apples or organic versus non-organic apples (which, of course, also implies a certain type of underlying power called economic opportunity). If we are effecting any kind change in ourselves or in the world around us at any time, we are using power.

So power is not inherently bad. All people have an innate sense of power, but some of us, based on history, social location, education, family background, economic situation, personality, and a host of other reasons, might experience a greater opportunity to wield power than others. It is horrible yet true that some people are more disenfranchised than others in our society—meaning some people have less ability to effect change, especially big change. To a vast degree, everyone in this whole world has power.

Power is kind of like money. Money is not inherently bad. It is a neutral tool that takes on the significance we ascribe to it. It acts in the ways we make it act. It takes on the meaning we give it. When everyone has enough, money is a wonderful tool of evaluation and exchange. It's the way we feed our families and build our society and create new things. But when a handful of people have much more than they need while others starve, money can take on a corrupt symbolic quality. People can grow to love money so much they mistake it for human worth. Historically, some people with great wealth have disregarded and dehumanized those without money, instead of working to make sure everyone has enough to live. In a state of imbalance, the use of both money and power can cause great suffering.

Despite the huge power imbalances in the world, all of us can, at the very least, exert power over our immediate selves. Yes, many factors are at work in our minds, bodies, and circumstances, but everyone can decide which words to choose and what actions to take. Every single person, in every single moment, has a degree of choice over how to use that power.

To stay healthy as human beings and to live in a peaceful and just world, we need to share power. Power is healthy, good, and right when it ebbs and flows, when everyone can participate, and when everyone can challenge each other.

Why?

Because when power is equalized, imagination, creativity, and innovation are unleashed. World problems get solved. Wars end. Justice reigns. Needs are met. Life becomes beautiful for all, not just for some.

This is Community.

Power Sharing in Action

Let's trace one amazing example of power sharing from ancient times to today.

Thousands of years ago, we as a human race invented an incredible system of power sharing called democracy. Democracy is based on the idea that for making difficult decisions, many voices are better than few. We created ways to remember our ideas about democracy (and many other kinds of knowledge) on scrolls made of plants and hides, and then we figured out how to remember our knowledge in an invention called books, made from trees.

But the process of making books by hand was slow and costly, so that only an elite few could access them. To make knowledge available to everyone despite their economic status, we invented machines that could print the books quickly and get them to many, many people. Having so many books was such a great thing that we started to create free libraries and schools. We looked for ways to share our knowledge with each other to a greater and greater degree.

Democracy went out of custom for a long time, but the knowledge of it in the books we printed sparked ideas in the minds of everyday people. We started experimenting with democracy again. At first, we weren't good at it. We copied the ancient tradition where only the elite could share voice and power. Such an approach was limited: it missed the contributions and geniuses of women and people of color, many of whom had been excluded not only from voice but also from education. Because our experiments lacked equality, they lacked justice. Democracy without justice does not facilitate the full flour-ishing of human dignity.

So we developed justice systems that could protect equality, the freedom of speech, the freedom of ideas, and access to education. As tech-nologies of power sharing continued to evolve and we learned it is better to enfranchise more people into democracy and opportunity, the world experienced an explosion of invention and industry. Why did this happen at the same time? Because a much larger pool of talent, from a wider range of perspectives, was slowly welcomed to participate in inventing things and solve problems.

We began to demand basic human rights for all, like reasonable working hours and children's right to education. We put an end to power-hoarding institutions like slavery and working-class oppression as we created legal protections and unions for everyday people. We began to share the vote; we started to allow everyone to participate in meaningful work of their choice.

We created new kinds of economic specializations that help us share resources more effectively. Industry and invention thrived. We sent human beings into outer space using pencils and yellow slide rules.

Eventually, our inventions began to outpace our brains' ability to remember and work. So we created complex, multifunctional machines that could compute solutions to problems. But these machines were cumbersome and expensive, and only an elite few could use them. Someone woke up one morning with the idea that just like mass-produced books, computing machines would be powerful in the hands of everyday people, so we found ways to invent smaller and more affordable machines.

When power-sharing machines were shared powerfully, we unleashed a fresh storm of innovation. One of these ideas was that our societies could benefit when these computing machines were connected. So we invented a new technology of power sharing called the internet. We found ways to make computing machines cheap enough for many to have in their homes. We put free computing machines in the free libraries and schools we had created long ago. We encouraged internet access in public spaces. In the internet age, one doesn't even have to be an adult or a citizen to share power. If we can access the internet, our human voice can be broadcast to the entire world. Each person can speak and create and challenge the status quo.

Once the internet was invented, an ancient idea was once again reinvigorated: sharing knowledge is the key to sharing power. Inspired by this conviction, we created a technology-powered power-sharing system, using the democratic values of co-creation and equality, to put all the information we know in one place. This system was named Wikipedia.

Wikipedia has become the greatest repository of human knowledge ever gathered in the history of the world. It is cultivated by volunteers from all walks of life, from all over the world, and it is completely free. Its knowledge can be accessed by anyone, no matter their status or income. It is one of the greatest marvels human beings have ever created.

Power sharing is *incredibly* powerful.

Domination: The Enemy of Community

Tragically, when humans gain a lot of power, we tend to want to keep it.

As our attachment to power grows large and in charge, it often shape-shifts into power's nasty cousin, domination. Domination is the kind of power that seeks to impose someone's will over another, through force or coercion. Domination may claim a narrative that it's acting "for the greater good," but it does not transform relationships for the better. It does not celebrate life or creativity. Its sole purpose is to impose its will and overpower others for its own purposes. It punishes people who don't bend to its wishes.

Left unchecked, domination's need for control is a bottomless pit of injustice and violence.[19]

Some might argue that domination has a place in our society. Take sports, for example. Yes, the point of friendly competition is to play one's best and to win—and, some would say, to dominate. But domination is not just winning; it seeks to win at any cost and therefore is unsportsmanlike.

Here are examples of what domination looks like:

- Domination in the world of business looks like chasing profits to the point of disregarding ethics and the needs of local communities.

- Domination in the world of parenting looks like overpowering a child and seeking to break their will.

- Domination in gendered relationships looks like one partner telling the other they can't make decisions because their gender is weak.

- Domination in religion looks like manipulative proselytizing, colonial missionizing, and ideological control.

- Domination in justice systems looks like locking human beings in cages for years over minor, nonviolent offenses and punishing them for life after they "pay their debt to society," while ignoring systemic issues like poverty, education, and lack of opportunity that facilitated the crime in the first place.

- Domination in politics looks like empire building, crushing anyone who stands in the way of a national agenda, and refusing to apologize for any damage that results.

- Domination in societies looks like one group claiming supremacy over others, whether overtly or subtly, and justifying exclusion or oppression on the basis of superiority.

Some of our cultures are so entrenched in domination, so familiar with its rule, that we can't even recognize it when it's staring us in the face.

It's important to note that being a strong person or having strong opinions doesn't mean someone is using domination. Advocating passionately in favor of an issue or standing up for one's self is not using domination. Domination is threatened by other people's power and seeks to stay in power *at all costs*. It doesn't like to share resources or space. It might even hurt others to protect itself. Domination is dangerously self-focused, so it blocks our capacity to empathize. It erodes relationships, especially relationships that challenge it. It takes advantage of fear and desperation to get what it wants.

Community and domination cannot coexist.

* * *

My parents like to tell a story from my childhood. I was too young to remember this, around three years old. One day they took me out to dinner and overheard two men in the next booth having a conversation. Actually, it was more like one man was talking *at* the other man—talking about himself for a long period of time. He was so loud and obnoxious that he seemed to be annoying everyone sitting at surrounding tables.

Apparently, Tiny Me watched this "conversation" unfold over the edge of the booth, and finally I had enough. I stood up in my seat, waved my hands just like the loud man, and shouted, "Myself, myself, myself!"

As you can imagine, my parents were mortified, but other people in the restaurant clapped and cheered me on.

This is a funny story, and I would be proud of it, except that throughout my entire life, any time I have started to get a big head about something, someone in my family has chuckled at me and yelled, "Myself, myself, myself!"

You could say that all these years, Tiny Me was guarding the entrance of my heart like a watchdog against the likes of domination.

Thank you, Tiny Me.

The language of domination is always "myself, myself, myself," spoken in a way that doesn't make space for anyone else. It lacks empathy or concern for the needs of others. It shuts other people down. It does not celebrate life and Community. Like a giant metal wrecking ball, it destroys life and Community.

Some people might say, "So what if I destroy Community? I am the only person in my world who matters." But by destroying Community, people using domination ultimately destroy themselves. They cut themselves off from meaningful connection and relationships. They flatten their emotional range and crush the things that make them human. Therefore, people using domination compromise their ability to be socially healthy.

People embrace domination for a lot of different reasons. Many times, they have been hurt or had their power taken away, and they vow never to let that happen again. Consider holding off judgment for how someone got there. What's important is what people do with the knowledge of domination once they have it. What's important is that while domination is cutting them off from Community, we choose to hope that in most cases they can be restored.

Before this can happen, we need to learn how to recognize domination. Let's take a deeper look at how it operates.

Domination Wears Masks

People love a good underdog story, like David and Goliath or the Tortoise and the Hare. Usually, we focus on the characters of David and the Tortoise—the wimpy, heroic underdogs who bested great big jerks, jerks too blinded by ego to see their own weaknesses.

Typically, the "bully" archetype—Goliath, the Hare—is our carica-ture of power. Goliath and the Hare were aware of and vocal about their domination—real tough guys. Goliath chose to go to battle against a kid, basically so he could show off. The Hare also was boasting of his abilities, acting like a jackass. They were myself-ing all over the place. When domi-nation acts like domination, it's pretty easy to spot.

But sometimes it's not easy to spot. Sometimes domination does not look like domination.

Domination is pretty dang slippery, especially in conflicted situations. We might not think domination is in the room, but it can hide. It can hide even when the person using power doesn't lord it over other people in a traditional jackass sense. In fact, the person using domination may even look like a nice and decent person despite having tendencies to dominate.

Domination hides when the person using power doesn't seem to understand or care about the consequences of their words. It hides when the person using domination somehow benefits, monetarily or otherwise, from not recognizing the consequences of their actions. And significantly, domination hides when it is supported and encouraged by larger social and political systems.

All of these factors add up to one thing: when someone is engaging in domination, that person is highly motivated to not *see* their domination or how it benefits them.

Domination likes to wear masks. Because it doesn't like to share, it doesn't like to be confronted; if confronted, it might be forced to share. There are many masks of domination, but five are especially relevant to our conversation around conflict: anonymity, benevolence, fragility, civility, and gaslighting.

We can see the masks of domination in the earlier story of Bob who hit your car.

Anonymity occurs when Bob simply denies hitting your car. He denies he is the problem and tries to shift the blame onto someone else. Anonymity, or being anonymous, means someone is hiding their identity. Bob is acting like an anonymous or neutral party by not wanting to be named or identified, even

though he was obviously involved. If Bob's domination can refuse to engage the problem, he thinks he won't be held accountable, and the problem will just go away. He pretends he's invisible and avoids taking responsibility.

Benevolence is the appearance that Bob maintains of being "one of the good guys." He panders to other people in power, as he did by being buddy-buddy with the cops. Bob seems to care only what powerful people think of him, not what the person he is hurting thinks of him. And you know what? Maybe he sincerely does believe he is a good guy. But he used his reputation as a weapon to protect himself and to hurt you. That's a power imbalance.

Fragility is domination's mask when Bob claims to the cops that you were the one hurting him, not the other way around. He points to the symptom of your anger to suggest *you* were the issue. He asks to be rescued from the imaginary threat he created in you. He pretends to be fragile. He is not.

Civility is a mask when Bob claims that you were speaking in an "aggressive" tone to him and therefore acts as if your claims are not credible. By acting like the more civilized party, Bob is suggesting that your response was too barbaric, too indecent, so you must be reined in. He plays to the cops' idea of what is respectable and decent to make himself look like a better citizen than you.

Gaslighting occurs when you later confront Bob and he tells you that you should thank him for not being more of a jerk and getting you into more serious trouble. He makes you feel confused, as if it was somehow your responsibility for the way the situation played out. By showing you he had even more power over you than you originally thought, he is intimidating you into going along with his strange, faulty logic.

Sharing Power vs. Benevolent Power

Some uses of power might look great on the outside but are actually that old benevolent mask of domination. Benevolence is one of the sneakiest masks that domination uses, so it's helpful to spend some time here.

Benevolence is the expression of being well-meaning or showing goodwill. Sometimes people in power don't realize they are using benevolence to hoard power instead of share power. On the surface, it looks like they are sharing power, but in reality, domination is still very much in control.

Benevolence can take the form of *distraction*. For example, if a chemical company spills dangerous chemicals into the ocean, they might distract by donating right away to a good cause, so they look better in the media.

Benevolence can take the form of *othering*. For example, a wealthy social club gathers blankets for "those poor people" in a town in South America. Instead of taking the time to get to know the people and what they need, they send a thousand blankets to a tropical location where people don't need or want blankets. The club didn't bother to build a relationship, because secretly they kind of believe those "other" people are not worth being in real Community with. The club members just want to feel good about themselves and see themselves as good people.

Benevolence can take the form of *tokenizing*. For example, a church invites Muslim neighbors from a local mosque to have an interfaith service. The Muslim neighbors show up, and they soon realize that they are the only non-Christians in the building, and the entire service is a Christian worship service with an "interfaith" label. It incorporates one Islamic prayer, but otherwise, little thought was given. It became clear the church didn't want to get to know the Muslims. As a result, the Muslims probably would begin to feel that they were invited so the church members can congratulate themselves for being progressive but that the church has no real desire to create long-term friendships. In this case, the Muslims were dehumanized into tokens of diversity, without any steps toward real Community.

Benevolence can also take the form of *infantilizing*. For example, a woman gives money to a man without a home, but as she gives, she doesn't treat the man like an adult or an equal member of society. She looks down on the man in need, not caring about his story, his struggles, the ways he can improve his life in the long term, or the legal and governmental obstacles to his journey. She talks to him condescendingly. So the old saying goes, "Give a man a fish, he will eat for a day. Teach a man to fish, he will eat for life." Infantilization is giving someone a fish, not lifting a finger to teach them to fish, and treating them like a child in the process.

Benevolence can also take the form of *neutrality*. Someone might want to seem like a good or moral or upright person by "staying out" of sticky or uncomfortable conversations. But when the person has significant power to make a change or influence others for the better, staying out of it is a form of domination. A stance of neutrality and silence in times of injustice benefits those who are dominating, not those who are being oppressed. Therefore, neutrality is a particularly common mask that domination views kindly.

In all, benevolent power looks like sharing power but in fact is often the enemy of sharing power. It's half baked, lazy, and often harmful. It doesn't make real change in the world. It doesn't build real, give-and-take relationships. It just props up and validates domination.

Dealing with Domination (without Using Domination)

Some people call domination "privilege." The idea of privilege, especially in terms of race, is attributed to an article written by Peggy McIntosh in 1990. [20] The central idea is that some people carry around an invisible backpack with privileges not afforded to everyone, like someone's ability to get good service at restaurants or be treated fairly by police because of the color of their skin. The invisible-backpack metaphor is a powerful image that has helped a lot of people begin to recognize inequality in the world.

While this is great progress, my problem with the word *privilege* is that the word itself is just too nice, too pretty. It sounds like someone giving a speech to a crowd of colleagues after winning an award; the speaker might say, "It's an honor and a privilege to be with you here tonight."

Whenever we use this word to describe social or economic systems— as in "I have racial privilege" or "I have gender privilege" or "I have economic privilege"—we're actually describing larger systems of domination where one group is somehow granted more special treatment than another. Calling privilege out is an important step for some of us in recognizing that the playing field is not equal; however, naming its reality was never meant to be the end of the story. Naming privilege isn't nearly enough to overturn domination. It exposes domination, which is important, but sometimes in a less helpful way than we think.

In a troubling sense, domination is so slippery that even when called out, it can grow stronger. Even if we don't want some people to have more privilege than others, saying the words "I have privilege" without taking more significant action can further entrench power imbalances. Sometimes when we say, "I have privilege" (or "I'm so blessed"), we don't mean, "Let's go change the world and make it so everyone has privilege." In other words, we don't mean, "Let's go make the word *privilege* obsolete." We mean, "I'm such a cosmic darling; thank goodness, I wasn't born like those people over there."

Even when we are trying to expose domination, domination still tries to find ways to hang on to its imbalance of power. It uses every possible means to make itself look good while clinging to its own internal sickness.

So how do we call power imbalance into account and also work for meaningful change? How do we confront domination and make it share without using force, or violence?

How do we overcome domination without using domination?

The only effective way to deal with domination must include three important steps. First, we need to disarm domination by identifying it. Then we need to create and model better ways of sharing power. And third, we need to change our larger systems so that power sharing is encouraged and protected over the long term.

Identifying Domination

Domination has to be identified in order to be disarmed. But it hates being identified. It will often rail against being identified; it will twist everything around on its head to make itself look good. Sometimes being identified even makes it stronger. Here are some practical ways we can deal with this challenge.

- **Speaking truth to power.** Speaking truth to power—a phrase used in human rights advocacy—is a perfect example of calling out domination. To illustrate what this looks like, let's explore the story of a derelict sea captain and a medal for bravery.

  Captain Pia Klemp has spent several years in the Mediterranean Sea, rescuing thousands of immigrants and refugees who were stranded and could not make it safely to shore. Her actions have been considered criminal in some European countries, and she has been threatened with a twenty-year sentence in Italy for assisting people who seek illegal passage.

  In 2019, the City of Paris decided to award her the prestigious Grand Vermeil Medal for bravery. Instead of claiming her award, Captain Pia formally rejected it with a scathing open letter written directly to the mayor of Paris:

  > Your police [steal] blankets from people that you force to live on the streets, while you raid protests and criminalize people that are standing up for rights of migrants and asylum seekers. . . . You want to give me a medal for actions that you fight in your own ramparts. . . . It is time we call out hypocrite honorings and fill the void with social justice.[21]

  The botched award made international news. Captain Pia weighed her personal power in the fight against domination and realized that rejecting this award was the loudest thing she could do to advocate for change.

  Sometimes speaking truth to power means rejecting benevolence and refusing to play by its niceties. We don't have to do this in a vulgar or mean way; as in Captain Pia's example, we can forcefully and articulately advocate for our cause while maintaining our own credibility and dignity. This is a great example of flipping the narrative of power and using domination-driven opportunities to speak on behalf of those whose voices have been silenced.

- **Laughter and satire.** Another vital tool in the fight against domination is laughter. Laughter helps us tell unpalatable truths and shed light on the absurd. From ancient times, court jesters have been the people who could say things in the presence of power that would get anyone else into trouble. Jesters got away with speaking truth to power because they could make people laugh, and it softened the blow. Today many comics play this role of using laughter to talk about "unspeakable" social, cultural, and political situations. Like the story of the emperor's new clothes, sometimes childlike laughter is the very thing needed to unravel lies that we are all pressured to buy into. We shouldn't underestimate laughter as a key social tool for addressing power imbalances.

  When we use laughter to challenge domination, it's important to make sure we are doing it in a way that maintains our credibility. We need to be as clever and as accurate as we can, avoiding pettiness and personal attacks that might make our people cheer us on but completely alienate those who disagree with us. An incredible ability of laughter is to unearth folly and wrongdoing and get our opponents to see the error of their ways. While sometimes the truths being told through comedy are too unpalatable even to laugh at, ideally, we hope give our opponents a chance to laugh with us so we can find our way back to each other. Comedy, theater, and satire are mediums we need to protect if we are to keep domination in check.

- **Public demonstrations.** There are many forms of public demonstration, which often get conflated, so let's take some time to learn the differences.[22]

  Nonviolent resistance (also called nonviolent action or civil resistance) is a form of protest that seeks maximum public attention while following all laws and avoiding any harm. The idea behind it is to disrupt cycles of violence—to be so peaceful and above reproach that protestors embarrass any domination force that would try to oppose them. For many decades and for many causes, from India's fight for independence, to the US civil rights movement, to ending South African apartheid, to protesting the Keystone Pipeline at Standing Rock, nonviolent resistance has been used to raise a huge red flag about the presence of domination. It takes many different forms, including sit-ins, marches, and any form of peaceful and law-abiding demonstration.

Nonviolent resistance is quite different from *civil disobedience*. Civil disobedience is refusal to comply with certain laws or rules of society to make a point that those laws or governments are corrupt. Some consider it the highest honor of the law to disobey bad laws. Henry David Thoreau claimed it is our duty to disobey when laws are wrong, so we don't become guilty of supporting injustice.[23] Nonviolent civil disobedience may include actions like illegally shutting down transit systems, staging school walkouts, and refusing to pay certain taxes.

Finally, *uncivil disobedience* is considered any form of protest that is violent or non-pacifist, though "violent" is a bit of a misnomer. Most uncivil disobedience seeks to prevent harm to living beings but is willing to violate what are considered "serious" boundaries or laws to make a point. Uncivil disobedience is the category into which destruction of property falls.[24] The Boston Tea Party, where colonists illegally dumped British tea into the Boston Harbor to protest unfair taxes, is a famous example of uncivil disobedience.

The success of protest is often measured by how much attention it is able to garner. There is a huge and ongoing debate about how to protest effectively and ethically, especially in a sensationalized media culture where peaceful resistance has become common and is often under threat of being ignored. For any form of protest you might use, carefully plan for the gains versus the costs and who will pay them. It is a good idea to consider clever and creative alternatives to any form of violence or destruction in order to find one that might have a similar impact as far as gaining attention but prevent damage from being incurred.

There are countless creative ways to confront domination, and every situation might require something different. Sometimes it's best to speak softly. Sometimes it's best to make a scene. There's no single answer.

Whatever means we choose, remember to be powerful and brave and articulate, but resist using domination in return. It's not only the message that matters; our methods are crucial. Trying to out-dominate domination only feeds domination; fighting violence with violence begets violence; cruelty begets cruelty.

The best way to confront domination in any capacity is to use strong, utterly empathetic, full-bodied arguments (see chapter 8) that state clearly what's at stake without personally attacking or demeaning others. As soon as we use personal attacks, we are using domination. Values like graciousness, ethics, dignity, and true compassion are things domination is allergic to. These are values that stand the test of time, values that show our cause to be righteous. In the many ways we shed light on the fact that domination fails to share power and fails to recognize the dignity of all, we must embody dignifying actions and language. If we don't, we side with domination, perpetuate its corruption, and destroy our credibility in working toward positive change.

Creating and Modeling Power Sharing

Humans learn through modeling. When we come out of the womb, we don't come out with little reading glasses and textbooks called *How to Be a Human*. We learn through watching other people do things like walk, talk, connect, and love.

If someone has known only domination, it doesn't really work to tell them, "Hey, you! Stop using domination." That person often doesn't know any other way to be in the world.

The only way to learn something different from domination is to either invent it or see it modeled. That takes a lot of creativity and patience, but creating or modeling is the only way for us to internalize another way of being.

Internalizing the idea of power sharing transforms us from the inside. It gives us an opportunity to see and practice power the new way. We should be teaching power sharing in our families, schools, places of work, religious communities, and civic centers. We should be giving ourselves opportunities to practice and make mistakes as we learn to collaborate against domination.

This kind of creativity often comes with risk. The following story tells of someone who risked their livelihood to share power.

There once was a man named Dennis, who helped found an electricity company. When the company started in the 1980s, it was common to run businesses according to a military-style hierarchical model where the people at the top were considered important and the people at the bottom were not. Springing from the grind of the Industrial Revolution, the "little guys" in the company were seen as mere cogs in a large, well-oiled machine. They were the expendable "human resources," expected to keep their heads down and obey.

Dennis watched workers slouch to work every morning, seeming to lack a sense of vitality at best, and at worst seeming outright miserable. It didn't seem fair to Dennis that executives were the only people allowed to enjoy their jobs and bring the full measure of their talents to work every day. It didn't feel right to sit in his ivory tower and have fun running a company while thousands of dispirited people "below" him would labor under a burden of drudgery. It felt demeaning and dehumanizing.

Inspired by his faith and upbringing on his family's farm, Dennis gathered a team of people and led a conversation about what kind of workplace they wanted. The word *fun* came up over and over, but not referring to the kind of fun associated with office pranks and Friday-night beers. The desire that emerged was that employees wanted a workplace where work itself would feel energizing and meaningful. Dennis started asking questions like "What would give all of my employees a sense of meaning?" His hunch was that when people feel a greater sense of power, work becomes more energizing and engaging, and this would create joy.

Dennis realized that in order to pursue this dream, he needed to invent some new ways to share power.

First, Dennis decided to reframe success for himself. Instead of a domination model of success that hoards all the important decision-making power, he decided he would consider himself successful if he made only a few important decisions a year. For him, being a great leader began to mean both delegating and sharing credit.

Then Dennis decided to reframe success for his entire company. He decided he would not just measure his company's worth by shareholder profits. Instead, he would measure worth by whether or not his company was a place where people were happy in their jobs. Profits would be secondary to the health of the corporate culture.

Next, he initiated a huge shift in company equality. He started to welcome people's ideas to make the company better. He let his employees know that anyone, regardless of status or position, could make a decision at any level of importance, so long as they did their research and presented it to the rest of the company for a vote. In other words, even a janitor who noticed the company needed a new machine could propose a major change or purchase.

To increase communication for these new ideas, Dennis realized he needed to have more contact with his workers. He removed middle managers and barriers that protected a strict hierarchy, making his organization flatter. Instead of avoiding his workers, he started interacting with them and accessed new and important information about all levels of the company.

As Dennis developed better relationships with his workers, he realized that many of the "little guys" had been locked into hourly paying jobs their whole lives. They often had to make difficult decisions about working nights, weekends, and holidays. This often came with a sense of shame and powerlessness, as they had to choose between family time and financial needs. He decided to give hourly workers the option to go on salary with benefits and stock options. He hoped this would create better income security and personal dignity.

While he was making these changes, Dennis didn't know what would happen. It was possible that these changes would lead to failure, and he would lose his company.

In fact, the result of all this risk taking was that employees got excited. Not only did they appreciate being appreciated and being trusted with big decisions, they were more invested, more engaged, and more alive. They voiced a greater sense of worth. They took more pride in their work. Employee turnover went down, as happy workers were less likely to leave. With so many decisions made by those with eyes and ears on the ground, the company avoided foolish overspending and unethical business moves. Within ten years, over 90 percent of the company's 40,000 workers had proudly chosen to become salaried. With such a healthy work environment, company productivity rose higher than thought possible. This created record long-term profits.

Dennis got to see firsthand that humans respond amazingly well to the basic justice of sharing power. His employees knew they mattered. They knew it because they understood that Dennis wasn't doing all of this just to make more money. He was doing this because he believed sharing power is the right thing to do. He believed that getting rid of domination is the secret to unlocking incredible health, creativity, and meaning.

Dennis Bakke's book about this experience, *Joy at Work*, has become a staple in business schools, teaching the power of equality in workplaces.[25] This story is an example of how modeling power sharing is vital to overcoming domination.

We can't just tell people what *not* to do. We have to show new ways of sharing power. If we don't have any models to follow, it's our responsibility to create them.

Fixing Systems

Once we call out domination and create and model new ways to share power, the ultimate goal is to address our systems that harbor domination and don't share power. The rules we create for ourselves, the rules we live by, can either help or hinder domination. Therefore, we need to take a good hard look at our systems of economics, education, criminal justice, business, city planning, politics, legislation and policy, medicine, media, earth care, human rights, and many others. It is possible to make these systems work better on behalf of us all, to make equality and power sharing the law of the land. It is possible to build a culture and a society that are more just, protecting many voices and many views.

What changes will we need to make to encourage using power in healthier ways? We owe it to ourselves and future generations to ask such questions.

Okay, but Whose Job Is It?

A while back, I was out watching a ball game and eating nachos with a couple of good friends, Jonas and Shelly. Jonas made a joke about one of the players needing to "lift up his skirts" so he could score points, implying the player was a weak girl.

Shelly looked straight at him and spit out the words "You're a misogynist." She seemed to be seething with resentment.

Wow, was it awkward.

On the one hand, Shelly was right: Jonas had made a bad joke. As a woman, I felt diminished by that joke. I don't know why Jonas said that. He is generally a good-hearted person and tries not to be a jerk. If Shelly had calmly explained to Jonas what bothered her about what he said, I'm sure he would have apologized and stopped making jokes like that. In my opinion, he's not a misogynist. He is usually highly respectful of women.

When Shelly snapped, it seemed like such an unnecessary and off-putting confrontation. I could sense Jonas getting defensive and shutting down. Sadly, their friendship didn't last long after that.

Maybe Shelly was sick of those kinds of jokes. Maybe she was tired of being a pushover and was finally standing up for herself the only way she knew how, and perhaps she overcompensated a little. Maybe she was having a terrible day. But with that one comment, Shelly lit a match and burned down a relationship that had taken years to build. If she had explained her feelings calmly, Jonas probably would have been receptive. She could have been a teacher, but instead she took a path of immediate gratification.

On the other hand, before you think I am telling women not to stand up for themselves, let's look at the situation with a lens of social responsibility.

How much patience should Shelly need to have with these kinds of statements? There are only so many "Oh, I was only joking" comments people can put up with before enough is enough. There are also only so many Bobs hitting your car that one person should have to endure in the world. How much tolerance for jackassery should less powerful people have to have?

In other words, whose job is it to regulate domination?

The less power someone has, the less they should have to be the one to have to fight for their rights. Less powerful people regulate domination only when they feel they have to. No one wants to have to say, "Hey, you hit my car! Please make it right!"

If Bob hits your car, it is Bob's job to call the insurance company and take responsibility. It is Bob's job to acknowledge the damage and do the right thing. It is Jonas's responsibility to consider the consequences of his words, not Shelly's job to educate him and keep him in line.

The more power you have, the higher your responsibility to regulate domination.

That's really hard to do, because domination has a nasty habit of not looking at itself.

I still forget about the dangers of domination sometimes. Though I grew up in a humble, lower-middle-class home and certainly know what it's like not to have enough, I can be kind of a loudmouth, unabashedly extroverted. I have caring parents who went to great lengths to put me through school, and my mother is so supportive she calls me her "shining star." I am a white woman, an author and business owner, and I have an advanced degree. While I am not wealthy by any means, and I've had to work hard, it's fair to say that in the context of my culture I have personality, family support system, ability, education, and political and socioeconomic power, including white privilege, to name a few.

If power is the ability to effect change in the world, I feel society ascribes to me a quite fair amount—certainly more than the average person globally. For those of us who grapple with privilege, the question that naturally follows is, "So what now? Should I feel guilty about the power I have?"

Before I address this question, let's zoom out on the larger picture.

When I began to learn about the history of my power, I began to realize that it has been generated at immense cost. My parents and grandparents sacrificed in creating a healthy family and saving every penny to give me a better life. My ancestors made sacrifices to emigrate from Europe in desperate circumstances, enabling me to have more opportunity. The sacrifices of innovators and businesspeople and scientists who took risks to build an economy mean I can enjoy unprecedented prosperity and technological advance. The sacrifices of women activists got me the rights to vote, own property, and have agency. The sacrifices of underpaid laborers who work tireless hours and thankless jobs make it is possible for me to have safe sanitation and inexpensive vegetables. The sacrifices of those who create and protect our nation's laws and freedoms benefit me. The sacrifices of teachers built school systems that I could grow within.

And with great heartache, I recognize the sacrifice of bodies: the forced labor and terror endured by slaves who built the physical and economic infrastructure of my country; the native peoples who were brutally cleared from their lands so my ancestors could settle it; the children and sweatshop laborers who are denied education and opportunity and work themselves to the bone so I can buy a three-dollar T-shirt; the refugees being displaced because deforestation and oil wars fill my house with furniture and my car with fuel. And on. And on. And on.

Did I personally ask or force any of these people to make any of these sacrifices? No. And yet I benefit from every single one. Any power I have emerges from the context of all of these other lives.

Any power I have been granted is way, way, way bigger than I. It's not "mine."

Choosing to move beyond guilt, I bow beneath the gravity of everything I have inherited. I take responsibility for the sins of the past. I make a promise to share my power so that future generations can know a world without domination—a world where equality and opportunity truly exist for all.

What does this promise look like in my day-to-day life? It means recognizing that since I am someone with a lot of power, it is scary-easy for me to walk into a room and use domination, gobbling up space that should belong to others. As I am someone socially granted a high degree of power, it is considered "normal" for me to speak loudly and freely while not having to listen to or learn from or see others. In any given situation, I can either amass power or share it; I can either smash Community or build Community. So I keep my eyes open. I practice the wisdom of knowing when to speak out and when to be silent.

If you think you have tendencies toward domination, it doesn't mean you are inherently a bad person. You've probably been taught that domination is your friend. If you've had a buddy-buddy relationship with domination, it means that you have more responsibility to learn how your power operates, where it comes from, and how it affects others. You are responsible to know the history of your power and why you have it. You are responsible to tell the truth and not deny ways you benefit from power imbalances. You are responsible to own the consequences that follow when you exercise your power.

And instead of trying to destroy power or even "use your power for good," you are responsible to do the thing that domination hates most: you are responsible to look for ways to share power, to create balance and equality, in big and small ways.

How do we share power? Here are a few ideas:

- Believe the best about people when they share their experiences of powerlessness.

- When you hold a microphone or are given the spotlight, invite others up and ask them to speak. Let people speak for themselves, unless they are physically unable to do so.

- Stick up for people who aren't being heard. Try to figure out why they aren't being heard. Build a relationship of equality with them, even if it's uncomfortable.

- Confront people who are spreading ideas that some people in this world are less valuable or less human. Work to take responsibility and authority away from people using domination, because people hoarding power are destroying others and themselves.

- When you give and help, give and help in ways that encourage the dignity and power of others. Give and help in trusting ways that put others in control of their own destiny.

- Be willing to look at ways your big power means that others have less.

- Consider how your norms, or sense of what's "normal," might not be the only norms worth taking seriously or giving rights to.

- When you come into conflict or difficult conversations, try to be the last to speak. Make sure everyone has the same amount of conversational "space." If someone seems to have less space than others, invite them to take up more space.

- Create ways to be the humble and secret champion of the less powerful. Help people climb the ladder and improve their situations without controlling their fate or expecting recognition.

- Understand how systems and institutions perpetuate domination. Use your voice, your habits of consumption and purchasing, your donations, your time, and your vote to fix those systems and make them more just.

Moving Forward

Power matters in conflict and impasse because the way it's wielded can lead to either justice or injustice, either peace or chaos. Wherever domination is present, injustice follows in its wake. In such cases, it is right and natural to protest, to explore the conflict that may arise. Especially when conflicts arise from power imbalances, it's imperative that we don't rush to a quick or cheap resolution. We need to understand what is actually causing the injustice; we need to understand how power is operating under the surface of conflict.

If you would like to think more deeply about the power you wield in the world, consider completing the Flower of Power exercise in the graphic at the end of this chapter. Tools like this can help us wrap our minds around

what kinds of power we have at our disposal and where we might be susceptible to domination.

If you don't have a lot of power in this world, you are probably well
versed in addressing power imbalances. If you take anything out of this
chapter, take this: It shouldn't be your job to fight for your rights. If you
choose to fight for yourself and others, that's great. But no one will fault
you for getting tired and overwhelmed sometimes. For the work that you
choose to engage in the fight against domination, thank you. The world
needs your testimony and perspective.

If you do have a lot of power in this world, to the point of being vulnerable
to using domination, I say this in all sincerity: though you may have won a
kind of genetic and social lottery, consider that those "winnings" don't belong
to you, even if you feel you have earned them. Those winnings are largely social
inventions, arising from much larger histories, and have an impact on us all.
Power imbalances come from somewhere and are often reinforced by systems
that cause pain and suffering. Someone always pays the price for domination
to exist. If you have more power, that usually means someone else in the world
has less. As you wrestle with this, remember that having a lot of power doesn't
mean you are bad or condemned. Don't get sidetracked by shame. Remember
that the more power you have, the more tremendous your responsibility to
call out domination, model new and creative ways of sharing power, and use
your power to fix broken systems that harbor injustice. Please don't waste that
chance. Grab the full faculties of your imagination, and get to work.

THE FLOWER OF POWER
— HOW VULNERABLE ARE YOU TO DOMINATION? —

ABLENESS
Are you a physically able-bodied person? Are you free of physical and mental health issues that make life complicated or challenging?

PERSONALITY
How powerful is your personality? Do people naturally defer to you? How "loud" is your voice?

TENACITY
How strong is your drive and work ethic to affect change? Do you have willpower and grit to overcome challenges?

RACE / ETHNICITY
Do you have racial or ethnic identity that is respected, or do you experience discrimination?

SUPPORT SYSTEM
How strong are your relationships with friends and family? Do they have your back and help you when you need help?

GENDER / SEXUAL ORIENTATION
Do you have a gender/sexual identity that is respected, or do you experience discrimination?

EDUCATION
Did you have access to good education? Do you have any degree or special training?

POLITICAL SWAY
Is your political party in power? How much do your political voice and actions count?

TITLE
What kind of occupation do you have? Is it highly respected or less respected?

ECONOMIC STATUS
How much wealth do you have to extend if you want to affect change? How easy is your life from a resource perspective?

INSTRUCTIONS

1. SHADE EACH PETAL FOR HOW YOU SEE YOURSELF

3 = lots of power   2 = average power   1 = little power   0 = powerless

2. ADD UP YOUR TOTAL

20 points or more   You are highly vulnerable to domination. You have the biggest responsibility to rein it in and actively look for ways to share power.

10 – 20 points: You are sometimes vulnerable to domination, but you also know what it's like to have domination wielded against you. You have a unique opportunity to disarm domination because you probably know it from both sides.

10 points or less: You are probably well versed in dealing with domination, and have a lot to teach. Keep up the good work.

Chapter 3 Reflection

1. If you could summarize this chapter in five words, what would they be, and why?

2. In what ways did this chapter challenge or reinforce the ways you think about power?

3. What do you think about the idea that conflict and power are closely related? Have you ever seen power play out in an interesting way during a conflict?

4. What masks of domination are the hardest for you to spot and confront? What are the easiest?

5. Have you ever experienced a time when someone used domination or when someone could have used their power well but didn't? What was it like? What about a time when you saw someone share power well? What were the effects?

6. What does your Flower of Power look like? How does it feel to share this with someone? Why do you think you feel this way?

7. What's the history of your power? Where does it come from? Who sacrificed to give you the power you have? Knowing this story, does it change the way you see your power?

8. What are ways you could better share power in your day-to-day life? What about ways you can work to share power in our larger society?

Part II

ENGAGING IMPASSE

- A case for why we need disagreement and how to disagree well

- Navigating tough emotions that come with impasse

- Tools for learning how to ask great questions

CHAPTER 4
Why We Need Disagreement
Leaping from the Trapeze

For two years, I cohosted a podcast on faith and culture called *Irenicast*, working under the name Mona. My cohosts and I had serious fun on this show, recording over one hundred episodes.

The thrill of being on air, sipping coffee, making corny jokes, and getting into wonderfully deep conversations was unlike any other experience.

We received a lot of positive feedback about the show, but one key criticism came up repeatedly: "You guys agree too much." Each time this issue came up, I laughed, thinking, "Look how smart and great we are. We are so unified."

Then the 2016 election hit, and many people including myself quickly realized we had been engrossed in a giant media bubble—a dangerous media bubble.

In my small way, I helped create the bubble. I'd had opportunities to invite guests onto the show who believed differently than I did. I could have engaged more diverse conversations and let myself be challenged. I could have facilitated more realistic conversation. But I actively chose not to.

Coming to terms with this put me into a tailspin. Why did I make those choices? In hindsight, I suppose I was afraid I wouldn't be able to defend my opinions. I was afraid of being made to look foolish. I didn't want to deal with disagreement. I associated disagreement with conflict, fear, and disappointment. It was too hard to engage.

Feeling empty and lost, I resigned from the show.

Perhaps few would fault me for not sharing the microphone, but in light of the new political landscape, I felt like I was part of the problem. I realized I had embraced the kind of intellectual hubris that would recognize only my own perspectives as valid.

I had missed something important: I missed the value of disagreement.

Since 2016, I have been exploring disagreement and the vital role it plays in shaping our ideas and relationships. I began to forge a different relationship with disagreement. I began to dream about replacing polarized ideological bubbles with vibrant communities that are strong instead of fragile—communities that can hold and sustain awkward and uncomfortable difference. I began to dream of communities that refuse to participate in shaming and shut-down culture, communities that have skills to handle disagreement in healthy, mutually beneficial ways.

In this chapter, I am going to try to convince you that we need disagreement. Feel free to disagree.

Four Reasons Why We Need Disagreement

Many of us don't know how to disagree well. We may even have a weird or even anxiety-laden relationship with conflict. And why should it be any different? If we don't grow up with healthy ways of dealing with conflict in our families, and if our role models only show us happy la-la harmony and don't show us how to really dig in and disagree, then where else do we learn?

Television and movies, probably. The thing is, conflict in entertainment is not only designed for a specific purpose (to move a story along), but also sensationalized; it's bigger and at the same time less complex than real life. For example, it might be comfortable for many of us to watch actors who play strangers yell at each other on set in a coffee shop, but in real life, strangers rarely yell at each other in a coffee shop. It would be super weird and extreme if that actually happened. The point is that conflict in entertainment is created to serve the entertainment and is often purposefully exaggerated. It is unreality, on many levels.

If we find that we are "bad" at conflict and if we lack important skills of navigating it, it's probably not our fault. We've had terrible examples. Significantly, we don't really get ways to practice conflict safely. And if disagreement has meant violence in our past, we may even experience physiological distress when it comes our way.

No wonder many of us find disagreement stressful, awkward, or even horrible.

Let's hold our realities, appreciate their weight, and then set them aside for a minute to consider a simple thought: Perhaps the models of disagreement we inherited are flawed. Perhaps disagreement is not inherently bad but actually plays an important role in our lives.

Here are four reasons why that might be true.

Disagreement Makes Us More Courageous

A while back, I posted on social media, "If you fear dissent, your ideas aren't strong enough." A friend of mine jumped on the thread and wrote, "I disagree," outlining some points of counterargument.

I'm a little ashamed to say that my first instinct was to be angry. I almost ignored her comment, but then I laughed at myself. My very idea claimed that dissent, a type of political disagreement, was good! So instead of shutting her down, I began my reply with, "Hey, thanks for disagreeing with me."

It felt strange—almost shocking—to say, "Thanks for disagreeing." It's uncommon to hear gratitude when someone disagrees. So often, disagreement is a threat. But the simple act of thanks paints disagreement in a totally new light.

Perhaps disagreement is the highest compliment. When someone takes the time to disagree, they didn't have to. They could have gone about their merry way, worrying about other things. They could have stayed silent in fear of rejection. They could have called names or acted out in anger.

Instead, they took the time to engage us and our ideas. That takes courage!

Disagreeing well always involves a level of risk. When someone disagrees without personal attacks, abuse, or name-calling, they are hoping the other party will engage them back and not attack or call them names. This exchange is tenuous and amazing, like two flying-trapeze artists jumping through the air, each trusting that their fellow artist will catch them.

Obviously, not all disagreement is done in healthy ways. Sometimes it's hostile and alienating. These days, anyone who sticks their neck out to talk about politics online, for example, might have a story about being verbally accosted. That kind of disagreement is not very productive; it just makes people hunker down in their trenches.

However, when disagreement has a posture of respect, power sharing, and truth telling, it's a deeply beautiful exchange.

When someone disagrees with us well, they are offering a kind of gift. The disagree-er is making time for us. They are investing, going out on a limb. It's an utterly vulnerable act. If someone disagrees, they are regarding their audience as a worthy conversation partner and opening up important lines of communication.

So perhaps the next time someone takes the time to disagree courageously, respectfully, and passionately, we can begin to recognize that behavior as a meaningful interaction, not a threatening one. Instead of reacting angrily or getting defensive, our courageous response can be "I see you, and I value the time and energy you are offering. I see the gift. Thank you."

Disagreement Makes Relationships Durable

Have you ever tried to use a rubber band that snapped and broke the moment you stretched it?

Rubber bands are useful to us only if their elastic is strong. If they dry out and break, they are no longer fulfilling their intended purpose.

Relationships are like this. Fragile relationships, or relationships that can't take the weight and stretching of disagreement, are like dried-out rubber bands. They aren't much help to us.

Most of us have experienced a walking-on-eggshells situation, where disagreement feels fundamentally off-limits. This usually comes with a sense of anxiety that if disagreement happens, the relationship could collapse at any moment. Fragile relationships can make us feel isolated and lonely, because we sense deep down that the bonds that are supposed to hold us might snap or dissolve under pressure. Fragile relationships do not make for a healthy support system.

If relationships can't be tested by conflict and disagreement—if we never get to see them stretched and bouncing back—we can't know where we stand with each other; we can't know that we are valued. Even if someone says, "You matter to me," if we have not seen that claim put to the test, we don't really trust that that person will stick with us through thick and thin. So we settle for brittle ties that come with insecurity and fear.

Resilient relationships are not forged by simply finding nice people to spend time with. Resilient relationships are forged when we are at odds, when we have to stretch for each other. Disagreement tests and solidifies our bonds and helps us get closer.

Actively caring about other people within disagreement is where Community happens.

Without disagreement, we don't have solid ground. We just have a pile of eggshells and broken feet.

Disagreement Makes Communities Healthier

Engaging disagreement can create unusual yet complementary bonds across difference.

Take, for example, my friend Cara. Cara is an extreme introvert, a super empath, meaning that she constantly absorbs all the emotional energy around her. She is one of the kindest and most considerate people I've ever met. Cara has told me that for much her life, interacting with other people has felt draining.

I, in contrast, am super extroverted. When I meet someone, my brain is racing around like a manic puppy, thinking, "New friend? *New friend???*"

By all accounts, Cara and I should not really click. We fundamentally disagree about whether people are or aren't threatening and draining. That's a pretty significant divergence.

Early in our friendship, we were able to identify something that helps us honor each other and value our relationship. Cara often experiences a high level of personal awkwardness in social situations. She is so sensitive to the energy around her all the time that a comment that feels mildly uncomfortable to me would feel painfully awkward to her. The situation would make her want to hide under a rock. I, in contrast, can be horribly brash and stampede through social situations without care. Cara's superpower is her consideration of others. My superpower is being able to walk into any room and feel comfortable. Cara's greatest weakness is being subject to awkwardness and debilitating shyness. My greatest weakness is lacking social grace and concern for others. Do you see where this is going? I need Cara's conscientiousness. She needs my ability to defray tension. She is my Consideration Hero, and I am her Awkwardness Shield. Our superpowers combined make us both stronger.

* * *

But what about differences that don't seem to connect—that don't seem complementary? When we get out of Pollyanna territory, sometimes we can't make heads or tails of disagreement. Our innate drive for resolution can lead us to seek conformity over "senseless" differences.

Let's consider cases where the lack of difference indicates danger.

In the 1930s, the United States was grappling with overfarming, erratic weather patterns, and mass soil erosion commonly referred to as the Dust Bowl. The US government decided to make a big push to revitalize the soil by encouraging farmers to plant a hearty species of plant called Japanese arrowroot. Tough and drought resistant, with trailing vines and beautiful purple flowers, it was marketed as the next great thing for farming and landscaping alike. Unfortunately, Japanese arrowroot was so hardy that it aggressively took over. It climbed over telephone poles and trees and houses and mountainsides. Once established, it was impossible to get rid of. Today, this vine, known as "kudzu," has been nicknamed "the plant that ate the South." From Texas to

Virginia are hundreds of miles of roadside stretches where kudzu is literally the only plant you will see, covering everything in the landscape to the point where highways look like they've been surrounded by sleeping green giants. The irresponsible introduction of this one little vine put hundreds of native species at risk, compromised ecosystems, and forever changed the beauty and biodiversity of the southern states.

In the natural world, when one type of creature takes over an ecosystem, the entire system gets out of whack. That creature might not have meant any harm. Kudzu isn't a bad or evil plant on its own. But its tendency to take over, its tendency to dominate and wipe out competition, prevents other creatures from thriving. For these reasons, the mere sight of kudzu fills many southerners with a great sense of loss.[26]

In other words, erasing difference is dangerous. It can even lead to death. In DNA, when any species lacks diversity in its gene pool and too many of the same individuals interbreed, harmful mutations and even extinction can follow. It's the same in our bodies. If we were to eat french fries and only french fries for every meal, we would eventually die of malnutrition. And it's the same in our markets. If a company becomes a monopoly and competition ceases, prices get out of whack; one unhealthy market has a negative impact on other markets, and the entire economy is worse off.

Over and over, our world teaches us that difference is good and right. Variety is not the spice of life. It is the meat and bones, the very thing that keeps us alive.

When it comes to healthy communities, humans also need difference. We need a wide range of other people and ideas to keep us balanced and healthy. When one idea or one type of person sweeps in and (intentionally or unintentionally) demands conformity; starts to police our thoughts, words, and feelings; or does anything else to try to erase difference and its associated freedoms like freedom of thought or freedom of expression, our communities fail to thrive.

Just as no creature in the natural world can exist without other plants and animals, no person is fully self-sufficient in our own understandings. We need difference. We need to engage difference deeply and broadly. We need to actively protect difference.

When we grapple with perspectives that are not our own, we gain wisdom, facts, stories, and ideas that not only strengthen us, but balance us.

Even if, within that difference, we find a painful impasse that we can't resolve, the process of appreciating difference helps us build better families, schools, businesses, governments, communities, and ultimately, better selves.

Disagreement Makes Ideas Stronger

When someone disagrees with us, it creates a space for discourse. Discourse is a specific type of conversation where differing opinions can be fairly weighted, challenged, and refined. In other words, discourse is like a mental gym; it's the space we create for working out in our minds. Disagreement is the resistance the weights provide—working our intellectual muscles, making our opinions stronger through a process of testing and refinement.

What, exactly, is an opinion? It's a familiar word, but hard to define.

There once was a point, in junior high, when I thought it was super cool to wear fruit stickers on my face. Every day I would collect fruit stickers from the oranges, apples, and bananas in my friends' lunches and wear them on my face. I also wore sunglasses with the lenses popped out way before the hipsters made that a thing. Back then, I didn't know the fancy French term *avant-garde*, I just did it because I wanted to. I embraced weirdness as only a prepubescent teen could.

My teachers begged me to stop putting the stickers on my face. It went on for months.

I suppose something inside me felt that breaking the mold in such a playful way tapped into some profound meaning of what it was to be human and alive. I still can't name that thing, whatever it was. Today, I miss the carefree, nothing-to-lose, no-one-to-impress, live-by-your-gut way of being in the world. Now as an adult, that's much harder to tap into.

Yes, there is a point to this story; stay with me.

What is an opinion? An opinion is a truth (lowercase *t*) told from one perspective. It is an extension of our core beliefs about the way the world works, built on top of all the facts, understanding, experiences, and assumptions we have ever known. Opinions are not necessarily provable or ultimate for all people for all time. In fact, they are usually hard to prove, but at the same time, they help us make sense of the world. They justify our actions and aesthetics. In other words, opinions help us express what we find good and beautiful—and cool.

Our opinions often come at the cost of precious time and energy. We form our opinions after studying, watching the news, living life, and hearing stories. We inherit them from our family and friends and the places we have lived. We even grab them randomly from other people's lunch boxes. We get wrapped up in our opinions; if we feel like we have found really good ones, we can even fall in love with them.

This is exactly why we should welcome disagreement. Because when someone takes the time to disagree with our opinions, they are giving us chances to test our opinions and even to talk more about them. What a great opportunity!

For most people, though, this isn't so rosy. Disagreement is hard to navigate because we all hold tightly to our opinions. It takes vulnerability and bravery to explore and test them.

There are many reasons why having our opinions challenged feels so threatening. Let's explore two.

First, we get attached to our opinions. We form emotional bonds with them. This is because our opinions arise from our experiences, beliefs, values, and assumptions about the world—which are packed with emotion and identity. A lot of people tried to get me to take those fruit stickers off my face. I was in love with my own cleverness, my own idea about how to live. I did not appreciate efforts to quell my spirit. When someone disagrees with our opinions, it can feel like they are attacking us, and it's hard not to take it personally. In addition, while on the surface someone might disagree with my opinions, they may actually be challenging my underlying values and beliefs—the things I hold dear and sacred in the world, the things I choose to accept or reject as moral, ethical, true, or beautiful. When our values are challenged in discourse, it can feel like an all-out assault on the very core of who we are.

The second reason it's hard to weigh opinions is that most of us are taught that smart, competent, healthy people don't change their mind very often; "healthy" people play by the rules. "Healthy" people have stable world views, not fickle ones. "Healthy" people are always right and never wrong; they don't grow or evolve or experiment. I believe this is the reason my fruit stickers bothered people so much, even though they weren't hurting anyone. Our collective desire for stability springs from that ancient existential fear of anomie, or chaos. From an early age, we are taught to believe that our societies will not be stable if people break social rules or are constantly changing their minds about things. Having stable ideas about the world supposedly allows us to make decisions and count on each other.

But what if this is a myth?

What if strong and reliable people are the *most* likely to change their minds, because their thirst for truth outpaces their fears? What if, instead of holding our opinions in a clenched fist, we hold them with an open palm, letting trusted conversation partners pick them up, feel their weight, examine them, and point out flaws we didn't see? This is not a sign of hating our opinions. It is sign of loving truth.

In the end, we might decide to keep the fruit stickers on our face; we might choose to keep our opinions. But when we let people challenge our fruit stickers, we grab opportunities to have wonderful conversations about aesthetics, human nature, values, beliefs, and even the meaning of life.

Here's some food for thought. Many communities and families have bans on talking about opinions related to politics and religion—two subjects that evoke strong emotions. Maybe these kinds of bans are not serving us. Maybe they are keeping our intellectual muscles weak, causing us to miss opportunities to understand and challenge each other. Maybe we could get good at talking about our opinions if we had more space to practice.

The Problem with "Civility"

At this point in the chapter, it would be so easy to say everyone should just go and disagree civilly, and—*abracadabra!*—we will have high-functioning communities.

While this might be a well-intended sentiment, the word *civil* has some major issues that are worthy of consideration.[27] "Civil discourse" means different things to different people. To some, being civil means something like being nice in public. To others, especially to people of color, the word *civil* evokes a complicated and violent history.

This section may feel intense to some readers, but please stay with it.

When Civility Is a Weapon

On the surface, the word *civil* is shiny and pretty. It may remind us of courtrooms, teacups, and powdered wigs. Dictionary definitions relating the word to "citizens," the "commonwealth," or "good manners" sound downright innocuous. However, history is fraught with examples of this word being weaponized.

For many centuries and in places all around the world, colonizers (people who marched into other people's land or resources and claimed it as their own) have used the word *civil* as a primary weapon of demeaning and punishing native peoples, especially people with darker skin, for their ways of being in the world. Colonizers commonly claimed that colonial ways of life were normal and "civilized," and the ways of life of native peoples—native customs, religion, knowledge, logic, institutions, traditions, government, social rules, language, celebrations, currency, technology, and art—were barbaric or "uncivilized." Colonizers used rules of civility to claim native peoples were "less than," in need of their help, or in need of being controlled, ruled, or mastered.[28]

"Civility" has been especially weaponized by white European Americans against Black American communities. From times of slavery, through Reconstruction, though Jim Crow, through the fight for civil rights, and now in the war on drugs and mass incarceration, black people have been denied human rights, education, economic opportunity, habitable neighborhoods, and access to political voice on the grounds that black people are (presumed to be) naturally less civilized and therefore need to be controlled. In conversations around race today, black voices are often silenced or not taken seriously because of the age-old domination myth that some black communication styles are "uncivil."[29]

Another example of a way the notion of civility has been weaponized is the treatment of Native American peoples. Friends of mine, Adam and Ben, directed an Emmy-winning documentary called *Dawnland*. The film tells the story of a Native American tribe in Maine called the Wabanaki who had a high percentage of their children forcibly taken away by the state. Some of the surviving Wabanaki children didn't know they were Native until later in life; many tell stories of horribly abusive treatment. This is not an isolated incident. In the last century, thousands of Native children have been separated from their families in the United States and Canada under governmental policies that sought to "civilize" new generations of Natives. High percentages of children were placed in foster care or boarding schools and taught to act, dress, pray, and speak as if they were white. They were cut off from their families and traditions in what can arguably called cultural genocide. After many years of pain, the film follows the Wabanaki tribe and the government of Maine seeking justice and healing through the first Truth and Reconciliation Commission on US soil.[30]

Examples like these are a testament to the dangers of civility—what it means and who gets to enforce it. Today, despite the word's troubled past, it's still common to hear *civility* used as a weapon in political conversations, usually with the intent of controlling or shutting down people. For example, if a speaker is exhibiting strong emotions like anger or grief to explain a problem, those who wish to stop the person from speaking might call them uncivil or divisive. If someone who is uneducated or poor doesn't use the "right" words to describe a problem, they might be called undignified or myriad other synonyms for breaking social rules or being "less than."

The word *uncivil* is often lobbed around to strip opponents of credibility, voice, and humanity simply because they aren't playing by the imaginary rules of the powers that be. Many other words are also used to represent civility in this way. *Decent, classy, refined, appropriate, educated,* and *proper* can all refer to not behaving according to arbitrary standards—standards that are commonly beholden to the tastes and preferences of domination culture.

Essayist Hua Hsa describes our present political moment eloquently:

> At its worst, concern for civility is a way to avoid having diffi-
> cult conversations at all. Today, the greatest structural driver
> of the civility wars is the Internet, where these two versions of
> the word collide. In the comparatively decentralized space, we
> have become compelled to take everyone's grievances seriously,
> even when those claims for civility and courteous debate have
> been made in bad faith. And, as the common ground between
> us seems to dwindle, *it has become easier to fixate on incivility*
> *than to reckon with whatever ideas rude language might describe.*
> Interestingly, the new civility troubles those across the polit-
> ical spectrum. For those on the right, civility is political cor-
> rectness by a different name, while those on the left tend to
> see it as a way of silencing dissent. What unites these inter-
> pretations is a shared suspicion that the rules of civility exist
> to preserve our hierarchies. (Emphasis added)[31]

In other words, it can be a cop-out to focus on civility instead of
the harder issues at stake, such as calling domination to account.

"What is civil?" is an incomplete question. The full question, the deeper and
often invisible question, is "*Who gets to decide what is civil?*"

*   *   *

What's at Stake

Before I was a trend-setting sticker wearer, I was a pioneer in entertainment.

When I was nine and my sister was seven, we entered our school
talent show. We put together costumes—neon parachute pants, ski
jackets, and sunglasses—and choreographed a truly cringeworthy
"hip-hop" dance to a motivational song. The chorus went:

> *Who made up the ru-ule*
> *You've got to keep up to be co-ool?*

The bridge of the song repeated, in a horrible Flavor Flav knockoff voice,
"Peer. Pressure. P-p-p-p-peer. Pressure."

We did not win the talent show.[32]

However, the hook of that song stuck with me. Who gets to decide what is decent? Different people define kindness, order, and decency differently.

Why does this matter? Because from the perspective of impasse transformation, both seeing and being seen are highly at stake in (who gets to decide) what is civil.

When Seeing Is a Stake

On the one hand, we might be *failing to see* someone's pain because that person is delivering it in a form that is not palatable to our senses or our definitions of what is normal and decent.

My sophomore year of college, tensions at school were high around race relations. In a courageous move, the school sponsored an assembly where four women of color were invited to speak about their experiences of discrimination on campus. Each woman expressed deep pain, and it seemed like it took a lot to speak out. One of the Latina women explained, with a fair sense of frustration, of anger, that she would not be returning to school in the fall because she had been so disappointed by our community. During her speech, at least a dozen different students in the audience stood up and walked out. Afterward, I heard others say this woman was "too angry," and they shouldn't have had to sit and listen to "that." Students started a Facebook group that was supposed to be a haven for "campus racists," and only when they were caught did they claim it was a joke. People threw food at the women in the cafeteria.

What strikes me about this memory is that none of the women who spoke at the assembly used foul language. They didn't name names. They didn't raise their voices. They were simply sharing their experiences, asking to be seen, and asking for change. Seemingly, even their controlled shows of emotion were interpreted by many as uncivil, and therefore unhearable.

Sometimes, telling the truth or calling for change simply isn't pleasant. Sometimes, truth doesn't fit into civility's constraints.

For those of us who embrace the idea that civility is king, if we care about justice, we need to work hard to resist demanding that someone "shape up" before we will make an effort to hear, understand, or empathize with them. Expecting people to shape up could mean a lot of different things: it could mean that to our ears someone is sounding too educated or not educated enough, too religious or not religious enough, too emotional or not emotional enough, too political or not political enough, too ethnic or not ethnic enough, too moral or not moral enough. Does this mean we should throw all our values out the window and pretend that communication differences don't matter? Of course not. It means that we should carefully weigh the person beneath the words, examining the expectations we carry with us as we listen.

When Being Seen Is a Stake

On the other hand, we might be failing to be seen by the people we want to be in conversation with because we are not taking our listener's needs or long-term consequences into consideration. In this case, we have opportunities to adjust the ways we communicate in order to be more effective with the people we want to engage (not just blow off steam for ourselves, though it is important to make time for blowing off steam). It may not feel like it in the heat of the moment, but we always have a range of options in the ways we choose to get our message across.

Sometimes speakers, activists, or artists strategically choose to use forms of communication that are not palatable, because they want to make a point. They want to send a loud message that we shouldn't have to play by the so-called rules of civility to have our basic human rights respected.

For example, let's say an artist creates paintings for an exhibit about sexism by using paint made out of cow manure. The artist is trying to express the visceral experiences of her reality as a woman. Art critics and anti-sexist groups might laud her, but taking such a strong split from common ideas of decency (manure evokes disgust for most people) might mean that the people she most wants to be in conversation with are probably not going anywhere near that exhibit. In fact, they might claim such an "indecent" exhibit is an example of how feminism is ruining society.

Was that art exhibit provocative? Probably. It is likely to be lauded by critics. Was it effective? It depends on who you ask. Perhaps the goal of art is to be provocative, and in that way it would certainly succeed.

The point is that when we radically depart from "civility," as defined by our intended audience, it's always a risk that we will be cheered on by people who already agree with us and ignored by those we are trying to reach.

Worse, we might even inflict lasting damage. When someone holds up a sign in public that says, "F*** [a political leader]," it might be cathartic for that person in the moment, but in the long run, it is likely to be bridge burning. Holding up that sign is not going to win over hearts and minds. It is antagonistic, punishing, and credibility destroying. There is good reason to believe it fosters resentment.

For those of us who fall into the "buck civility" camp, that's laudable, and there is certainly a place for that kind of work, especially when civility is being used to prop up domination. But we need to figure out what outcomes we really want, think carefully about the long-term consequences of our performativity, and plan for the impact it has on our relationships.[33] As we exercise our power to try to make the world better, we always have the choice to be strategic about the ways we perform.

In Sum: Civility and Impasse

Our relationship with civility is incredibly significant when it comes to impasse. If we choose to engage this idea in any way, we must remember a few key points:

- The word *civility* comes with a host of hidden meanings, many of which are rooted in domination. Understand that this word means different things to different people.

- The rules of what is considered "civil" are not accidents. They come from history and culture. What is considered "normal" or "appropriate" communication is usually determined by the culture most using domination. Someone always gets to decide and enforce civility.

- As a result of the rules of civility, someone is usually silenced.

- As a result of focusing on the rules of civility, we can be missing bigger and more important issues.

For these reasons, instead of using the term *civil discourse*, we might choose to focus instead on "courageous dialogue." Courageous dialogue is the respectful, full-bodied, sharing of hard truths. Courageous dialogue lets people be where they are instead of policing the ways they are being. Courageous dialogue listens to the issues beneath the expression and focuses on true understanding.

When we disagree and meet each other in impasse, each of us has a responsibility to examine and understand the rules we bring to the table so that we can see, be seen, and share power effectively. We are responsible to be aware of our expectations and what we are bringing to the table.

Why is it so important to be aware of our expectations? Because at the very foundations of our thinking and acting in the world, we can hold war in our hearts and not even know it.

War in Our Hearts: Challenging Us-vs.-Them Thinking

> Many people were dying on the other side of the chasm, but Kaladin didn't feel a thing for them. No itch to heal them, no desire to help. Kaladin could thank Hav for that, for training him to think in terms of "us" and "them." ... Protect "us," destroy "them." A soldier had to think like that. So Kaladin hated the Parshendi. They were the enemy. If he hadn't learned to divide his mind like that, war would have destroyed him.
>
> —Brandon Sanderson, *The Way of Kings*

Us-versus-them thinking is a mind-set of warfare. Using this mind-set, we regard our fellow humans as "those people over there"—people who are separate from and oppositional to us, who do not hold a stake in our life in any way and therefore do not have to matter to us. Us-versus-them thinking does not facilitate cooperation or empathy.

Us-versus-them thinking has two faces: covert and overt.

The covert version of us-versus-them is *othering*. To "other" means to consider someone so different from us that they become unrelatable. When we "other" someone, we highlight the differences between us and that person in a way that distance ourselves from them. Whether we start degrading or idolizing someone, whether we shame them or put them on a pedestal, we are building a wall that prevents meaningful connection. We are creating excuses for not having to empathize or treat them with equality. We start to lose sight of their full humanity.

The overt form of us-versus-them is *demonizing*. Demonizing is turning people, in our minds and in our language, into demons—into utter threats. When we demonize, we go the full extent of denying them humanity, logic, reasonableness, freedom, or choice. Demonization is fueled by the idea that the person in question is an enemy to me and mine.

Othering and demonizing are dangerous games. Both go beyond a good and natural instinct to stay safe; they are used to justify beliefs and actions that break Community. Both lead to punishing and even violent behaviors toward others, seeking to wield control over, and ultimately annihilate, perceived threats. Both tend to see "us" as overly angelic and make us less likely to see our own shortcomings because we are so busy rallying against "them," who seem to embody all the bad.

The opposite of us-versus-them thinking is *humanizing*. Humanizing is a process that intentionally and profoundly chooses to recognize the basic human dignity of others, even if they don't treat us or themselves this way. Humanizing holds the following values:

- I am human, you are human, and therefore we are equals.

- I want to hear about the experiences that have shaped you.

- Even if I strongly disagree with your ideas, I believe you have good intentions. I will trust you mean well until I have concrete reasons to believe otherwise.[34]

- I will set aside personal attacks for the sake of building a relationship.

- Even if I don't like your truth, I believe we both seek truth. I will try to understand your truth.

- I will welcome the challenge of exploring different ways of thinking, hoping that we will sharpen each other.

- I will thank you for taking the time and effort to disagree with me. It means a lot.

How to Disagree Well

When two parties approach disagreement in a way that is hostile—using us-versus-them thinking, being argumentative, and demanding an immediate end to disagreement—conflict nearly always escalates. Nothing gets accomplished. People just talk (or yell) past each other, use domination, or even destroy each other.

When two parties approach disagreement in a way that values and welcomes disagreement, when they approach the conflict in a way that is dialogical and cooperative, they may never, ever agree. But they will be more likely to have a productive conversation that leads to greater understanding and empathy. They are more likely to learn from each other and challenge each other. They may not resolve anything, but they will accomplish something equally, if not more, valuable: they will see each other.

Recognizing Many Ways to Disagree

There's not a single way to disagree. Based on individual personalities and communication preferences, and based on the context, situation, and set of issues, healthy disagreement might take a lot of different forms. We each have different styles in the ways we handle disagreement, meaning we each have unique approaches to dealing with conflict. Some of us are natural avoidants, some are brawlers, and some are devil's advocates, to name just a few.

Without trying to fit everyone into the same box, this chapter offers a framework to help us determine which styles of handling disagreement will be more or less helpful, depending on the person and the circumstance. While there's not a single "right" way to disagree, some approaches may be more appropriate or effective in different situations.

While we each have go-to styles of disagreement, we may each feel more or less comfortable disagreeing, depending on the types of disagreement we are facing.

Though it may not always feel like it, we each have a choice for how and what we engage. What's important to understand about disagreement styles is that we aren't locked in to just one; we can actually learn multiple styles and use the one we want, depending on what's needed in any given situation.

Many Styles of Disagreement

Depending on the situation or your personality, you might approach disagreement differently in different contexts. Most of us have a "go-to" style of dealing with conflicting views. Do any of these feel familiar?

– Less Productive for Community –

 AVOIDANTS are widely uncomfortable with conflict and seek to minimize or bypass dealing with it. Avoidant styles might try to shift focus or use humor to lessen the tension in the room.

 BRAWLERS hold animosity at the center of their approach. They are often aggressive and accompanied by open hostility or resentment toward another party. Brawlers come in with the proverbial "guns blazing," ready for a fight.

CONCILIATORS seek resolution and peace quickly, which in some cases can miss out on opportunities to discuss and learn new and difficult things. They are similar to avoidants but use swift action to avoid the tension of conflict.

DEBATERS in many cases have developed healthy ways to discuss differences, using persuasive speech free of personal attacks. Debate allows two parties, in a structured setting, to weigh the merits of different arguments in order to test their validity. It has limitations, however. Debate is generally competitive and can lead to a focus on winning instead of listening. Often people get sidetracked by delivering "zingers" and coming across as intelligent to those around them. Debate also tends to neglect emotions, personal experiences, and heart-intuition, which are important sources of knowledge. Lastly, as some people are better at debating than others, debate can create counterproductive power imbalances.

– More Productive for Community –

DEVIL'S ADVOCATES believe that sometimes it's helpful just to disagree more, for the sake of the idea or conversation. Usually someone will announce they are playing "the devil's advocate." It should be noted they are not actually in cahoots with the devil.

COOPERATIVES seek to establish common ground and work together to navigate the conversation. Cooperative styles engage deep conversation and sharing power. They don't back off of difficult subjects or resort to cheap peace.

They focus on the journey of learning and insight through discourse, instead of the destination of resolving. They do not back down from making a good argument, but they also don't see their conversation partner as an opponent or enemy. They approach disagreement as a kind of partnership.

Just because you have a "go-to" style, you don't have to use it. You can always learn to use other styles of engaging disagreement. We are all learning, all the time. Practicing is okay.

Many Types of Disagreement

Before we start disagreeing with everyone, it may be helpful to review different types of disagreement and the nuances that distinguish them. When we are disagreeing, identifying the source of the disagreement is incredibly helpful to figure out where, exactly, the fault lines lie.

BELIEF DISAGREEMENTS arise when people hold different beliefs about the nature of being and reality. These can be some of the hardest disagreements to navigate, because they are generally faith-based rather than factual. If I believe that the deity Snorklag the Cosmic Toad told me to read every book written by Kurt Vonnegut by the end of the year, but you doubt that happened, you and I would be likely to get into a long, speculative, theological conversation. Disagreements about belief often fall into impasse territory.

FACTUAL DISAGREEMENTS often deal with trying to come to a consensus about which facts are, in fact, fact. This deals with credibility of source. If two parties can't agree on which sources of information are reliable, they won't make much progress. Questioning the validity of wide- consensus facts is a dangerous game. If facts can't be established, there is no way to establish common ground, and communication fundamentally breaks down. Calling credible news "fake" is an assault on discourse; calling opinion-based news "factual" is just as much of an assault on discourse. Eroding the idea of facts inhibits our ability to establish common assumptions, communication, beliefs, and courses of action.

POLICY DISAGREEMENTS spring from different views about how rules or law should function. They can be as complex as formal disagreements taken to the highest court in the land, or as simple as a friendly fight about which way the toilet paper should go on the roller. The rules of how we engage the world, including etiquette and ethics, fall under policy. A significant type of policy disagreement is Dissent. Dissent means holding an opinion that is not in the majority or is not an officially held position. Early US Americans were expressing dissent when they wrote the constitution and advocated "no taxation without representation," in opposition to British colonial rule. Dissent is the bedrock of democracy and revolution. It is what generally advances human and legal rights. As people organize and dissent against oppressive legal and authoritative structures, revolutionary change often follows. Dissent has a political connotation but could also be used to describe holding a minority voice within any institution.

RESOURCE (OR SCARCITY) DISAGREEMENTS are disagreements over how resources or power should be allocated. Scarcity describes a state of lack, for example, not having enough food to go around, and nearly always results in conflict and disagreement about how to allocate the resources that do exist. There is also a notion of "false scarcity," a state where people are encouraged to fight over the illusion of a lack of resources or power, but in reality, there is plenty to go around. Usually when this happens, a third party is benefitting from the perception of scarcity. For example, diamonds are not actually as scarce or as precious as jewelry companies would have people believe. Many diamond companies intentionally control the supply to affect prices. False scarcity, whether cultivated or not, fuels land conflicts, labor disputes, and inflation.

SEMANTIC DISAGREEMENTS arise when two parties disagree on the definition or use of words. Language is complex and can be incredibly muddy. Sometimes words are muddied intentionally to manipulate a situation. Famously, you may remember when Bill Clinton said under oath, "It depends on what the definition of 'is' is." Semantic disagreements include what is considered offensive and politically correct—what rhetoric is acceptable and unacceptable.

VALUE DISAGREEMENTS are different from religious and policy disagreements in that they stem from what we hold most dear and value in the world. Values are our highest-order Meaning-Making principles that drive our loyalties and decisions. There is certainly crossover; for example, if you are very religious, you might say your highest value is to love your neighbor because God commanded it. Values come with taboos; they are not just what we embrace, but what we reject. Often, taboos are a point of impasse, as they are more controversial in nature than positive values.

Five Principles of Disagreeing Well

When it comes to healthy disagreement, or disagreeing well, there might not be a magic formula, but there are principles we can follow. Here are five principles for healthy disagreement.

1. Relationship Is More Important than Resolution

Going back to the central idea of this book, approach the disagreement as if it's an impasse. Instead of marching into a situation with an agenda to resolve things, try to suspend the desire to change the other person's mind. Pretend, temporarily, that you can't change the situation. Focus on understanding them deeply—on seeing them—and do your absolute best to be seen and understood. The time for resolution or seeking agreement may come, but right now, the most important goals are understanding the nuance of your conversation partner's arguments, assessing the relationship, and figuring out the mechanics of the difference. When we lay aside combativeness and hear each other out, even if it's uncomfortable, we engage a highly effective strategy to prevent miscommunication that may exacerbate the situation. It helps us gain important information and details that we might have otherwise missed.

2. Find the Iron Calm

To approach a disagreement well, we have to practice emotional regulation. A dear friend of mine named Katie is a pastor and social worker in an underserved neighborhood that experiences high rates of poverty. She has a difficult job and has tireless love and dedication for the hundreds of kids she works with, most of whom have been through a lot. She once inspired me by sharing one of her coping techniques. She calls it the "iron calm." Whenever her situation is chaotic and she feels like control is slipping from her grasp, she just becomes the iron calm. She centers, stills, and strengthens herself in the middle of chaos, imagining she is immovable.

The best thing you can do in a difficult conversation around difference is to just sit in that iron calm. Remember your center. Remember that no one can force you to think or believe a certain way. No one can change your values and beliefs but you. You are always in control, and you can always decide. If you find your iron calm, you will be able to go into situations of disagreement and be okay.

3. Call for Courageous Dialogue instead of Civil Discourse

Civil discourse is often focused on the rules of propriety and stuffing people into boxes before they will be heard. Courageous dialogue, on the other hand, means focusing on the person beneath the words and making room for a wide range of emotional and experiential expression. It extends freedom and hospitality, shares power, and honors dignity. It says, "I am willing to be uncomfortable, so I can hear your truth. I will try to empathize, not enforce or control." Courageous dialogue seeks to understand hard truths that might not be palatable. It wants to dig down into the underlying causes of conflict and impasse. Courageous dialogue may be awkward, but it is the heart of Community.

4. Be the First to Leap

Be the first person to leap off the trapeze, the first to act in courage in order to build stronger relationships. A while back, I had a particularly painful run-in with an in-law over religious differences. When we met afterward to try to smooth over the intensity of the conversation, I started to say that perhaps we shouldn't talk about hard things. Before I could finish, he jumped in and said, "You matter too much to me to just talk about the weather. You matter enough to me to talk about the hard things." Between the two of us, he was the first person to leap! He said loud and clear that an eggshell relationship was not going to cut it. He took a risk in this. I was tempted to walk away and say, "Nah, this isn't worth the pain and inconvenience." My in-law taught me how to love better in that moment. When we make a choice to be the first to leap off the trapeze, we make our relationships and communities stronger, and we show leadership.

5. Have a QUEST Conversation

Disagreeing fruitfully is more than just talking at someone. It involves steps, repeated many times. When this process is practiced, the conversation becomes more effective. Thinking of the conversation as a spiral, where the center is growth and deeper understanding, QUEST[35] conversations help us move inward, toward each other and toward making disagreement productive:

- **Question honestly.** Ask your conversation partner open, curious, honest questions about their reality and how they see things.

- **Understand deeply.** Hold the things your conversation partner says. You don't have to believe what they give you or accept it as true, but you do try to understand where they are coming from.

- **Explain effectively.** Offer your truths and experiences, in the full strength of your conviction and to the best of your ability. Offer in a way that is bridge building and constructive, not shaming, attacking, or expecting conformity.

- **Sift gently.** Sift through everything you hear and decide what you think is valid or not valid, true and not true, good and not good. Figure out where the true points of disagreement lie. Do this in a way that holds an open hand to the fact that you don't know everything. Be gentle with yourself and your conversation partner.

- **Tweak accordingly.** As you gain new information and understanding of nuance, and especially if you realize there is a better way to look at things, you are allowed to adjust your questions and opinions. This is the mark of a strong thinker.

- **Repeat.** Let the conversation continue through these steps, again and again. Don't pressure yourself or your conversation partner to find resolution. If resolution comes naturally, it will arise on its own. Focus instead on seeing and being seen, on building trust and a spirit of cooperation. A resilient relationship is the ultimate goal.

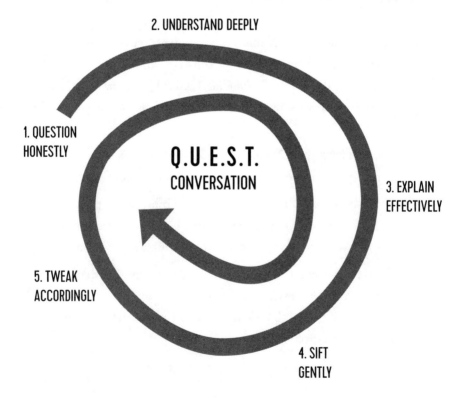

2. UNDERSTAND DEEPLY

1. QUESTION
HONESTLY

Q.U.E.S.T.
CONVERSATION

3. EXPLAIN
EFFECTIVELY

5. TWEAK
ACCORDINGLY

4. SIFT
GENTLY

SUMMARY: Disagreement May Be Challenging, but We Need It to Thrive

I hope this chapter didn't pressure anyone to *like* disagreement. Even people who navigate disagreement well—people who have great conflict transformation skills—may always feel nervous or even a sense of dread when they happen upon disagreement. These folks choose to engage because they know disagreement is healthy and creates opportunities for growth. In those difficult moments of confrontation, it's the steel of our nerves and the love in our hearts that ultimately put disagreement in its rightful place: as a vital and beneficial part of being in Community. Based on our personalities and past experiences, we may never love disagreement, but we can learn to value it because it makes us, our families, our communities, our ideas, and our imaginations stronger.

Chapter 4 Reflection

1. What is your go-to style of disagreement? Are some types of disagreement easier for you to engage than others?

2. Share a time you or someone you know went out on a limb to build community. Did it work?

3. Share a time you experienced a fragile relationship. Why was it fragile? What do you wish would have been different?

4. When have you watched a community diminish or reject difference? How did it play out? What were the consequences? What could they have done differently?

5. When is the last time your ideas were made stronger by the feedback of another person? Or when is the last time you were able to offer constructive feedback and it made a positive impact?

6. What's your relationship with civility? Are you someone who embraces it, rejects it, or something else?

7. What is the hardest part of overcoming us-versus-them thinking? Are there any times when it's good to be in a mind-set of war? When does it get the better of us?

8. After reading this chapter, do you see disagreement differently?

CHAPTER 5
A Guide to Great Questions
Common Cures for Loud-Thought Syndrome

Hey, what's up. I'm your Brain! You should really eat a sandwich. So guess what, I know about all kinds of things, and I like to think about things and tell people what I think, and every time someone says something it reminds me of everything I know, and what's that smell by the way? But yeah, just to remind you, I am frickin' fascinating, do you know what I mean? ... do you? ... hey ... excuse me, PLEASE EAT A SANDWICH!

One of the reasons I started writing this book was a question from a guy named Steve. Steve and I were getting to know each other over burgers at a networking lunch. Without pretense or a sense of competition, without expectation or pressure, Steve asked me a phenomenal question:

"What's the one thing in the whole world you are most passionate about?"

No one had ever asked me that—not the way he asked. I got the sense that he genuinely wanted to know. I said, "I'm not sure" several times. He waited for me to think. He was so patient and so curious, I started to open up. "You know, in the past," I told him, "I've been really interested in conflict."

"Wow, that's really interesting! Tell me more."

I shrugged. I didn't know what more to say. "Well, we're bad at it, in this country. Um—I've been through a lot of conflict. I feel there is a need out there to help people talk to each other. Beyond that, I have no idea."

Steve asked, "So how can you help people deal with conflict? If money were no issue you, how would you pursue that? What would you bring to the world?"

I said I didn't know. He said it was okay. He encouraged me that it was a great pursuit. He said if I ever wanted to kick around ideas, he was always happy to help.

At the time, I had zero answers. But Steve's wonderful question asking started me on a path that resulted in this book and a greater sense of personal purpose.

The reason Steve's questions started me on an important path was that his questions were about me, not him. He put thoughts of himself aside for a few minutes to take the time to *see* me. In seeing me, he asked me to *see* myself. Even now, I feel a deep sense of gratitude that Steve did that for me.

All too often, we focus only on telling. When we focus only on telling, we don't connect fully with our fellow humans. We also miss out on opportunities to gather new information about the other side of the issue that might change the way we see our side.

Asking great questions is not about telling or taking, it's about giving. It's giving opportunities for exploration, insight, and friendship.

Asking great questions is an art.

Is It Okay to Question?

Asking questions, for some of us, might be scary. For those of us who have been rejected or punished for asking, it might seem like a threatening activity.

Whether or not we let ourselves ask questions is, in itself, a question.

Here is a mental picture that might be helpful as each of us thinks through our relationship with questions. Every person, at birth, inherits a vault. This is not a vault we can see with our human eyes. It's intangible, holding all the invisible things we have inherited: all the ideas, attitudes, beliefs, values, biases, and loyalties we have been handed. Our family, role models, community, and culture all deposit things inside the vault. Let's call it our Paradigm Vault.

Though we have largely inherited the contents, our Paradigm Vault belongs to us, not to anyone else. Each of us has a right and even a responsibility to open our vault and sort through what's inside.

If we choose to open it, we might find priceless treasures, we might find trash, or we might find toxic sludge. Most of us find sludge, trash, and treasure all mixed in together.

A lot of people don't want to take a good look inside their vault. They know the vault is there, but they are perfectly fine with leaving well enough alone and accepting it all without question. Other people try to toss out the whole thing and start from scratch.

Maturity means sorting through our vault. It means holding tight to the priceless intangibles that we've been given—the things that make life meaningful and worth living—and gently disposing of what we don't find to be healthy. For example, we might choose to keep "God is love" but get rid of "It's okay to hit people who make me angry." Maturity also means finding new treasures to add and working to pass down positive beliefs, ideas, and loyalties to others.

Whether or not we choose to open our vault comes down to a basic human right known as curiosity. Curiosity is a set of skills that might come more naturally to some than to others, but one thing is certain: curiosity is a decision. Do we choose to be curious? Are we ready to face the necessary action that might come as a result of being curious? Do we have the courage to question even the ways we question? How well does our curiosity about our own selves translate to curiosity about others?

Before we engage in difficult conversations, it's important to go through the process of sorting through our vault and knowing what's in it. That way, when we get to a place of trying to *see* someone else, we will have already practiced seeing ourselves.

The bottom line is this: it's okay to question. It's okay to question ourselves and others, to peer deeply into the inner workings of how we function as humans and how we relate to each other. Some would even call questioning one of the greatest joys and responsibilities we can know in this life.

Asking deep questions doesn't mean we are throwing out the whole vault or trying to throw out someone else's. It doesn't mean we are being disrespectful. Asking questions means we are holding our past, present, and future with honor. We are showing honor to others. We are practicing wonder. We are being fully alive.

Six Guidelines for Asking Great Questions

The rest of this chapter is devoted to the art of asking great questions. The following six guidelines can help you practice this art.

1. Quiet Loud Thoughts

In college, I had a super-talkative friend named Aaron. Sometimes conversations with Aaron were a lot, but he was a good friend, so we hung out. One day, we were sharing a meal at the cafeteria, and I noticed a curious pattern. Aaron would ask me a question, but as soon I would start to answer, he was already telling me what he thought about the question or switching to a different topic.

After about a half hour of this, I broke in: "Hey, Aaron?" "Yeah?" he answered. I asked him casually, "Do you feel like you have, like, loud thoughts?" He started laughing and replied, "I've never put it that way, but yeah. Yeah, I definitely have loud thoughts."

Since that day, I've called this phenomenon Loud-Thought Syndrome.* It's what happens when you are so engrossed in what's going on inside your own head that it's hard to slow down and really listen to the person you are talking to. We all have Loud-Thought Syndrome sometimes. It's a common human behavior.

---

* Not a real syndrome.

The thing is, great questions and loud thoughts don't work together. Loud thoughts block the ability to see someone else, because we are too focused on our own brain.

Loud thoughts can be about anything—balloons, camping, adding jelly to the grocery list, pre-twentieth-century dental health, that one time I saw Patrick Stewart at the airport.

Our thoughts can be loud on a regular basis, let alone when we are talking about difficult or controversial issues. With regard to impasse, when we hold strong opinions about the topic at hand, it can be intensely challenging to quiet loud thoughts. News articles! Experiences! Beliefs! Sometimes our opinions so desperately want to be heard that, while the other person is talking, our thoughts are lining themselves up like paratroopers, preparing to parachute in from above.

The danger in not quieting loud thoughts is that we miss things. We are likely to misunderstand our conversation partner's stance because we don't hear everything they are saying. If we don't slow down, quiet down, and listen, we are much more likely to speak off topic or in circles. We miss opportunities to speak directly to the most important parts of the conversation.

So the first step in quieting loud thoughts is to take a deep breath and say, "Self, it's time to chill." As you ask your mind and body to calm down, recognize you are in control. Don't get preoccupied with the worry that your thoughts will leave or won't be available when you need them. Your thoughts are still there. You still know what you know; you still think what you think. There is still space for you. You are just making space for someone else too. Space is good. Occasional silence is good. Slowing down is good. Making space, really seeing the other person, is the only way we can ask great questions.

2. Study Your Intentions

One of the most helpful skills to learn for asking great questions is the ability to look at our own intent before we open our mouth. Why? Because our motivations and approach will leak out. Our intent will be spotted—quickly. No matter what we think of our conversation partner's opinions, that person is not dumb. Most people can spot BS right away. Most people know a blow-hard when they see one. Take it from a fellow blowhard.

We humans have been communicating our whole lives. While we may not always agree on language, most of us are very good at picking up on subtle cues that show a person's intent. Because asking questions puts us in a vulnerable position, our hearts leak through when we ask questions. Our motivations poke their little heads out like meerkats awaiting a storm.

So before you ask a question, ask yourself: What's my intention with this question? Am I trying to . . .

- Show off my knowledge?

- Avoid looking dumb?

- Make someone else look dumb?

- Get this person to admit something?

- Cope with my anxiety as I open up an uncomfortable topic?

- Control the conversation?

- Get this question over with, so I can keep talking?

Most of us have had intentions like these more than once. No one is a perfect question asker. But the clearer I am about my intentions, the closer I can get to a great question.

If we are feeling confident or uneasy or any strong emotion, we can't just force ourselves to feel something else. The best way to handle our intentions is to be bold. Since we aren't fooling anyone else with the subtexts of our questions, we might as well just own our intentions. Go ahead and lead with your motiva-tion and approach before asking the question:

- Trying to show off my knowledge → owning it

  "You know, I've studied this topic a bit, so I want to ask you about ___."

- Trying to avoid looking dumb → owning it

  "I don't know much about this. May I ask a dumb question?"

- Trying to make someone else look dumb → owning it

  "I respectfully disagree; an article I read said otherwise. What do you think?"

- Trying to get this person to admit something → owning it

  "I would love to hear you talk more about ___."

- Trying to open up an uncomfortable topic → owning it

  "I'm not sure how to ask this. May I ask an awkward question?"

- Trying to control the conversation → owning it

  "Can we switch topics? I would love to hear more about _."

- Trying to get this question over with, so I can keep talking → don't own it

  (Holy lack of curiosity, Batman! You are missing an opportunity to learn.)

Intent will not only shape the way I ask, but also shape my ability to listen and learn from my conversation partner. Intent affects my ability to co-create a reciprocal space—a space of true seeing and understanding. Sharing my intent keeps my language accountable and makes sure I am speaking for myself, not anyone else. Plus, if I am wrong in any way, I lower the chance of a "gotcha" moment if I'm upfront about where I'm coming from.

3. Ask from a Place of Genuine Curiosity and Power Sharing

When you ask a question, are you trying to get your conversation partner to a certain destination, like a rat in a maze? Or are you genuinely curious and open to what they say?

This is so important that I would like to say it again.

Are you asking a question that *already knows*, or one that *wants to learn?*

If you already know everything, what are you even doing here? Go drop that knowledge on the world!

Presumably, some readers just put down the book at this point. You are still with me, awesome.

Here is what I know to be true. I have met many smart people—people who teach at the most exclusive universities, people who work to cure cancer. I have met brilliant poets and artists. The most brilliant people will tell you the secret to brilliance, the secret to true wisdom, is never letting go of childlike curiosity.

When we lean into the fact that we do not know, when we lean into the fact that there is a vast world of knowledge and understanding we do not yet have, we grow. Great questions can only come from a place of curiosity. There are three components of a great, power-sharing question.

A. Great Questions Contextualize

No one can know everything, and no question asker speaks for everyone. We all have biases and core assumptions built on what we have experienced and learned—a big old heap of biases. Biases help us interpret the world and stay safe (for example, eating lead is dangerous; I am anti-lead). They can also be limiting (for example, eating broccoli is dangerous; I am anti-broccoli).

Before you ask a question, it's important to contextualize—that is, to explain where you are coming from:

"From my perspective, I understand ___. Can you share your take on that?"

"Growing up, I experienced ___, which leads me to wonder ___."

"I read an article about ___; does it have anything to do with what you are sharing?"

Contextualizing your perspective shows that you don't presume to be unbiased; you recognize that you don't know everything. It shows that you understand that your context matters in the formation of your beliefs and opinions. It's much easier to have a conversation with someone who doesn't presume a sense of ultimate authority.

B. Great Questions Are Open

A great question is open, meaning there is no agenda laid out. It's different from a leading question, which presupposes a certain set of answers and can shape responses.

Leading Question

"Hey, Angie, I see you have that big concert coming up. OMG, are you nervous?"

"Bah! I wasn't nervous, but now that you said that, I am!"

Your question plastered your assumptions and fears onto Angie, and now she is shutting down and diving into her Fear Bunker. Smooth moves, Ex-Lax.

Open Question

"Hey, Angie, I see you have that big concert coming up. How are you feeling?"

"You know, I'm really excited! Thanks for asking. I did all the choreography myself, I'm really proud of it."

Your question let Angie speak for herself and opened up more conversational possibilities. You built a bridge and validated her. You created a more interesting and meaningful discussion. (*High five!*)

Open questions let conversation partners answer and feel however *they* want. Open questions let others "be where they are," so to speak.

Leading questions are more controlling. They either pressure the other person to agree, or they force a contradiction. Leading questions lead to yes-or-no answers, not discussion full of nuance and complexity. Leading questions are often aggressive and can even tap into using domination, or trying to control someone else through force or coercion.

Open questions share power. The artful question asker asks questions from a sense of equality, with control ebbing and flowing.

That doesn't mean you can't be specific when you ask great questions. It means you don't anticipate a certain answer when you ask. It means that you work for a larger variety of answers than yes or no.

C. Great Questions Reciprocate

Have you ever tried to play ball with a ball hog? Ball hogs don't pass the ball back. This is the same feeling when the question asking in a conversation is one-sided. It feels imbalanced; there is little sense of play, no back-and-forth.

Many times, people ask questions because they want those same questions asked of them. It's a wonderful practice to reciprocate questions. In other words, throw the ball back.

For expert-level question asking, you can ask the same question back to that person but put a spin on it—ask it in a different and more nuanced way, using information you picked up during the conversation.

This does two great things. It cuts in half the work of coming up with good questions, since you get to use questions twice (score for lazy people!). It also makes your conversation partner feel heard and understood. That's an exponential win.

4. Listen to Your Gut

Once a coworker called me to ask a small question she could have easily found out from looking online. I was a bit miffed. During the same week, this happened a few more times, and eventually I started to get truly annoyed. There was no reason she needed to keep bothering me. I don't like talking on the phone, so it was extra uncomfortable.

After the fifth time she called me, something in my gut told me something else was going on. I called her back. "Mary, are you okay?" She replied, "Why do you ask?" I said, "Because you sounded a little sad." She burst into tears and told me she was going through some difficult personal things and didn't have any support. She asked me how I knew to call her back, suggesting that maybe an angel had told me to do it. I didn't want to correct her, but it wasn't an angel. It was just me, finally listening to my gut. Mary wasn't calling me all those times to get information. She called because she was alone and needed human connection. She was needing to feel like she mattered to someone. She was reaching out, even if she didn't realize it. When I stopped long enough to look past my own loud annoyance, my gut was pretty intelligent about what was really going on. I wish I had listened to it sooner.

In difficult conversations, our guts have super listening powers. If you pair that with a great question, you can take the conversation to a deeper level:

"I am sensing ___ from you. Is that true?"

"You sounded ___ when you said that. Am I reading that correctly?"

"Am I right to say that you're telling me ___?"

5. Get to the Heart of the Matter

When I think about great questions, I picture the Tin Man from *The Wizard of Oz*. It's a weird analogy, but stay with me. When Dorothy first encounters the Tin Man, he is completely rusted over and unable to move. Next to him sits an oil can, but he can't reach it. All he can do is mumble something from behind a rusted jaw. "Oil, please!" Dorothy jumps in to help, grabs the oil can, and oils his joints.

Now, what if Dorothy had just put oil on his arm bone, or his head, or shinbone? It would have made him shinier but wouldn't have helped him move. She had to put the oil into the joints, into the partially hidden, connecting spaces.

Great question askers do this. When they approach an awkward and difficult conversation, they ask themselves, Where is the most effective place to put my energy? What should I focus on here? What connections can I make to open this up and make it more fluid? How can I take us closer to the heart of the matter? Great questions help people make interesting and significant ties between ideas.

"I heard you say ___, and I also heard you say ___. Do you think those are connected?"

"I want to circle back to something you said earlier that felt important."

"Help me understand how these things are related."

One technique you might use for getting to the heart of the matter is the "child's why." Children ask why all the time because they are trying to learn how ideas connect. They are trying to learn what core assumptions and beliefs support the subject at hand.

What is the chain of events that caused someone to have this idea? What are the invisible things beneath this idea that support it? Sometimes, we look too much at results instead of causes. The question of "why" is a question of causes.

"What is ___ based on?"

"What comes before or beneath ___?"

"You said the issue was ___, but it sounds like it might go deeper than that."

6. "Getting Real" Takes Trust

We have to earn the right to "get real," or be transparent about sensitive matters. Especially in situations where we wield a lot of power, but even if we don't, we are not entitled to ask vulnerable questions until we build trust.

Great questions are willing to lean into awkward or uncomfortable places for the sake of the strength of the relationship, but they do not ignore boundaries. Great questions are courageous but not to the extent of being nosy.

Once you build trust with someone and you are both able to start letting walls down, you might be granted the right to ask open, curious, contextualized, humble questions that are controversial in nature.

"What's it like to have your experiences in the world?"

"What's it like to overcome the hardship you named?"

"May I ask something I've been curious about for a long time?
And please know I mean no offense."

What if your conversation partner doesn't want to answer? No problem. Great question askers are always respectful in times when people don't feel comfortable answering.

THE MIRRORING TOOL

How do we know if we are getting to the heart of the matter? A great rule of thumb is to practice a technique called mirroring.

Have you ever held up a mirror next to another mirror? Suddenly, dozens of mirrors come into view, stretching into infinity. Mirroring takes place when we repeat back what we've been hearing and then ask for feedback to make sure we are on the right track. In other words, imagine two mirrors: the mirror we hold up, reflecting/recapping what we've heard, and the mirror we ask our conversation partner to hold up to our mirror, giving feedback on our reflection.

Mirroring helps the person we're speaking with feel more understood and connected. It also helps prevent miscommunication and helps us refrain from speaking for our conversation partner.

For example, Juan is pouring out his heart to Angelo. Angelo holds up the first mirror when he says, "I'm hearing you say that your mom isn't doing well and can't support herself. You seem really worried about her. Is that right?" Juan holds up the second mirror by saying, "Yes, that's exactly right." Angelo goes on, "You didn't say this exactly, but what I understand from everything you've said is that you are worried about your ability to support her, since no one else in the family can. Is that true?" (mirror 1). Angelo might say yes or no (mirror 2); either way, Angelo's answer pushes the conversation closer to the heart of the matter. This process helps increase depth, understanding, and most importantly, accuracy.

SUMMARY: Artful Questions Can Be Life Altering

With this understanding, consider that asking questions is not a sideline or something to just get over with. Questions are the center of conversation and discourse, the center of human connection.

Let yourself practice asking courageous, open questions. Remember, this is an art. As with any art form, you are allowed to practice. You don't have to be good at asking questions right away. Most of us certainly have yet to master it.

If you are used to being heard, perhaps it's a good idea to practice asking more questions— especially asking people who don't get to speak as often.

Finally, an important caveat to this chapter is that some people, depending on their social location, may be in the position of always asking and listening, rarely being invited to share their story. If this sounds more like you, you may already know the art of great questions. Perhaps you can practice sharing more instead of asking or waiting to be asked.

Chapter 5 Reflection

1. Which do you find yourself doing more often: asking or being asked questions?

2. Do you feel you have really taken the time to explore your Paradigm Vault? Why or why not? If you have, what's something in there you decided to keep? What's something you decided to discard?

3. What do you find is the hardest part of asking questions? What parts do you want to be better at?

4. What's the best question you've ever heard? What made it great?

5. What's the worst question you have ever heard? What made it bad?

6. Have you ever asked or been asked a life-changing question?

7. What questions do you wish people would ask you?

8. What questions do you wish you could ask?

CHAPTER 6
Dealing with Feelings
Too Many *%$@! Blue Cars

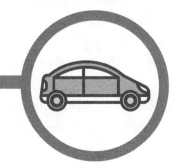

Feelings play a huge role in impasse and difficult conversations. Conflict without anger, fear, or sadness is a cakewalk to navigate. Most of us can do that. The hardest conflicts can come with a piñata of complex emotions. One little whack, and who knows what feelings will come tumbling out.

People who transform conflict have often done a lot of internal work to learn a set of skills known as emotional regulation. This doesn't mean repressing, stifling, or ignoring important emotions. It means being aware and in control of emotions so they don't get the better of us, especially when the stakes are high and situations get tense. Emotional regulation comes more naturally to some people than others, based on differences in personality, family, communication styles, and background. It can take a lot of practice to get good at emotional regulation. And that's okay.

To be honest with you, I don't like talking about feelings. Most of the time, it's hard for me to explain my emotions to others, let alone to myself. It takes a lot of concentration and hard work for me to figure out what feelings I experience. I envy people who have an easy time saying what they feel. It's just not easy for me.

Because I'm so bad at feelings, I've done a lot of thinking about them.

In this chapter, I offer a guiding metaphor for understanding emotions that has helped me tremendously. I cover techniques for navigating our own difficult feelings, as well as ways in which we can support others effectively as they cope with their difficult feelings.

Please be advised that I am not a licensed clinician, nor is this intended to be a clinical reference. This chapter is based on my personal experience and research and forms the basis of how I deal with emotion in conflict. Hopefully, it will give you some new ideas to think about.

Finally, because this chapter discusses emotional self-regulation, it may not be helpful if you are someone who struggles with self-regulating emotions due to a diagnosable condition that requires professional support. If that is your experience, I hope you don't feel pressure to make this chapter "work" for you, but I do hope you still feel included and accepted in this conversation. If this material is not useful to you on a practical level, perhaps it can at least offer you language for educating those who don't have a frame of reference for what you have been through. Thank you for walking with me in this journey.

Emotions: Us Taking Care of Us

Growing up, I believed we got to pick and choose our feelings. Feelings were things I was supposed to war against and master; I could learn to turn them off at will.

I don't believe this anymore. I've learned that feelings are things that happen *to* us. Wouldn't the world be easier if everyone could decide how to feel all the time? That's just not the way it works. Accepting emotions as a natural part of life is one of the hardest things to grapple with as a human.

Although I can choose how to *interpret* my feelings and how to *act* on my feelings, ultimately I cannot choose how to feel. As I breathe my breath and blink my eyes, I feel my feelings. They are part of my physical, chemical, and psychological makeup as a person. If all of this is true, judging ourselves for having emotions doesn't make a lot of sense.

While feelings are real, in that we experience them on a visceral level, they are not always *true*. Sometimes feelings can be misdirected. Sometimes they can go haywire. Sometimes they can be nurtured and blown out of proportion. Sometimes they can take over and tell us how to think. They can even keep us from thinking!

Several years ago, I was going through a rough spot in a former relationship. For weeks, I was doing my usual thing—avoiding my feelings. Then one day, I was driving to the store to get groceries. As I pulled up to a stoplight, I suddenly became *furious* that there were too many blue cars at that intersection.

They were all blue! I was enraged.

Obviously, that reaction made zero sense. Nothing traumatic had happened to me involving a blue car. What was really happening was that my relationship was in trouble, and I was refusing to deal with it. The cars did nothing wrong. I was unraveling.

When we don't deal with our feelings, they don't just go away. They squirt out somewhere else.

Ew! That's gross, but hopefully you will remember that, the next time you experience something like getting angry at blue cars for no reason.

Meanwhile, here's some food for thought: What if certain "negative" emotions, like anger and frustration, are not inherently bad? What if they play an important role in our lives?

Consider the possibility that emotions are simply our mind and body taking care of itself. Feelings are us, taking care of us.

Philosophers, psychologists, scientists, and theologians have spent millennia debating the complex nature of emotions and the relationship between our bodies, hearts, minds, and even souls. Much of Western thought has leaned toward the idea that these "parts" of us are separate—an idea known in philosophy as mind-body "dualism."[36] However, neurological research in the last century has demonstrated that humans are way more internally connected than we realize.[37]

We really don't have separate parts of us, like a part where thinking happens or a part where love happens. Our minds and bodies are completely linked in a beautiful dance of intelligence and instinct. Instead of having a mind and a body, separate from each other, we have a "mindbody." What is happening in our mind is connected to our body, and what is happening in our body is connected to our mind.

Our mindbody as a whole is hardwired for one purpose: to help us survive and thrive.

When we talk about emotions, I invite you to think with me about the "mindbody": our full selves, interlaced, inseparable. Learning to think this way helps us put off judging our emotions as they come up, which is highly valuable in difficult conversations. When we respect the intelligence and interconnectedness of our mindbody, we can learn to listen to our emotions and deal with them in better ways.

And most of all, we can be gentle with ourselves.

The Two Rivers of Feelings

By and large, human beings have two sources of feelings that inform and act in our mindbody, like two rivers that feed into one lake. Both of these "rivers" are complex systems built into who we are as humans. They are designed to help us cope with the world. They are part of us for good reason.

The first "river" is our *self-protection system*—our fight-or-flight response. In the Self-Protection River, our adrenal glands emit chemicals to prepare us for any situation where quick action is needed.[38] This self-protection system is a fast system, rooted in our very good and natural drive to survive and avoid pain. This river can change quickly, moment to moment, depending on what's going on around us. If you could see this river, it would be calm one minute and raging with white-water rapids the next. "Fast" forms of anger, fear, anxiety, and disgust stem from the Self-Protection River. When we are dealing with conflict and impasse, the Self-Protection River often is working whenever our heartbeat rises. We might experience the rush of relief and joy when our Self-Protection River is not needed, because in that moment we feel safe and secure and happy. In this case, this river bubbles along contentedly. But make no mistake—the moment it senses danger around us, it will respond.

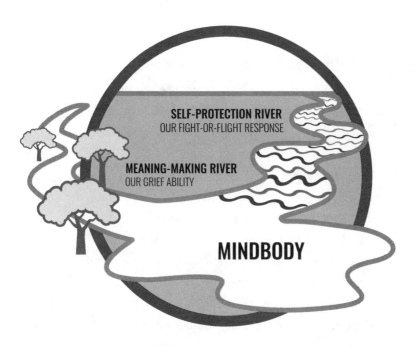

SELF-PROTECTION RIVER
OUR FIGHT-OR-FLIGHT RESPONSE

MEANING-MAKING RIVER
OUR GRIEF ABILITY

MINDBODY

The second "river" is our *meaning-making system*—our grief ability. Grief is how we deal with the unacceptable, how we re-create meaning after meaning has been shattered.[39] We grieve for many different reasons, not just after physical death. Grief is a slow and sidewinding process, sometimes stretching out over the course of years. If you could see this river, it would be deep and barely inching along; it would be covered by dark trees that block out the sun. It would probably wind around in big loops, because it is anything but a straight line. The Meaning-Making River does not respond to what's around us. Instead, it can shape and change what's around us and influence how we process it. "Slow" forms of anger, sadness, disappointment, disillusionment, and some forms of depression belong to our Meaning-Making River. Our Meaning-Making River doesn't just hold negative emotions; it is also the seat of our loves and loyalties, the deepest, slowest, long-term feelings that constitute our sense of meaning and purpose. When we are dealing with conflict and impasse, the Meaning-Making River is working most strongly when our heads and hearts hurt. Whenever we do the hard work of making sense of things or coming to terms with hardship, this river is at work.

Navigating the Two Rivers

These systems, these two rivers, are independent of each other, but they often flow simultaneously in difficult conversations. When both rivers flow strongly at once, it can result in a big confusing whirlpool of emotions in our mindbody.

The Self-Protection River

If you've ever had a panic attack or saw red during a fight, you know the intensity of the Self-Protection River. In conversations with my family, even peaceful conversations, where I felt boundaries were being crossed, I have had panic attacks that have involved hyperventilating and a crazed desire to run away.

Once, during an argument in the car, I was so desperate to escape the conversation that I panicked and began opening a car door *on the freeway*. Did that particular conversation put me in physical danger? In hindsight, no, but at the time, the conversation was tapping into something so painful, and the emotions I experienced were so intense, that it felt like a physical affront. My self-protection system had taken over in an effort to protect me, but it was misfiring. The flight response I received—trying to open the car door—was nearly beyond my control, nearly beyond rational ability to talk myself down. It was almost system override. I remember looking at my hand pulling the door handle and thinking, "Oh, my God! What am I doing?" Thankfully, my good sense kicked in before I was out of the frying pan and into the fire.

How It Works

The Self-Protection River is a set of survival skills. It is the body's ability to kick us into fight or flight, as needed, to keep us safe. Sometimes it's a subtle experience, other times an overwhelming experience. This system uses several tools to protect us:

- **Anxiety**, a general "sixth sense" of dread that something is wrong, is our first alarm that we should be on the watch for danger.

- **Disgust** involves feeling repulsed or repelled by dangerous or untenable ideas or circumstances or by the breaking of boundaries or taboos that we believe keep us safe.

- **Embarrassment** is the immediate, visceral response to feeling too vulnerable or boundary-less.

- **Fear**, the apprehension or terror that we are not safe or that things we rely on will fall apart, motivates us to take action— to either fight or flee.

- **"Short" anger** is anger that boils up in our adrenal glands to help us respond to threats and move quickly when action is needed.

The Self-Protection River is fast. It can kick in and disengage within a span of seconds or minutes. As far as energy is concerned, it's a shallow river; it doesn't take a lot for it to flow swiftly and then slow down again.

When our Self-Protection River kicks in—when we see red and hear that internal voice screaming either "Run!" or "Fight!"—we are often unable to gauge how rational we are being, due to chemical and psychological manifestations in our mindbody.[40] Because the Self-Protection River, also known as the sympathetic nervous system, is housed in our "lower," pre-language brain,[41] it has a special ability to override our rational mental processes. Why? Self-protection doesn't have time to be rational! Its only job is to help us survive.

When we feel that urge to fight or flee, it means the system is doing its job, but sometimes it can do its job a little too well. If this system is overfunctioning, we might be experiencing fight or flight to an irrational degree; we might feel threatened to a degree that doesn't quite make sense in that moment. When we feel as if this might be happening, it's helpful to learn how to nonjudgmentally reconnect with ourselves and learn how to slow down to examine the information our river is giving us.

Tools and Techniques

When conflict arises and we feel our Self-Protection River turning into white-water rapids, what do we do? Here are some useful tools for emotional regulation of the Self-Protection River. These are tools that help me self-soothe.

In psychological terms, self-soothing means gently taking control back from our self-protection system and inviting ourselves to calm down before things go haywire.[42] By self-soothing, we push the pause button on our sympathetic nervous system and activate the opposite system: our parasympathetic system. The parasympathetic system is known as the "rest and digest" system. It lowers our blood pressure, increases our immune systems, and chemically helps us think more clearly.[43]

The following tools are just for you; you don't have to let anyone know you are using them. One idea may resonate with you more than another, or you don't have to use any of them. Maybe you can come up with your own way to self-soothe. These are just examples that I hope will be helpful to you.

- **Feel it, cool it (helpful for fight).** In the heat of the moment, when your self-protection system is raging, stand very still, and let yourself feel the feeling. Let it course through your body; don't fight it. It will begin to diminish in intensity when you acknowledge and honor it.[44] This works for two reasons. First, your self-protection system is trying to help and needs to be heard, even if it's misfiring. Second, the fear of the emotions is often stronger than the emotions themselves. If you fight against those fight feelings—if you try to force yourself to stop feeling or if you judge yourself harshly for feeling—those feelings will often get stronger and take over more intensely. Instead, close your eyes, and let yourself feel the raging river. Let yourself feel the anger and intensity. Thank your body for sending you important information. Once you have felt the river for a few moments, imagine those feelings getting a little slower and a little colder, until instead of having hot-lava anger, you have "cold anger."[45] Cold anger is the experience of taking something destructive and turning it into a useful tool for change. Instead of a volcano, cold anger is a river that cuts through stone. Once your anger is cold, make a plan of positive, productive action. If you don't know what action you can take, gather some people you trust, and figure it out.

- **The safe blanket (helpful for flight).** Imagine the best blanket in the world. Imagine its feel, its weight, its color, and size. Got it? Now, pretend that the blanket has magical properties: it can keep you safe from words. As long as you are under that blanket, the words that fly around you don't make any impact on your mind-body. If you are in the middle of a conversation and things go beyond discomfort and into unsafe/panic/flight territory, silently wrap that invisible safe blanket around you for a while. Feel its warmth and protection. Feel its texture against your hands. Sit under it long enough for you to remember that you are, indeed, safe; you will get through this. You can keep the blanket on or take it off when you feel better.

- **The soul garden (helpful for fight or flight).** When emotional storms are raging and you feel powerless over your emotions, you can always go to your "soul garden." Your soul garden is the deepest, innermost part of your heart, where no one else is able to go. It is a space you share only with yourself, at the center of your being. What does it look like? You get to decide! Mine is a beautiful, secluded green space filled with musical instruments, a giant buffet of food from around the world, and the comfiest couch I've ever sat in. Your soul garden doesn't have to make sense. It doesn't have to resemble any place you've ever been before. It gets to be a place that brings you joy and peace, right in the middle of your being. No one else is able to visit the soul garden; it's just for you. Next time you find your self-protection system starting to go into overdrive, just head into your soul garden for a minute, and take a couple of deep breaths. Remember that nothing and no one can ever harm the center of your being except for you, because you are the only one who can go there.

- **The ground circle (helpful for fight or flight).** If you feel scattered and hyped up to the point of not being able to think straight, draw an imaginary circle on the floor, a few feet wide. Now pick a word. This word should be something you need in that moment; maybe it's *clarity* or *stability* or *strength*. The word should be whatever it is you feel that you most need at that time. Once you have your word, write it inside the circle, and then imagine yourself stepping into that circle. Stand there, right on top of that word, and feel the word connecting you to the ground. Feel it seeping up through your feet. Take some slow deep breaths, drawing the word up through your whole mindbody. Once you start to feel as if that word is beginning to become part of you, you can exit the circle any way you please. You can step out respectfully, you can jump out, or you can do the hokey pokey—whatever feels right.

The Meaning-Making River

If you've ever found yourself coping with loss, wondering what your purpose is, struggling with change, being unsure about the significance of life, had your beliefs shift, or been forced to find a new normal, you have experienced the Meaning-Making River.

After my divorce, I went through a strange process of trying to start my life over after so many of my dreams had broken. When I first got divorced, I expected to cry all the time. While there were tears, there were also a lot of things I did not expect—things that were much harder for me to deal with than crying. I experienced depression, a strong urge to push people away, and most difficult, a constant mental fog, as if my brain wouldn't work right. I remember one particularly bad day, I was sitting in the school library, trying to get through some of the 500 pages a week I was assigned to read for grad school. I could look at the words on the page, but I couldn't comprehend them. During a four-hour study session, I was only able to read two pages. I sat in the library's wooden chair and sobbed in silence. Eventually I gave up, went home, and crawled into bed, feeling utterly incompetent.

That experience was a wake-up call that I needed help. I decided to join a divorce support group. When I went to my first meeting, it was comforting to hear I wasn't the only one experiencing low productivity. Every single person in the group expressed having a hard time focusing. Everyone talked about how, for months and even years after loss, they found it hard to do things that used to be easy, like working or spending time with friends. One man even lost his job because he was still grieving heavily after a year. According to his boss, his inability to "move on" became a professional liability.

Why do our brains get foggy when we grieve? It's because our Meaning-Making River takes a ton of our energy to run. When we struggle to make meaning after many kinds of loss, we have difficulty with the basics of life—getting out of bed, brushing our teeth, and eating food—let alone having to make decisions or do more complicated tasks. All of our resources are going toward trying to heal and make sense of senseless pain.

In all, finding ourselves on the Meaning-Making River can be a strange, upside-down experience.

How It Works

Meaning making is a process we go through when, after change, loss, or hardship, we have to find a new way to make sense of things. When we make meaning, we are trying to discover or build significance and purpose for our role in the world. Often, we have to go through this because our old ways of making sense have fractured or simply aren't working anymore.

For these reasons, meaning making is incredibly hard. Some people find it disorienting or even scary. It can feel as if we are tossed up into the air with no certain landing or as if the very ground beneath us is shifting.

Usually, meaning-making involves some kind of grief.

What is grief? Grief is the process of learning to live again after being forced to accept the unacceptable. Often when people talk about grief, they talk about the "five stages" (denial, anger, bargaining, depression, acceptance), as if this is a linear process. The five stages of grief is a model developed by psychologists Elisabeth Kübler-Ross and David Kessler.[46] These experts carefully explain that grief phases are not a straight line. Instead, grief often looks a lot more like a giant, frustrating squiggle. Going through it takes a lot of courage.

GRIEF IS A COMPLICATED PROCESS
—NOT A STRAIGHT LINE—

Humans grieve for a thousand different reasons. The most prominent association of grief is physical death of a loved one. Some cultures have beautiful grief traditions; people are encouraged to grieve and given plenty of time to do it. In the United States, the grieving party usu-ally gets a funeral, a couple of days of bereavement leave from work, and an outpouring of condolences and casseroles, but that's about it. After those first couple of weeks, most of us find grief culturally awkward. We don't know how to act or what to say in the presence of grief. We offer thoughts like "I'm sorry for your loss," as if it's somehow the person's fault who is offering those sentiments.

That's pretty meager. In the same token, death receives more acknowledgment than other significant processes of grief. Some losses—losses that shape us and deeply affect us—remain totally ignored. There are so many sources of grief they are almost too numerous to count:

- Grieving the death of dreams

- Grieving a relationship that will never be what we need it to be

- Grieving when someone you poured love into fails or betrays you

- Grieving that a community or nation isn't what it should be or isn't what we need it to be

- Grieving that someone you love struggles with the horrors of addiction

- Grieving that someone you love is incarcerated—alive and well but socially dead

- Grieving the loss of a job or retiring when that job gave you identity and purpose

- Grieving becoming a parent prematurely or grieving not being able to be a parent

- Grieving the loss of a pet, a pure-hearted soul who was there for you unconditionally

- Grieving loneliness when you don't want to be alone but can't change it

- Grieving illness or loss of opportunity

- Grieving the sheer brokenness of the world

We all grieve, all the time. Chances are high that any person we meet on the street is dealing with loss and disappointment and trying to make sense of life after the loss. This is a great reason to simply be gentle with people and with ourselves in difficult conversations and in life. You never know what someone is going through, and you never know how much of their energy for basic tasks is going to run the deep river of grief.

The meaning-making system offers several tools that help us rebuild our lives:

- **Sadness**—being overwhelmed with unfortunate or regretful circumstances—recognizes the loss and mourns its tragedy.

- **Disappointment** occurs when we recognize that dreams are dying or have died. Figuring out how to manage expectations moving forward is a large component of disappointment.

- **"Long" anger** is a profound sense of the world not being right, not being as it should be. Long anger is a powerful motivator for seeking justice.

- **Shame** is a sense of vulnerability, weakness, or impurity in our identities.

- **Disillusionment** may feel like a permanent sense of brokenness or meaninglessness. It recognizes and seeks to come to terms with the fact that old structures of meaning are no longer functional and new structures are needed.

- **Numbness** happens because meaning making is so draining on our internal resources. Therefore, we can often lapse into periods of numbness when the mindbody needs to take breaks from processing in order to recuperate. The schedule for these times of rest is decided by the mindbody. We cannot turn numbness on or off. The mindbody's intelligent systems decide when we are ready to feel or not feel.

- **Depression** as part of grieving processes is a form of long, slow-moving sadness that has a component of restfulness. (Some forms of depression are clinical, to the extent that they deal with chemical imbalances in the brain.) Rebuilding is a slow process. Sometimes our bodies need to just be allowed to sleep, eat, and be. People experiencing the depression of grief may oscillate between feeling sad, disillusioned, and numb. That is the mindbody in rebuild mode; it is the Meaning-Making River moving very slowly. Eventually, as we heal, meaning-based depression passes. It should not be rushed.

The Meaning-Making River—that slow, dark river of grief—takes a ton of our resources to run. The ways we make meaning in the world touch on so many of our structures of belief and so much of our understanding. It is a monumental effort to heal from when some part of ourselves or our world has broken. It takes a lot to rebuild hope. Meaning making calls on our mindbody to reprogram, to function after a huge chunk of us has been lopped off and swept away, usually against our will.

Is there a right way to grieve? Yes and no. While it's true that people grieve in different ways, there are indeed healthier and less healthy ways to grieve. The

Meaning-Making River runs so slowly and deeply that it contaminates easily. When we dump buckets of resentment, bitterness, or scorn into the river, or when we can't find a way to forgive, our grieving processes can become toxic or stagnant, and as a result, our ability to make meaning can become skewed. It might not feel like we have a say over our grieving processes, but we do have some control. It's important that we do our best to grieve well.

Tools and Techniques

How do we make meaning and deal with grief in healthy ways? Beyond recognizing that grief is a process designed to help us, I invite you to consider three tools I developed in my own journey with grief.

- **Float and honor.** Imagine yourself floating down the Meaning-Making River in a boat, furiously trying to paddle to get to the end. You are straining, sweating, and desperate to get it over with, trying to force your way out of the river and out of grief. Now imagine yourself pausing. Imagine yourself taking the paddle out of the water, sitting back a little, and looking around you. Take in the trees, the air, the touch of breeze. Now feel that current pulling you along. You don't have to do the work. The work will get done. Your job is to rest. Sometimes you need to take the paddle out and steer the boat around a rock or a branch. But mostly, your job is to let that river carry you. Let it do its job. Your job is to rest. Take this moment to honor your mindbody for all the hard work it has been doing.

- **Befriend the bees**. Some experiences of grief are so painful and so present that it's almost like a cloud of invisible bees that are constantly stinging you. No one else can see these bees. They just fly around your head, bringing pain and agitation, disrupting your ability to function. Why are the bees there? They might seem like predators, but the pain you're experiencing is the result of your mindbody trying to heal an open emotional wound. In this light, perhaps you can see the bees working on behalf of the

Meaning-Making River, trying to pollinate the garden of your mindbody, getting you ready for a new sense of purpose and normalcy. But the process feels awful, and sometimes you can only focus on the pain. Imagine yourself talking to the bees. "I know you guys are here to help me. Maybe we can work together, instead of fight. I will try to treat you gently. I will try to be your friend." If you let the bees do their job instead of shooing them away—if you let grief be present with you instead of resisting it—the stinging might feel a little more bearable. When you accept the bees, you accept your grief as something helpful, even though it hurts. And you hold the hope that while today you feel void, someday, with the passage of time, things will make sense again.

- **Boulder, brick, pebble.**[47] The initial phase of grief is like carrying a boulder everywhere you go. It's heavy and cumbersome, and it seems to draw attention to itself at all times. It's exhausting to lug around. You can't do anything without considering how that boulder fits into the picture. Over time, after a lot of grieving, that boulder will shrink into a brick. The brick is still cumbersome but less so. It doesn't get in the way as much, but it's still there, and it's still a significant part of your life. Eventually, after more time, that brick shrinks into a pebble, and you will carry that pebble with you for the rest of your days. The pebble will always remind you of what you went through; it will always remind you of the pain it took to forge you into the new version of yourself. That pebble is a testament to your survival. If you carry a boulder, trust that a day is coming when it will begin to feel like a brick. Hold that image in your mind: the lightness you will feel, the hope that it won't always be this hard. If you carry a brick, trust that a day will come that it will become small enough to slip into your pocket. Imagine the day you will feel hopeful about rebuilding your life; imagine the day you will be able to move on. It will come. If you carry a pebble, go out and find the people carrying boulders, and be the support you wish you would have had.

Dealing with Discomfort

As mentioned at other points in this book, transforming conflict and impasse comes with feelings of discomfort. Discomfort isn't itself a category of emotion; it can be tied to a lot of different factors. Sometimes it can be hard to figure out if being uncomfortable is just plain old awkwardness and being new at something, or whether it's actually a sign that one of the rivers is flowing strongly. Here are three questions to ask when you feel discomfort.

Am I Safe or in Danger?

First ask, "Am I safe or in danger?" Sometimes we feel like we are unsafe, physically or emotionally, and we forget that we are in control. There are two alternative reasons for feeling unsafe in a conversation: we are unsafe and feel unsafe, or we are safe but feel unsafe.

If we are not safe, because someone is threatening us physically or being emotionally manipulative, we should probably not continue the conversation. If we are feeling that trauma reaction begin—that sickening bubble of panic, rational or irrational, as if we are spiraling out of control—it's time to take care of ourselves. It's perfectly okay to say "I need to take a break" or "I need to stop talking about this right now. Let's plan to revisit in the future."

At other times, our Self-Protection River starts to run fast when we actually aren't in any danger. Sometimes the act of talking about tough things just gets us physically worked up, and it feels like panic. In this case, if we are still firmly in control of our mindbody and are in a rational enough state to understand our Self-Protection River might be giving faulty threat signals, then the level of discomfort we are feeling is okay. For example, let's say someone at work always bullies me whenever I talk about the environment. Bringing up this particular issue always causes nasty run-ins. Later on, when I talk to a different person about the environment, it's likely that my Self-Protection River will kick off a fight-or-flight response because I associate the topic with hostility. However, I am aware enough to understand that this is not my coworker I am speaking with; this is a totally different person and a different situation. The sense of agitation I feel is real, but it is not something I need to act on. Though my Self-Protection River is telling me I should be uncomfortable and even run away, I understand on a deeper level that I'm safe.

As long as you feel in control and understand there is no real danger, it's okay to sit with the discomfort.

Am I Being Stretched or Threatened?

Assuming you are safe, you can ask the next question: "Am I being stretched or threatened?" Being stretched by entertaining new ideas, cultures, or beliefs that we don't agree with is an awesome endeavor. It's one of the best things about engaging conflict. As long as no one is controlling us or forcing us to change our beliefs, there is generally no harm in just weighing an unfamiliar idea and testing its merits. However, if foul play is at work—if domination is at work and you are under emotional, spiritual, or physical threat—the discomfort you feel may be your Self-Protection River trying to protect you. In this case, walk away. Establish measures of precaution, and safeguard yourself and anyone else who may be negatively affected by this person.

Am I Challenging or Am I Using Domination?

Finally, ask yourself, "Am I challenging the other person in healthy ways, or am I using domination?" It's great to share your beliefs, values, and ideas with conviction. However, it's easy to cross a line from sharing to pushing, seeking to change or control others until they agree. In this case, our conversation partner will probably start to send us signals that they don't appreciate it. The discomfort you feel here is your internal monitor trying to tell you to back off, take a breather, revisit your emotional regulation, and look at ways you can better share power. Giving people space and freedom to make up their own minds is healthier for both of you and healthier for the relationship. It also increases the chances that they will listen to your perspective, because they don't have to spend time and energy being afraid of domination.

The Two Rivers in Action

Valerie has a sister named Elena, who doesn't treat her very well. Valerie finds herself on edge around Elena and feels a disorienting set of emotions whenever they are together. She doesn't really know why.

Using the two-rivers theory, we can begin to unpack what's happening. We might even be able to predict what will happen if the sisters have a confrontation.

Valerie's Self-Protection River is probably a rushing torrent, as Elena often crosses boundaries and throws jabs out of nowhere. Whether Valerie recognizes it consciously or not, her intelligent fight-or-flight system is working hard to prevent further harm. Valerie's mindbody has identified her sister Elena as an unsafe person and is putting up defenses left and right. Valerie might bounce between anger, fear, and anxiety as her self-protection system does its job. She might sometimes feel like fighting and other times feel like running away.

Since the two sisters haven't had a good relationship for a long time, when Elena happens to do something nice, it's likely Valerie will feel *more* anxiety. Even friendly interactions make Valerie feel confused and disquieted, because Elena has taught her, over the course of many years, to wait for the other shoe to drop.

Valerie's Meaning-Making River is also overflowing when she is around Elena, and even when they are not together. After a lifetime of trying to have a good relationship, Valerie is realizing this may never happen. They *should* have a good relationship, but they don't have what families have on TV. They are not best friends or even friends at all. How does Valerie deal with that fact? It breaks her heart. It doesn't make sense. Valerie will probably grieve the loss of that hoped-for relationship, even though her sister is alive and well.

Let's say Elena does something hurtful to Valerie, for the 8,067th time, so Valerie decides to confront her. If Valerie hasn't taken the time before the difficult conversation to work on emotional regulation, to sort through all of her layers of feelings and deal with them, one of two things is going to happen. One possibility is that as soon as Valerie opens her mouth, both rivers of emotion will come pouring out, causing a flash flood of external chaos, probably in the form of a nasty blow-up with Elena. Or Valerie will dam up her feelings inside, and they will contribute to self-destructive problems in her mindbody, which could lead to illness, depression, or addiction.

Feelings that aren't dealt with can cause explosions, implosions, or both.

It is totally unfair that Valerie has to deal with any of this. Elena is the aggressor, lacking care or concern for how her actions affect her sister. It shouldn't have to be Valerie's job to take responsibility for this. Yet because she can't change Elena, and because she wants to be a healthy person, Valerie chooses to work on what she can: she engages her mindbody's intelligent processes and works to partner with the two rivers for her own health and well-being.

We Deal with Feelings Differently

It's important to understand that we all have different relationships with our two rivers. Some of us may love and embrace them; some of us may resent and ignore them. What we share in common, for the most part, is that we must all deal with our feelings the best we can, and that might look different from person to person. As we navigate our feelings, we need to remember that the ways we choose to engage our rivers have downstream effects in the lives of others.

Identity, Expression, and Personal Preference

Few of us are comfortable with the idea of other people thinking we are weak. Some of us go to great lengths to avoid it. We often work hard to keep up the appearance that we are fine.

To avoid coming across as weak, we often show emotions on the outside that are a "harder" version of what is happening inside. In other words, when someone is outwardly angry, often they are inwardly afraid. This is the fight response of our Self-Protection River. Other times, when someone is outwardly uncomfortable, they are inwardly experiencing anxiety or full-blown panic. In difficult conversations, this response is entirely common. This is the flight response of our Self-Protection River. When someone is expressing outward apathy, often they are going through an inward grief process. This is the Meaning-Making River at work.

Sometimes we experience one river, one system, a lot more than the other. If we lose our job unjustly, we might start extreme-sport rafting down the Self-Protection River. If we lose someone to death, our Meaning-Making River will be flowing dark and strong.

The way we deal with emotions can also depend on our personalities. Some people are much more comfortable engaging one river more than the other.

Someone who is a more driven, or type A, person might be a lot more comfortable attending to their Self-Protection River. When they feel things, they turn that energy into forward motion and general busyness. They won't slow down long enough to look at their grief side. They don't want to engage directly in meaning making. Their busyness can be an attempt at making meaning through chaotic action.

Someone who is naturally more introspective, or type B, might be more comfortable attending to their Meaning-Making River and have a hard time finding the motivation that the fight-or-flight system provides. This group may tend to get bogged down in melancholy and do not like to engage the action of their fight or flight. All they might want to do is float. Floating can be an attempt to run away or escape through inaction.

I have been in both of these places at different times of my life. From personal experience, I have been happiest and felt most balanced when I've learned to recognize and honor both rivers at the same time.

It's the Ciiiiiircle of Striiiiiife

When we don't honor our two rivers, we aren't just affecting ourselves. Remember Valerie? Let's imagine she is your dental hygienist. The day after Valerie confronts her sister, she is scheduled to clean your teeth. Can you guess how that intense conflict might affect her focus at work? If she doesn't know how to navigate that situation and deal with her feelings, it's likely she will make mistakes and hurt someone else—in this case, you in the dental chair. Maybe after a horrible teeth cleaning, you are in a foul mood, and you go home and lash out at your kids. Then your kids turn around and bully other kids—and on and on it goes.

When we don't or can't work through our issues and feelings, we often send ripples of pain through our community. Therefore, it is in our collective best interest to learn how to deal with our feelings and not run away from them.

It's also in our best interest to learn better ways to care for others as they deal with emotions.

Trauma and the Two Rivers

Trauma is the experience of events that are so horrific or disturbing that they change or alter our mindbody in some way. Much has been written on trauma and emotion, and there are phenomenal resources out there to help anyone who experiences trauma or post-traumatic stress disorder (PTSD).[48] In terms of the two-rivers metaphor, it's important to understand that while trauma can dam up the Meaning-Making River and prevent future healing or forward motion, its most significant impact is on the Self-Protection River, to the point of permanently changing the way it works.

For those who have not experienced extreme trauma, our Self-Protection River day to day normally looks like a babbling brook with occasional whitewater rapids when a legitimate threat sounds off. For those of us who have trauma, our Self-Protection River looks like whitewater rapids at the drop of a hat and like full-blown waterfalls in especially triggering environments.

Neurologically speaking, for someone with trauma, their fight-or-flight response gets short-circuited, and they are literally and physically, from a brain function and chemistry perspective, less able to parse what is a real threat versus a perceived threat. They may seem to overreact to small things or become afraid much more easily than an average person. They often experience "hypervigilance," which is a sense of being overly alert and on edge, and are unable to stop feeling this way. They also lack an ability to concentrate. Control over their mindbody and their memory function is compromised to the point of shutting down, detaching from reality, or having full gaps in their memory. In some cases, people with long-term trauma can act in reckless or self-destructive ways, hold negative or irrational attitudes toward themselves or others especially as relates to traumatic events, and in some cases report being unable to experience positive or happy emotions. For many reasons that include emotional, physical, and neurological causes, it's often hard or even impossible for people with trauma to explain or work through what happened to them, unless they get professional help.[49]

Please remember that if you see someone struggling to self-regulate their emotions or calm down, it's likely they may have had experiences in their life that physically and emotionally prevent them from doing so. "Calm down" is the last thing people need to hear when they can't. Educating ourselves on the way trauma works is incredibly important. It's also important to learn how to use the word *trauma* in a clinical sense, not flippantly, so we can be sensitive to those who are deeply affected by it.

If you think you or someone you know is dealing with trauma, there are amazing resources and professionals whose sole job it is to help you manage what you are experiencing. Notably, you might look into an emerging form of psychological care called cognitive behavioral therapy (CBT),[50] which has a high success rate in helping people learn to cope with trauma and PTSD.

Supporting Others Who Experience Difficult Feelings

Conflict and impasse can dredge up old wounds that come with strong feelings. There will be times in life when emotions are difficult because someone else is having them. When we see someone else feeling strongly, it's natural to want to help somehow.

First, I want to stress that being supportive does not mean setting aside boundaries. We need to put on our own oxygen mask before we help others. This section presumes that you are in a good place to help others; it presumes you understand and practice emotional regulation.

Importantly, we can't do emotional work *for* someone else. We can't actually feel what they feel or deal with it on their behalf. We can only be supportive.

Being a Non-Anxious Presence

There is a wonderful concept from the discipline of clinical counseling, pastoral care, and chaplaincy called "non-anxious presence." Our first goal in supporting someone experiencing hard emotions is to simply and profoundly set aside nervousness and become still, soft, and quietly strong. Of course, we can't just turn off anxiety like a faucet. But there are definitive steps we can certainly take to be a non-anxious presence so we can help and support others as they do the work of strong emotions.

1. Make It about Them

When you seek to support someone going through difficulties, the first step is to stop doing anything that draws attention to yourself. Stop talking about yourself, stop referencing yourself. Don't apologize or talk about how awkward you feel. Don't try to defray tension or "make it better." This is about them. Your goal is to let them talk. Making them feel understood is like giving them medicine.

2. Sit

Just sit with them. Be. Breathe. And then *be* some more. If that's hard to do, you can pretend you are a giant, solid tree. Stretch your roots into the ground, and show that person quietly that you are being solid so they can fall apart. For any tension or anxiety you feel, imagine yourself taking it from the room and sinking it through your roots into the ground. Offer your trunk so they can lean on you. Stretch out your branches to offer them shade and rest. And then let the wind move through your leaves. Let there be quiet. Quiet is healing. It's okay if things move slowly. When you slow down, ground yourself, and breathe, you remind the other person to slow down and ground themselves and breathe. You are showing incredible strength and leadership.

3. Let Them Lead the Conversation

Don't direct. Let them talk about whatever they want to talk about. Focus on asking open questions, but don't force them to answer. If they want to be quiet, then be quiet. If they want to talk, let them talk. Let them know you aren't talking because you want them to have plenty of space to talk, even with big silences in between.

4. Show You Understand

Empathy starts with your eyes. Speak with your eyes before you use words. Let your eyes show someone you care about them, that you seek to feel their pain.

If you must speak, validate their experience to the best of your ability, without telling them you know how they feel. You can't know how they feel. But you can say you hear them: "Wow, that's terrible." "Yes, I can understand how hard that would be." "No, you're not crazy. I would feel that way too." "I can see it from your perspective." "Everything you are saying makes sense." From time to time, repeat what you hear back to them. Do not speak for them or put words in their mouth. Listen deeply and be specific about what you hear.

Regarding physical contact, if you normally engage in physical contact with this person, if it's a close relative or partner, then use it. If it's someone you wouldn't normally touch, then it could be distracting or interpreted wrongly, so avoid touching.

5. Don't Fix It!

Don't even try to fix it; just don't. If they need advice, they will ask. You can certainly process with them and ask open questions, but what they need from you right now is not a solution. They need the medicine of someone understanding them. Before anything needs to be fixed, they need to know they are not alone.

6. Offer to Help Plan Further Action

After someone pours out their heart and the conversation is winding down, if you think the situation requires further action, then ask, "Can we find a time to make a plan?" While you don't want to fix things at that particular moment, you can make a plan to work on it in the future. You can set up a time to meet and talk through options, to weigh pros and cons. You can offer to help find a

How to Be A "Non-Anxious Presence"

—TO SUPPORT SOMEONE THROUGH DIFFICULT EMOTIONS—

Being supportive does not mean setting aside boundaries. We need to "put on our own oxygen mask" before we help others. This section presumes that you are okay and in a good place to help others.

1. **MAKE IT ABOUT THEM** and don't draw attention to yourself in any way. Don't ask them to take care of you. Right now, this is about them.

2. **SIT.** Just sit with them.

3. **FOLLOW THEIR LEAD** for the tone and flow of the conversation. Ask questions.

4. **SHOW YOU UNDERSTAND.** Empathy starts with your eyes. From time to time, repeat what you hear back to them. Do not speak for them. Listen deeply.

5. **DON'T FIX IT.** If they need advice, they will ask.

6. **OFFER TO HELP MAKE A PLAN,** at the end of the conversation, if any further action is needed.

7. **FOLLOW UP MORE THAN ONCE.** Ask them how they are doing within a couple of days. Ask what you can do to help.

REMEMBER:

- **NO ONE LIKES TO BE PITIED.** Empathy means "being alongside as equals."

- **BOUNDED CARE IS OKAY.** Be honest with yourself and them about how much care you are willing and able to give. Help find other help. It's healthy for both of you to diversify support systems.

- **LET THEM RECIPROCATE.** in giving you care if they want to, even if they are going through something really hard. Sometimes when people grieve, it helps them to give back so they don't feel too needy. Let them help you.

- **WATCH FOR DESPAIR AND THE LOSS OF A FUTURE STORY.** Don't hesitate to ask for the help and advice of a professional caregiver if your gut tells you to.

helping professional they can speak with. If they don't want help, don't force the issue. You have already helped immensely by being a non-anxious presence.

7. Follow Up

A day or two after you talk to the person dealing with tough things, send them a text, call them, or even send a card to let them you know are thinking about them. Let them know you are honored to be there for them. Ask them how they are doing and if they need anything. Sometimes after people are really vulnerable, they might get uncomfortable around the person they opened up to. So it's important for the longevity of your relationship that you send a strong, ongoing message that you think well of them, that things are good and not weird for you. Assure them that the friendship is important to you. Let them know you are there for them, and you aren't going anywhere.

Some Further Guidance

As you practice being a non-anxious presence, here are a few more things to remember:

- **No one likes to be pitied.** Empathy means being alongside as equals. When you look down on someone for struggling, you aren't being vulnerable or honest about your own shortcomings and struggles, so in a way, you are claiming to be superhuman. That's not fair or right. We all struggle; we all learn. We are all human.

- **Bounded care is okay.** If things go well, that person might begin to lean on you a lot. You need to be honest with yourself and them about how much care you are willing and able to give. You are allowed to tell that person what your limitations and blind spots are. In fact, it's better for both of you to diversify support systems, to find more than one source of support. It's not healthy for you to be the only source of care this person receives. Seek out resources and support groups to help share the responsibility of caring for that person, and seek the advice of a professional caregivers if needed. A lot of help exists out there.

- **Let them reciprocate in giving you care.** When some people lean on you, it helps them to be able to give something back to you. Some of us are taught that care and love are transactional; we fear that the person giving us care has too much power over us or that we will be in their debt, and it makes us uncomfortable. It might feel strange, but let the person you are caring for help you in return or give you gifts (within reason). It's their way of making the relationship feel balanced. Accept the gift, and make sure to assure them in many ways that they are not a burden and don't have to give you anything to deserve care.

- **Watch for the loss of a future story.** Sometimes people can grieve so hard or be so depressed that their idea of meaning breaks, and they might give up. If you hear someone say they are losing hope—if they stop talking about the future, if their perceptions of reality begin to get skewed, if they start giving away precious belongings, if they talk about harming themselves, or if they speak fatalistically in any way (as in, "There's no point in living" or "After I'm gone ..."), seek professional help *immediately*. This person might not be planning to take drastic action right now, but they might be on that path. Don't accuse them, judge them, or roughly force them to take action, because that might drive them away, but gently and firmly get them into the care of a helping professional. If you need advice, you can personally call the National Suicide Prevention Lifeline (+1 800-273-8255), explain the situation, and ask them what you should do. This is not something either of you should navigate alone. A lot of help is available to them and to you.

SUMMARY: A Celebration of Emotion

If emotions are hard for you, I applaud you for making it through this chapter. I hope the "two rivers" model is as helpful to you as it is to me. Remember that emotions are good; feelings are us taking care of us, even though they sometimes misfire.

Honor your mindbody and its processes. Remember that no one is perfect at dealing with emotions. We are all learning and practicing.

If you have ever been shamed for having emotions, wipe that guilt off like a bird turd, and throw it away. Your mindbody is good just the way it is. The information it sends you is for your benefit. Your two rivers might misfire every once in a while, especially if you have been through a lot in your life, but they are not your enemy. They exist to help you thrive in full humanity and purpose. You have the capacity to learn emotional regulation in a way that honors the intelligence and beauty of your mindbody.

You also have the capacity to be an incredible friend and caregiver, an empathetic and effective conversation partner, someone that people feel safe opening up to. Your experiences, as hard as they have been, speak to your intention to be healthy and expand your capacity to love.

Though this capacity may have come with pain, the person you choose to become is a remarkable creation.

1. Did this chapter reinforce or challenge the ways you think about emotions, self-protection, and meaning making? How do you see emotion the same way or differently?

2. We all have a relationship with our own emotions. What is yours? If you're not sure, say the phrase "I am an emotional being" five times. The first time, say it as if you are sad. Then say it angrily. Then say it happily. Then fearfully. Then numbly. Which one felt the most comfortable? Which one felt the least comfortable?

3. Which emotions in other people are you most comfortable being around? Which are you least comfortable around?

4. When difficult conversations happen, what are you usually feeling? Do you have any tips or tricks for working through those feelings?

5. Share a story of your experience with the Self-Protection River (fight-or-flight response).

6. Share a story of your experience with the Meaning-Making River (grief ability).

7. When was a time you were able to be a non-anxious presence for someone? What was it like?

8. When was a time someone else was able to be a non-anxious presence for you? What were the short-term and long-term effects?

Part III

TRANSFORMING IMPASSE

- Unpacking the role of assumptions in our structures of meaning

- Expanding rhetorical and communications skills

- Bringing more resilient communities to life

CHAPTER 7

Assumptions and the Awesome If

Singing to Worms

I love the coziness of a fresh Christmas tree in the house. Several years ago, I didn't have extra money during the holidays and wasn't going to be able to afford one. However, to my sheer and utter delight, I won a real, full-size tree in a raffle!

Ecstatic, I called my then-boyfriend and said, "Peter, you're never going to believe this! I just won a real Christmas tree! Will you come with me to the tree lot and help me pick it out?"

He replied angrily, "I am *not* coming!" and hung up the phone.

I was stunned. This was totally out of character. I called him back and asked what was the matter. He just kept saying he wasn't coming.

Begging and pleading, I finally convinced him I couldn't manage on my own. He ended the call with a gruff, "Fine," leaving me to stare at my phone and wonder what kind of monster hated Christmas trees and whether I would be able to stay with such a man.

Peter met me at the lot, marched out of his car, grabbed the first tree he could find, and said, "This one." At this point, I was too taken aback to argue. I just wanted to get home before he changed his mind.

We made it back to the house and tensely set up the tree in the living room. After an hour or two, I said gently, "Hey, I'm not sure what happened back there. Please help me understand."

After a long pause, he told me that in his family growing up, picking out a Christmas tree was a guaranteed fight every year. Unable to make a group decision, every member of the family became furious at each other. It was always frustrating and sad for him.

I thought back to memories of my family picking out a tree. It was one time all year we *didn't* fight. There was peace on earth and silver bells, and tiny Christmas angels descended from heaven and flitted around the living room as we unpacked floppy boxes of homemade ornaments.

Christmas trees were utterly magical for me but full of pain for him.

In this situation, Peter and I had different core assumptions about the way the world works and what we expected to happen. Based on our family systems, our experiences, and observable patterns over time, we both developed emotional associations; Christmas trees had become totally different symbols to each of us, causing us to develop totally different and very strong opinions about the tree. These associations were so strong they nearly caused a full-blown impasse.

While on the surface, it might seem that Peter was being mean, he was also willing to overcome his beliefs and painful memories for my sake, because he cared about me.

Everything considered, that's surprisingly loving.

Our Structure of Meaning

Each of us has a structure of meaning. A structure of meaning is the web of ideas and truths that are connected inside our hearts and minds.

At the center of who we are, we hold our *core beliefs*—what we understand reality is.

OUR STRUCTURE OF MEANING

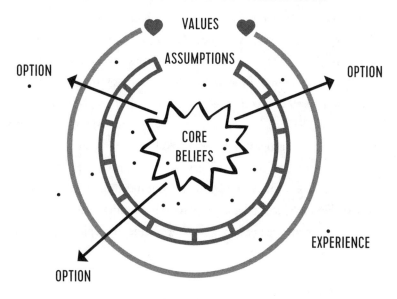

Oranges: I believe oranges are real.

Wrapped around that are *assumptions*—things we accept to be true, based on our beliefs and reinforced by our experiences, that we don't spend a lot of time proving. We just take assumptions as given.

An orange is an orange because I've seen an orange, I've held an orange in my hand. I was taught to call it an orange. I assume oranges are safe to eat, because someone fed them to me. When I eat them, I don't die. I am told they are nutritious, and I assume that is correct information, even though I can't personally prove it, because I am not a scientist.

Around our beliefs and assumptions—our view of reality and truth— we build our *values*. Values are our sense of what makes reality meaningful.

I value oranges because I value survival and health. Oranges are nutritious and delicious, so they help me achieve my goal of well-being.

Out of all of this spring our opinions—our views and judgments about how the world should work and how people should act. Our opinions pass through all the other layers of our structure of meaning and are shaped by each level.

Oranges are good! Everyone should eat them.

The takeaway here is that opinions don't happen out of thin air. They are linked to a huge unseen web of how we understand reality. Since opinions are linked to our entire structure of meaning, every opinion we hold is actually the tip of an iceberg. A ton of other things are going on below the surface. Therefore, in difficult conversations, when people talk about "differences of opinion," it's a mistake to engage only the opinions themselves ("I won't eat oranges"; "Oh, yeah? Well you're wrong") while failing to engage the why—all the beliefs, assumptions, and values that support the opinions. If we want to be effective communicators in difficult conversations, seeking to gain a deep and full understanding of someone's truth in order to see them, we need to make ample time for exploring the whole structure of meaning.

How Structures of Meaning Work

Our structures of meaning like to be "internally consistent," meaning that all the different parts—our experiences, beliefs, assumptions, values, and opinions—connect and rely on each other. Change one piece, and other pieces will likely change. In other words, a structure of meaning is like a close-knit group of kids on the playground. They are friends and want to play nice with each other. They don't like to contradict, so they often will shift to try to accommodate each other.

For example, let's say I believe the following:

Ghosts are real. (belief, based on experience or not)

Ghosts can mess with me. (assumption, based on evidence or logic)

Safety is important to me. (value)

Therefore, holding a séance to contact the dead is a really bad idea. (opinion)

What if we change one piece in a structure of meaning? Other pieces will likely change:

Change of Core Belief

Ghosts are not real. (change of core belief, based on experience or not)

If ghosts aren't real, they can't mess with me. (assumption, based on evidence or logic)

Safety is important to me, but in this case, there is no danger. **(value)**

Therefore, séances don't do anything; we could hold one or not hold one. **(opinion)**

Change of Core Assumption

Ghosts are real. **(core belief, based on experience or not)**

<u>Ghosts can't mess with me.</u> **(change of assumption, based on evidence or logic)**

Safety is important to me, but in this case, there is no danger. **(value)**

Therefore, séances aren't dangerous. We could hold one or not hold one. **(opinion)**

Change of Value

Ghosts are real. **(core belief, based on experience or not)**

Ghosts can mess with me at any time. **(assumption, based on evidence or logic)**

<u>Safety is less important to me than sheer curiosity.</u> **(change of value)**

Therefore, a séance is a great idea! **(opinion)**

While our structures of meaning like to play nice, sometimes they do contradict. Occasionally, one piece shifts but others don't or can't shift in response. When our structures of meaning contradict within us, it causes a phenomenon that psychologists call cognitive dissonance. This is an experience of inconsistencies between our beliefs and actions, our assumptions and values, and so on.[51] It can feel utterly uncomfortable, confusing, and even senseless. For example, if a person who struggles with a gambling addiction values providing for his family and believes gambling is wrong but gambles anyway, he will probably experience cognitive dissonance in which his beliefs and values are in conflict with his actions. Whether consciously or subconsciously, most of us work to resolve cognitive dissonance, even if that means telling ourselves things that aren't true. The man in our example might try to relieve the dissonance by telling himself that while he believes gambling is bad, someday he will win the jackpot, and his family won't have to struggle anymore. He might try to convince himself that ultimately he gambles *because* he loves his family.

Cognitive dissonance can also occur when we learn new information or have an experience that challenges what we thought we knew to be true and right. For example, Ana believes being gay is wrong and that gay people are corrupt and licentious. One day, she meets a gay person named Leslie, who seems incredibly kind and moral and upstanding. When Ana meets Leslie, she gains new information that not *all* gay people are a certain way; here is living evidence. Ana will probably experience cognitive dissonance, because her beliefs and assumptions are suddenly at odds with her new experiences.

Shifts in our structures of meaning are a big reason why learning new information or meeting people who are different from us can feel threatening. Sometimes everything we thought we knew and believed to be true feels like it's falling apart. Big internal changes within our structure of meaning have an impact on the very center of who we are, the center of our identity. It can be extremely disorienting.

If you are going through this or know someone who is, remember to be patient with yourself and others in this process. Changes in our structures of meaning are a natural part of personal growth, but they can be painful and challenging, and they may take a long time to sort through. When someone is in the midst of this kind of transition, they don't need shame or judgment. They need support, kindness, and importantly, safe spaces to process what they are going through.

Introducing Assumptions

When we are working with difficult conversations, it's vital to be able to tell the difference between a belief, an assumption, a value, and an opinion. Knowing how these things are unique can help us understand not just what people think, but also why they think it.

Beliefs are fundamentally unprovable and don't need logic or evidence to be valid. While there are many different understandings and histories of belief, most people define belief as something based on faith—an idea or conviction beyond the realm of logic or evidence.[52] Beliefs are powerful and lie deep in the center of our identity and sense of safety and order. They constitute the very core of our structure of meaning. Beliefs are so powerful that we are more likely to agree with people who say they hold the same beliefs as we do, even if we might otherwise disagree with them. This phenomenon is called "belief bias."[53] The fact that we naturally favor beliefs doesn't mean beliefs are bad. On the contrary, many people hold them in high esteem and find incredible life and purpose within them.[54] That's why it's important to be very careful if we are tempted to challenge someone's core beliefs. When humans experience having their beliefs under fire, the most common response is to batten down the hatches and cling even harder to what they believe, even if it causes cognitive dissonance. Therefore, in most cases, it's not fair or right or effective to challenge someone's beliefs. People should be free to believe whatever they wish.

Sitting just outside our core beliefs are our assumptions—the basis of our values, opinions, and actions. Assumptions and beliefs both make up the deepest parts of what we hold dear, but unlike beliefs, assumptions *can* be proven or disproven. Because they are so central, having our assumptions challenged can be downright unnerving, but challenging them is totally fair in difficult conversations. Therefore, understanding what assumptions are and how they work is an important skill to learn.

Faulty vs. Core Assumptions

Almost invariably, whenever anyone says the word *assume*, someone in the room chimes in with that classic dad joke, "Remember, when you assume, you make an ass out of you and me" (Ass + U + Me—get it?).

Yes, true; sometimes our assumptions can betray us and lead us to false conclusions. For example, I see someone sitting on their porch during a workday. I could assume they don't have a job. However, maybe they work from home. Maybe they work the night shift. Maybe they are taking a sick day. Maybe they are on their lunch break. Maybe they are waiting for a ride to work. Maybe I was reading into that situation based on the way the person on the porch looked, how they were dressed, or what their house looks like.

We make assumptions all the time without realizing it. Making a *faulty* assumption, like assuming we know the life of the person sitting on the porch, means we are passing judgment based on incomplete sets of data. Faulty assumptions occur when we fill in gaps of our understanding with guessing and bias. That means we may be wrong, often.

Avoiding Faulty Assumptions: Giving the Benefit of the Doubt

When my partner and I moved into our first apartment, I decided to start a worm composting bin, good little hippie that I am. Worm composting involves putting a small population of worms in a bucket and feeding them organic food scraps. The worms turn the scraps into garden fertilizer.

One Saturday morning, I went out digging in the backyard that we shared with a few other apartments. I was really getting into the worm hunting, turning over rocks and leaves, finding tons of worms, and getting covered in dirt. Sometimes I sing while I work, and on this particular occasion, it seemed appropriate to sing the theme from Charlie and the Chocolate Factory: "Come with meeee / and you'll be / in a wooooooorld of pure imagination . . ."

In the midst of my revelry, I looked up and saw one of my new neighbors watching me from the patio, about twenty feet away. I froze, realizing that she definitely just heard me singing to worms. I gave her an awkward wave, and she waved back and walked inside, looking amused.

When I saw her a few days later, I introduced myself and apologized for what she had to see. She answered with a smile, "Oh, don't worry about it. I figured you had a good reason."

My neighbor could have assumed I was off my rocker. Instead, she chose to recognize that she probably didn't have all the information.[55]

We make faulty assumptions when our interpretation of the world is incomplete. The opposite of making a faulty assumption is giving the benefit of the doubt. Because no person is omniscient, our assumption structures are a lot less like granite and a lot more like Swiss cheese. Giving the benefit of the doubt means we recognize that we are not perfect interpreters.

In those moments when we are tempted to make an assumption and pass judgment, what might it mean to hold off and ask ourselves, "What don't I know yet? What space can I make for the benefit of the doubt?"

When we do this, we are seeking a fuller picture of reality. We are starting to see.

Core Assumptions Are Different

Making a *faulty* assumption is quite different from holding a *core* assumption. A core assumption is something we can safely accept to be true. Core assumptions are the "rules" we live by (whether we realize it or not). These kinds of assumptions aren't things that make an ass of us. They are things we use, appropriately, all the time. Most of the time, they go unsaid.

Flibbins McGlib is a sailor. He just told you he plans to "sail around the world." When Flibbins tells you this, he probably won't spell out all his beliefs and assumptions. But it's still true he has a whole structure of meaning under his plan to sail. Here's what Flibbins would say if he explained it all:

Core Beliefs

I believe the earth exists and humans are free to travel it.

Core Assumptions

I am told the earth is round. Though I've never been to space and looked at the planet with my own eyes, it seems reasonable to assume that this is correct information, based on gravity and the curvature of the horizon.

The buoyancy of water will support the weight of a ship and my body in it. Sailing ships is mostly safe. I've sailed before, and I lived.

Since the earth is round, I don't have to be afraid of falling off the edge if I try to sail around it.

Values

We need to understand the earth. It's my job to help explore it.

Opinion

It's a good idea to sail around the world.

Action

Bon voyage!

To function in the world around us, we all hold gobs of foundational assumptions that help us make sense of things. Most of the time, we accept them as fact and don't worry about proving them. "Two plus two always equals four" is a foundational assumption that we can pretty much bank on. If two plus two occasionally equaled five, the world would cease to function. Anything built on basic mathematical principles could not operate—computers, streetlights, planes, money, geometric angles, light waves—pretty much life as we know it.

How do we know that two plus two equals four? I have never personally proven, through complex mathematics, that it's true. But sometime, somewhere, smart mathematicians did, so I trust them.

A foundational assumption is like a belief in the way it sits at the core of how we think and operate. Unlike a belief, foundational assumptions *can* be proven through one of two ways: logic or evidence. We can reasonably take a foundational assumption as a given, because 1) it's constructed through airtight logic (reason, critical thought) or 2) someone somewhere proved it (scientific process, simple observation).

Sometimes assumptions masquerade as beliefs so they can't be challenged. For example, suppose someone claims, "I believe women are less intelligent than men; it's just what I believe." This person might be claiming the clemency of faith that can't be proven or disproven, but they are actually talking about assumptions. It's totally fair to ask them what they are basing this on and to offer evidence, studies, and logic demonstrating reasons to the contrary. "Believing" in inequality is a totally different kind of claim than saying, "I believe in God" or "I believe in karma" or "I don't believe in life after death." If a claim is within the realm of what we can prove or disprove, it's based in assumptions, not beliefs.

Unlike faulty assumptions, which always get us into trouble, core assumptions can be wrong, faulty, neutral, or positive. We need core assumptions to function in the world, or each of us would spend all day staring into telescopes and making calculations to prove things like "the sky is blue" over and over and over. Foundational assumptions let us accept certain things as fact and move on.

Foundational assumptions can also be true and faulty at the same time. One of the most famous examples of a true-yet-faulty assumption is found in the US Declaration of Independence: "We hold these truths to be self-evident that all men are created equal." Holding something to be "self-evident" means the writers of the declaration were saying they weren't going to mince words proving this idea; they were taking it as a given that "men are created equal." There's an appeal to this. Yes, all men are created equal. That is sound logic and very hard to disprove. But at the same time, there's a faulty side. The writers weren't using the modern, universal definition of the word *men*, as in the human race. They actually meant free, property-owning, male citizens. At the time the declaration was written, many believed that women and enslaved people were not capable of citizenship and democracy because they weren't educated, and they weren't educated because it was widely assumed that they weren't mentally capable of being educated. This chicken-and-egg cycle of faulty assumptions and dehumanizing beliefs was propped up like a house of cards for many years. It would take decades of careful activism, personal sacrifice, and multiple constitutional amendments before the domination hidden within that one little core assumption could be called into account.

Can you imagine, then, how different history would be if the writers of the declaration had instead penned the words, "We hold these truths to be self-evident, that all human beings are created equal"?

Excavating Core Assumptions

Why do core assumptions matter so much? In difficult conversations, it's easy to talk about oppositional opinions. It's often easy to talk about beliefs and values, because many of us spend a lot of time figuring out what we believe about the world and what gives life meaning. Talking about core assumptions is much more challenging, because assumptions are usually hidden. They have to be excavated, the way an archaeologist digs through layers of rock to see what's below. Carefully excavating assumptions is very important in difficult conversations.

So how do we "establish" our core assumptions? Don't we hold too many assumptions to count? Yes, but only a handful will be relevant for any given conversation. When we establish assumptions, we are trying to explain to our conversation partner which specific core assumptions make up the basis for the opinions we hold in the conversation. We are trying to be aware of how we know what we know. (Is my assumption logic-based, evidence-based, or both? If it can't

HOW WE KNOW WHAT WE KNOW: THE TWO TYPES OF CORE ASSUMPTIONS

Two types of core assumptions relate to how we know what we know.[56] An *a priori* (Latin for "what comes first") assumption describes what we can know apart from direct experience—what we can safely deduce from reason and logic.

Today is Sunday, so it can't also be Wednesday.

It's wrong to punish innocent people.

2 + 2 = 4.

An *a posteriori* (Latin for "what comes after") assumption describes what we know from the experience of our senses, including all scientific knowledge, because it can be tested.

This book is a book because it looks and feels like what I've learned a book looks and feels like.

Without love, I become sad.

Plants use sunlight to grow.

We all use both of these types of assumptions all the time, and each kind has pros and cons. One is not necessarily better than the other. An *a priori* assumption is harder to prove, because it's based on abstract principles and logic, not on what we can see, feel, and touch. An *a posteriori* assumption is not always 100 percent valid, because our senses and experiences can sometimes betray us.

When we talk about assumptions and investigate them, it's a good rule of thumb to be aware of what kind of assumption we are dealing with, so we can track how we know what we know.

be proven or disproven, it's a belief.) We are trying to compare our core assumptions, figuring out how much common ground we share and where we disagree. This means asking someone why they think what they think. What are the reasons? What is their evidence? What is their logic? What are their experiences? Excavating assumptions means not assuming we know the answers. It means asking a ton of questions and then using what we learn to connect the dots and get a sense of someone's whole outlook. It means seeing them.

Once we have established our core assumptions, our communication will improve, because we know where each other is coming from and we don't have to keep explaining what we take as given. From this point on, the conversation can be more nuanced and fruitful.

Excavating Assumptions: The Awesome If

"The test of a first-rate intelligence is the ability to hold two opposed ideas
in mind at the same time and still retain the ability to function."
- F. Scott Fitzgerald

One of the most powerful tools in engaging difficult conversations is what I call the Awesome If. The Awesome If allows us to temporarily jump out of what we know to be true and use our imaginations about what we would think or how we would feel *if* we held different beliefs, assumptions, or values. Part of maturity is learning how to honestly and openly explore someone else's truth without having to accept it as our own. Being a powerful thinker doesn't require that we have a fancy degree attached to our name. Being a powerful thinker requires an ability to grapple with paradox—to understand why someone thinks the way they do without having to agree with them or feel threatened by the differences we find.

The Awesome If is more than walking an hour in someone else's shoes (which we know is impossible). It means trying to understand and interpret their structure of meaning, trying to imagine life and reality from their perspective. This tool helps us humanize, contextualize, and empathize with our conversation partner, leading to a productive conversation.

The Awesome If Has Five Steps

1. Learn your conversation partner's backstory.

2. Excavate their structure of meaning.

3. Use the Awesome If, imagining what it would be like to have their experiences.

4. Identify what you think is valid in their structure of meaning.

5. Dig into nuance.

Here is a scenario. Two people meet at a work party. Laura, a company accountant wearing a green dress, is a democratic socialist. She believes our country should share resources in order to wipe out poverty. She feels strongly that capitalism is dangerous if left unchecked.

Eric, an account executive wearing a bespoke blue suit, believes we should be a totally free-market society with no social safety programs (welfare, food stamps, etc.). He assumes that people who participate in safety net programs are lazy. He says he doesn't want to share with people who won't "pull their weight."

Laura and Eric are in for a huge disagreement, right?

Engaging the Awesome If, Laura is going to try, with honesty and curiosity, to picture herself having Eric's beliefs, assumptions, and values—the things that sit beneath his opinions.

To do this, she needs to gather more information. Time to excavate.

First, Laura needs to learn Eric's backstory (step 1). After forming some great questions, she learns that he grew up with an abusive alcoholic father; his family made terrible financial decisions and was perpetually on welfare because his parents were dishonest about their ability to work. She learned he was afraid to ask for things he needed, like new shoes for school. She learns that Eric put himself through college by working two jobs. She learns that he is proud of what he has accomplished, despite the lack of help from his family. Having had to work so hard, Eric has a low tolerance for what he calls excuses. He says he is proud to live in a country full of opportunity for anyone who works hard enough. He believes he earned everything he has, and social safety net programs create unhealthy dependency, as happened in his family.

At this point, Laura is able to dig into Eric's structure of meaning (step 2). She might start to have some thoughts about it—for example, that although Eric has had a hard life, he still has a lot of power automatically granted to him because he has light skin, blue eyes, and an athletic male build. She suspects that Eric's personal charisma and Romney-esque hair probably made him some friends in high places who opened doors for him. She silently questions whether he was perhaps too hard on his parents, who suffered from addiction. Though he had a rough experience of safety net programs, she believes he is painting people on welfare with a brush that is much too broad.

Laura has very strong opinions and is feeling some strong feelings. At this point, she has three choices. She can walk away. She can lash out at Eric, label him, and demand that he change his mind. Or she can use the Awesome If.

Using the Awesome If (step 3), Laura tries to imagine—while not losing sight of her own experiences and emotions—what it would be like to have a life like Eric's. *If* she were Eric and those experiences had shaped her, what might life be like? She imagines herself as a little child, sitting in her room, needing new shoes for school but knowing her family can't afford them because of alcohol abuse, too afraid of her dad to ask. She imagines herself earning that college degree against many odds, after years of sleepless, work-filled nights. Would she grow fond of capitalism and the new future she was able to forge through it? Though Laura might sharply disagree with Eric's ideas and think he is wrong, where can she give him some credit? How can she extend a hand of friendship and understanding? How can she see him?

She realizes he probably did work very hard. He probably did overcome a lot of pain and negative role models who did very little to help him grow.

So Laura chooses to validate (step 4) her conversation partner. "You know what, Eric, it sounds like you had a difficult upbringing. That can't have been easy. Though I don't agree with a lot of your views, I do agree that working hard and taking advantage of the opportunities our country affords is important. Based on your story, I can understand why you may have arrived at your beliefs."

At this point, Eric is confused, because he was expecting a liberal-versus-conservative brawl, replete with name calling and defensiveness. Instead of being blasted or shamed, the experiences and the values closest to Eric's heart are being validated. His opinions are not being accepted; Laura is still definitively disagreeing with him. But she is showing him that she recognizes and respects his right to have ideas. She is showing him that she recognizes his structure of meaning is internally consistent. And, above all, she is showing him that she values him as a human being.

The Awesome If gives the benefit of the doubt. It trusts that people's experiences are valid, no matter what they choose to make of them.

USING THE "AWESOME IF"

A PRODUCTIVE CONVERSATION happens after building trust, respect, and cooperation.

5. Dig into **nuance**. Discuss specific points of disagreement and invite courageous dialogue (respectful sharing of hard truths).

4. Identify what is **valid**. By giving credit when they make a solid point, and by naming the things you both agree on, you show that you are reasonable.

3. Use the **Awesome If**. Try to imagine what it would be like if you were in their situation and had their experiences. By expressing empathy, you show that you really see them.

2. Excavate their **structure of meaning**. By studying how their beliefs, assumptions, values, and opinions interconnect, you show that you want to understand them, not judge them.

STEP 1. Learn your conversation partner's **backstory**. Understand how their experiences have shaped their views. By humanizing their perspective, you show them you care about them as a person, not that you just want to win.

THE INCREDIBLE IMPORTANCE OF
GIVING CREDIT WHERE IT'S DUE

Many times, when we are in conversation with someone with whom we deeply disagree, it can be easy to oppose or reject every single thing that person says because we don't like what they stand for.

We often approach conversations like this because the views of our conversation partner make us angry or flustered. We fear that if we validate *anything* they say, we have to agree with them on *everything* or give over too much ground.

Refusing to give credit where it's due causes a lot of harm.

Most arguments contain a kernel of truth; their claims are based on some kind of logic, facts, grievances, or pain. There is some good reason the person is passionate. Sometimes those reasons are understandable, even if we don't come to the same conclusions.

When we refuse to acknowledge that kernel of truth—when we refuse to give credit to the good reason someone is passionate—we send a message loud and clear that our commitment to opposing them is stronger than our commitment to truth and reason. When we close ourselves to the idea that our "opponent" could make good points or have something valuable to say, we heighten antagonism and defensiveness. Collaboration is far less possible through this approach. Teaching each other becomes impossible as strong emotions flare and block our ability to learn.

Instead of opposing 100 percent of what your conversation partner says, consider that it's much more effective and fair to look for opportunities to make statements like these:

"You know, I actually agree with you that ___ ."

"That's an excellent point. I hadn't thought about it that way."

"I didn't realize that was the case."

"That sounds like a hard experience to go through. I can see how it might have affected the way you see things."

"I don't agree, but I could see how that would make sense."

Being willing to say these things builds trust, and trust lowers antagonism, increasing the chances we will be heard. We can still disagree strongly, but we are showing that care about cooperation and understanding, not just winning.

Giving credit makes all the difference in courageous conversations.

What Laura did when she validated Eric's experiences was invite him to cooperate with her. She put aside us-versus-them thinking and created a space where the two of them could begin to build trust and share with each other openly, without threat. When Laura used the Awesome If, Eric discovered she is not hell-bent on attacking him. By validating him as a person, she showed him that she is reasonable and wants to give credit where it's due.

Once Laura has established trust, she can probably open any door of conversation, and it will not be contentious. And hopefully, Eric will be more likely to listen to anything she has to say from this point forward.

That is the power of the Awesome If.

Are Laura's interactions with Eric manipulative? No. She is showing basic human empathy and hospitality. Laura isn't forcing Eric to trust or engage with her. She is simply treating him with respect and choosing to believe that he means well. She is inviting him into brave talk.

Once Laura and Eric have established cooperation, she may be invited to challenge Eric's opinions in a productive way and vice versa, but she still needs more information. She needs to understand the nuance (step 5) of his core assumptions.

The claim that concerned Laura the most was Eric's statement that "anyone can achieve anything in our country if they work hard enough." Eric seems to assume that everyone has equal opportunity. Laura strongly disagrees and thinks that such opportunity should exist for everyone but only actually exists for some people.

Instead of blasting him, Laura knows she still doesn't have the full picture. Without hostility, she asks Eric open questions about his views on systemic inequality and discrimination, like racism, sexism, and ableism. Laura might learn that Eric doesn't think inequality is real and doesn't care about it. Or she might learn that he is passionate about fighting inequality and believes that "dependency programs" like welfare actually perpetuate it. This nuance is small, but it's a highly important distinction, opening pathways to very different conversations.

Laura has the wisdom to understand that she is not a mind reader. She understands that people who believe differently than she does are not a monolith or a flat caricature. She can't know what Eric thinks until she asks. Unless she meets him on a human level, establishing trust and collaboration, she can't get to the point where she can really start to differentiate small and important nuance. By engaging her imagination, asking questions, and paying attention to important details, she leads a more productive conversation, because she finds out specifically where the points of disagreement lie. By using the Awesome If, Laura gives herself a much better chance to challenge Eric meaningfully, in a way that he might be open to really considering her perspective. She can ask him to see her as she has seen him. That makes Laura not only a more effective communicator, but a leader.

The Awesome If is essentially what it means to give the benefit of the doubt, both to others and to ourselves. The benefit of the doubt means that we suspend judgment because we don't and can't know everything. We offer our conversation partner trust that they are basically a good person, doing their best, unless we gain solid evidence to believe otherwise. We are choosing to make room for them to surprise us, challenge us, and even teach us. When we build this kind of resilient relationship in the ways we treat our conversation partners, even those who we vastly disagree with, we open the door to courageous dialogue—the respectful sharing of hard truths.

SUMMARY: Understanding Assumptions Is Worth the Effort

Do we have to learn to examine and establish assumptions? Do we have to use the Awesome If? Of course not. We are all free to see things only from our own perspective. But if we don't engage this kind of thinking, we are missing out on chances to expand our imaginations and hearts. Trying to understand different perspectives is one of the most amazing abilities we have as human beings. It is the very source of empathy.

In times of conflict and strain, it is a balm to the human spirit to look at someone who has had a very different life than we've had and say, "I can't fully know how you feel. But I can try to understand."

Chapter 7 Reflection

1. Has any part of your structure of meaning ever shifted? How and why did it change? Did it cause cognitive dissonance? What was the result of the change?

2. When is it hardest to give the benefit of the doubt? When should we withhold the benefit of the doubt? When should we make sure to give it?

3. Share a time when premature assumptions got the better of you. What was the result?

4. Who in your life seems to have core assumptions that are very different from yours? How did you learn about that person's assumptions? What kinds of assumptions do they hold that you don't quite understand and would still like to excavate?

5. Do you have any core assumptions that are unusual or unpopular? If so, what beliefs, values, or experiences do they relate to or spring from? Is each assumption *a priori* (based in logic) or *a posteriori* (based in evidence)?

6. Can you think of a situation where the Awesome If would be helpful? How do you think it would help?

7. Share a time someone made you feel totally seen and understood. How did they do it?

8. Share a time you were able to make someone feel seen and understood. How did you do it, and how do you know you were successful?

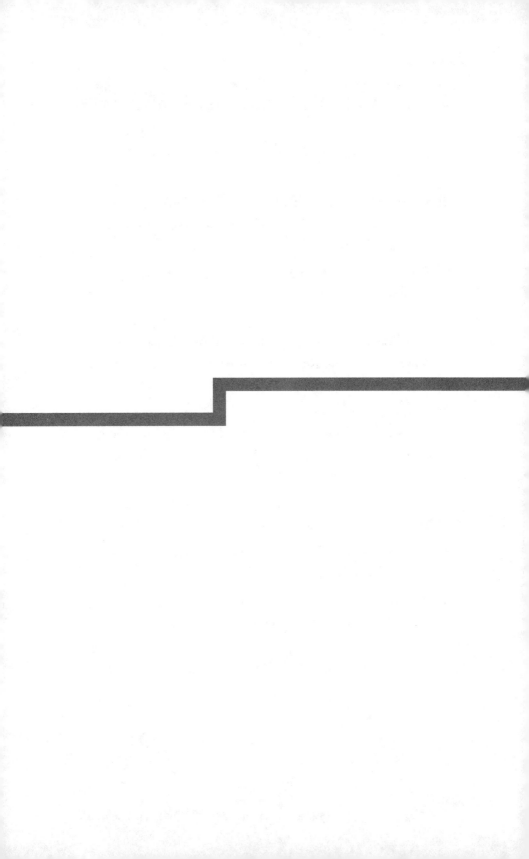

CHAPTER 8

Build a Better House

Rhetoric and Argumentation
for the Rest of Us

We can't transform impasse without a two-way conversation. This means both seeing and letting ourselves be seen.

We've talked a lot about seeing. But letting ourselves be seen is sometimes an even tougher challenge.

Letting ourselves be seen means being open and sharing our heart with the world, doing everything we can to be understood. It means refusing to launch verbal grenades, speak in sound bites, or take shortcuts that can muddy the water. We don't have to be the smartest or most educated people of all time, and we don't have to be nice or meek, but if we want to transform impasse, we do need to learn to be articulate. We need to become effective communicators.

To become an effective communicator, it's helpful to take a dive into the study of rhetoric.

An Introduction to Rhetoric: A Fancy Word for a Simple Idea

Rhetoric is using language toward any desired effect. It means trying to change something or someone in the world using words. By this definition, rhetoric is a way we use power.

Rhetoric can be overt and open, like a middle-school election poster that says, "Vote for me because I will put vending machines in every hallway of the school." Or it can be covert and subtle, like a breakup where the person ending the relationship gives the reason that "it's not you, it's me." Rhetoric can even be manipulative, like a news story that bends the truth to get a rise out of people:

Mayor Embroiled in Scandal!

This week, an exclusive look at CoffeeGate. Tuesday morning, June 7, the mayor broke from her usual route to Jenny's Diner and purchased what can only be called a fascist cup of coffee from a corporate chain. Members of the town were aghast. . . .

Rhetoric is the power of persuasion, for better or for worse.

If we believe we have good ideas about the world, it stands to reason that we should represent them well. This chapter focuses on the responsible rhetoric, because there will come a time in every difficult conversation when it's appropriate to represent our beliefs, assumptions, values, and opinions.

Before we explore persuasion further, let's back up and look at how language works.

"Use Your Words" Ain't That Simple

The biggest reason communicating is so hard is that words mean different things to different people. Many of us act as if communication works this way:

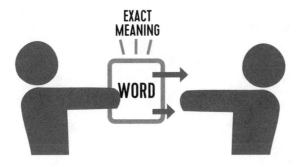

But actually, it works a lot more like this:

When we use a word, we can't magically transfer our exact intended use of the word to the person listening. Language, meaning, and interpretation are a negotiation. It's not a simple math equation: "Marco gives Sarah IdeaX. Sarah now has Idea X."

Communication is a complex back-and-forth process. The person listening is interpreting everything we say, filtered through their own system of meaning, their own understanding of language and context. Even when two people are speaking the same language, they aren't. Not really.

Just take the word *green*, for example. It seems like a straightforward word, right? But someone using the word *green* can refer to any of the following:

- A color—*I'll have a green one.*

- Being full of plant life—*It's so green out there.*

- An area for playing golf—*I'm on the green.*

- Environmental friendliness—*Let's go green.*

- Being new at something—*He's pretty green.*

- Being jealous—*She's pretty green.*

- Being seasick—*They're pretty green.*

- Money—*Let's see some green.*

To communicate anything at all, even "simple" ideas that seem straightforward, we need to take into account that the context of the word matters, the intention of the speaker matters, and most importantly, the hearing and interpretation of the listener matter greatly.

Is your green my purple? What if I am color-blind? What if I hate the color green and you love it? What if I grew up in the middle of New York City, but you grew up in the woods?

"Green" has a history of interpretation, with many connotations. Its meaning varies based on the larger context and can be significantly affected by the experiences of the speaker and the listener.

All words are symbols, and all symbols are imbued with specific meanings by each person who recognizes the symbol as a particular something. In other words, words are often shape-shifters. Words mean what we want them to mean. We do our best to negotiate a common understanding, but there will always be slight to major variances in interpretation. The word *green* is a simplistic example; think about how this might apply to words like *fair, right, moral,* or *good.* A variety of meanings and interpretations can become quickly complicated.

The most important thing to remember is that every word we use is both an individual thing and a collective thing at the same time. I could decide to start calling potatoes "rock cookies," but no one else would know what I was talking about. I would have a very specific individual interpretation but no collective reference (no one else in the world knows what I am referring to). Each of us has an individual interpretation, and the sum and variety of all those interpretations add up to a common understanding. Communities and societies do a lot of work over long periods of time to negotiate the meaning of every word we use.

Communication Differences Matter

Not only do words have variety in meaning, but everyone has different norms and expectations when it comes to communication. These differences, large or small, can make or break conversations.

During my sophomore year in college, tensions flared on campus between the predominantly white student body and the minority student body of color. Faculty members were attempting to facilitate dialogue, so they hosted a seminar on race.

During the seminar, a black staff member named Rodney offered an insight about intercultural communication that really stuck with me. This lesson was when I first began to understand how much communication differences matter.

Rodney pointed to a black student in the front row and said, "Hey, Ernie, let's pretend you got a bad grade on a paper. I'm going to speak to you about it in two different ways, and you tell me which was more respectful." The student agreed.

The first time Rodney spoke to the student, he was very polite. He said in a soft tone, "Ernie, what's up, man. Hey, I noticed you got an F on your paper. I really need you to focus and try harder. Can you do that for me?"

The second time, he used a stern, aggressive tone. "Listen up. You got an F. Okay? You really messed up. You need to get it together—now."

He asked the black student which statement was the most respectful. The student picked the second option.

I was totally surprised by this choice; I felt *sure* the first one was better.

Rodney explained that in some communities—for example, in some black communities—speaking softly and being polite can be seen as condescending, as if the person being reprimanded is an inferior. He explained that this represents a strong black cultural value of equality. Being expressive and direct means the speaker sees the person who messed up as a peer. An in-your-face style of speech is a way for the speaker to show that power is equalized between them.

As a white student raised in a soft-spoken home, in that moment I was able to recognize for the first time that the indirect, less expressive, less confrontational way I learned to communicate isn't the only way. It isn't the gold standard. It is one way, among many ways. I was comfortable with my way, and I preferred my way, because I grew up with it.

Other people are comfortable with other ways of interacting. It might be somewhat of a shock for some of us to realize there is no single "best" or "right" way.

As I began to think about it, I realized that even within my own immediate family, each of us has slightly different comfort levels for how direct, expressive, or abstract the conversation should be. Some of us rather enjoy having more of an in-your-face conversation about hard issues; when others of us hear loud, firm voices, it makes us feel threatened and want to shut down.

In big and small ways, we all communicate differently. Truly understanding another person, *especially* in difficult conversations, requires taking the time to orient to their communication style. As we interpret their words and intentions to the best of our ability, we should be aware of how we are communicating. In any given situation, we might also ask ourselves if there are any ways we can adjust for maximum understanding and connection.

Understanding Communication Styles: Sun, Moon, Dawn, Dusk

So how exactly do we unpack communication styles and navigate their impact? In recent years, cultural-communication experts have identified several key dynamics that help us understand the norms and expectations we each hold as we communicate. These dynamics show not only our personal preferences, but also the values and priorities that underlie our communication styles. [57]

We each have comfort zones, or go-to ways of relating with other people. These preferences are influenced by a wide range of factors, including our personalities, our unique body chemistries, the ways we were socialized in family and school and friend groups, our educations, any personal traumas or victories we have experienced, our media consumption, and significantly, our larger social, ethnic, and political contexts. Even two people in the same family with the exact same upbringing may come to have very different preferences for what "good" communication looks like.

Our challenge is to wrap our minds around a vast range of styles, holding an understanding that no one style is better than another. The "What's Your Communication Style?" tool presented here can be helpful for understanding our personal communication styles in relation to others' styles.[58]

All communication styles are equally valid, but they do have some important differences. Sun-style communicators are direct and focused on tasks, order, and results. They tend to be less expressive, more abstract, more focused on authority, and more punctual. Moon-style communicators tend to be indirect and focused on relationships, principles, and descriptive language. They tend to be more expressive, more focused on group decision making and equality, and more fluid in respect to time. Of course, most people will not be only sun-style or only moon-style. It is possible to be dawn-style—someone who leans toward sun in action (operational) but has moon tendencies in the way they think (philosophical). Or a person can be dusk-style—someone who leans toward moon operationally but has sun tendencies philosophically.

Anyone who is comfortable working in both sun and moon styles is a flex-style. Those who become flex-style communicators do so for many reasons. Some personalities are simply more prone to flex; flex communication is also learned through external contexts, such as having to navigate the rules and norms of a majority culture as a minority.

WHAT'S YOUR COMMUNICATION STYLE?
— SUN, MOON, DAWN, DUSK —

Instructions: For each line, mark which box, left or right, feels most true
and comfortable for you. If both options feel equally true, mark both.

☀   **OPERATIONAL**   ☾

Abstract ideas and theories are most comfortable	☐	IDEAS ☐	Concrete ideas and stories are most comfortable
Being clear and using words to say exactly what is meant are the best interpretation	☐	CONTEXT ☐	Nonverbal clues and reading between the lines are the best interpretation
Being sober, calm, and understated is most comfortable	☐	EXPRESSION ☐	Being passionate, demonstrative, and vivid is most comfortable
Embracing confrontation is most comfortable	☐	CONFLICT ☐	Avoid confrontation is most comfortable
Negative feedback is best direct	☐	EVALUATION ☐	Negative feedback is best indirect

PHILOSOPHICAL

Focusing on the task is most important	☐	TRUST ☐	Focusing on the relationship is most important
End results are most important	☐	MOTIVATION ☐	Principles are most important
Hierarchy and order are most important	☐	LEADERSHIP ☐	Equality is most important
Protecting the individual is most important	☐	DECISIONS ☐	Protecting the community is most important
Time and schedules are linear and fixed	☐	TIMING ☐	Time and schedules are flexible and fluid

SUN-style = 6+ sun   DAWN-style = 3+ sun operational, 3+ moon philosophical
MOON-style = 6+ moon   DUSK-style = 3+ moon operational, 3+ sun philosophical

FLEX-style = 3+ comfortable with both sun and moon

Sun-style: Direct + task-/idea-focused communicators
Moon-style: Indirect + relationship-focused communicators
Dawn-style: Direct + relationship-focused communicators
Dusk-style: Indirect + task-/idea-focused communicators
Flex-style: People who can adapt their communication style depending on who they are speaking to

Adapted from Erin Meyer, *The Culture Map: Breaking through the Invisible Boundaries of Global Business* (New York: Perseus, 2014).

These styles are not meant to be hard-and-fast rules. They are meant to show that when we communicate, most of us are primarily comfortable in a certain way of being in the world that might be different from our neighbor's way. We each have a set of priorities that are oriented toward a certain set of ultimate goals and values. It's important to remember that being a task- or idea-focused person doesn't mean relationships aren't important, and being relationship focused doesn't mean tasks or ideas aren't important. Sun-style people, though direct, have the capacity to be gentle, and moon-style people, though indirect, can be assertive. We might have tendencies and comfort zones, but we can adapt if needed.

Here's an example. Wei, a moon-style communicator, just bumped into his friend Dave, a sun-style communicator. They chat for half an hour, and at the end, Wei walks away happy. His ultimate orientation—spending time with Dave—was satisfied. Wei feels connected and at peace. Dave, however, feels unsettled and frustrated. In Dave's ultimate orientation toward tasks and ideas, the half hour he just spent with Wei felt like a waste because they didn't get anything done or exchange any important information beyond surface-level chitchat. Dave and Wei may be great friends, but their communication styles are significantly different, and it sometimes causes friction.

Let's say Dave, being such a direct communicator, feels he should explain to Wei that he doesn't like small talk. Dave feels like this information will strengthen their relationship. Wei, a moon-style communicator, is an indirect and nonconfrontational guy; hearing this feedback is hurtful and confusing. How could Dave be so unhappy with their friendship, when it brought so much joy to Wei? How is Wei supposed to act around Dave now?

Instead of confronting Wei, it would be more effective for Dave to be more proactive in future conversations. As points of conversation, Dave could take the initiative to bring up ideas and tasks that are important to him, while at the same time enjoying Wei's company. Wei could recognize that Dave's sun-style communication means Dave is highly focused on tasks, so Wei might suggest they plan an activity where they can talk while they are doing something else, like bowling or volunteering. Hopefully, the increase in time together while accomplishing a task will allow them to go beyond small talk and connect a little deeper.

When both friends learn to take each other's styles into account, they can meet in the middle and both get what they need from the relationship without expecting each other to change the way they operate or the things they prioritize.

Once we recognize that communication differences are common and natural, we can stop judging which is the "right" way to communicate. We can learn to spot and negotiate differences instead of fighting them. We can even learn to appreciate what each orientation brings to the table, building beneficial relationships with people who operate and think differently than we do.

This frees us to focus on what it means to deeply understand. And it frees us to make sure we are doing everything in our power to be understood. One significant tool we can use here is called accountable language.

Keeping Language Accountable: Using "I-Speak" instead of "All-Speak"

Holding language accountable involves taking responsibility for the effects of language *and* for the claims that lie beneath our words. Accountable language is a profoundly important practice in difficult conversations and can make a world of difference in outcomes.

A while back, I was moving from Boston to Tennessee with my partner, Corey. We decided to sell most of our furniture to make the move easier.

Corey owned a big leather easy chair that I did not particularly love, especially because one of the arms was broken.

We must have had nine different conversations about this chair. Every time it came up, I would say something to the effect of "If you fix the chair, I'm on board with keeping it."

Finally, he threw up his hands and said, "Do what you want! I don't want to fight with you about this anymore. You already decided to sell it, so just get it over with."

I was totally caught off guard. First of all, up to that point, I didn't realize we were fighting. I thought we were just sorting through options. Second, I never said I had made a decision to get rid of it. But that's what he was hearing. We were definitely not on the same page.

So I replied, "I'm going to say two things, and you tell me if they are the same or different."

"Okay."

"One: If you fix the chair, we can keep it. Two: If you fix the chair, I am on board with keeping it."

He said, in his mind, those two statements were exactly the same.

I explained that to me, these statements were totally different. In the first statement, I would have been speaking for both of us (all-speak) and making the decision on my own, without him. In the second statement, I was expressing my opinion (I-speak) and trying to share power by making a decision together.

As we kept talking things out, it suddenly dawned on me that the chair might mean more to him than to me. I asked him, "Is that chair special to you?" He replied crisply, "Look, if you want to get rid of the chair, fine. It's just a chair. We can get rid of it if you hate it that much."

Sensing frustration, I made sure to let him know that he is more important to me than the chair. If the chair was important to him, I would be open to keeping it. I just wanted to talk it through.

It wasn't until this point in the conversation that tension started to decrease, and Corey felt comfortable opening up. He explained that the move we were planning felt incredibly stressful and uncertain. Having one familiar piece of furniture in the new place sounded nice. He said he knew it was silly to keep a broken chair, and maybe someday we could get rid of it, but it was comfortable, and it made him feel better to think of it in the new house. He calmly restated that we could get rid of the chair if I truly felt strongly about it; in this way, he showed leadership and compromise, which made his case even more appealing.

I could completely relate to his feelings of stress and uncertainty. His argument was understandable. It didn't change the way I felt about the chair. I still strongly disliked it. But the way he felt—his reasons for keeping it, plus the values and emotions behind those reasons—was totally reasonable and valid.

In the end? I told him if that's what the chair meant to him, then yes, I would agree to keep it, broken arm and all. He met me halfway by putting it in his office, so I don't have to look at it. Hooray!

Using accountable language helped us transform impasse and animosity into a moment of deeper relationship and better understanding. It helped us share power and make a truly joint decision. Taking responsibility for language helps us transform conflict and make our relationships more resilient.

Many wise people throughout history have discovered the power of accountable language. Take Benjamin Franklin, for example:

> I made it a rule to forbear all direct contradictions to the sentiments of others, and all positive assertion of my own. I even forbade myself the use of every word or expression in

the language that imported a fixed opinion, such as "certainly", "undoubtedly", etc. I adopted instead of them "I conceive", "I apprehend", or "I imagine" a thing to be so or so; or "so it appears to me at present."[59]

In other words, Ben began speaking more openly, with a little less confidence, making sure to say things only from his own perspective, softening grand, sweeping statements. In this writing, he goes on to list several benefits that come from approaching conversations this way. Accountable language opens conversations to exploring a wider range of possibilities, makes conversations more pleasant and cooperative because he was helping his conversation partners to feel more comfortable and validated, and allows both him and others to make mistakes, to be wrong, or even to switch sides without shame.

It is incredibly important to take responsibility for our own experiences in the world and to resist trying to speak for everyone else. That doesn't mean we can't be confident or authoritative. But it does mean staying firmly rooted in our own context and in our own limitations of knowledge.

Let's see how doing this can make a huge difference in the way conversations play out. Watch what happens when we make language accountable:

Amber: "The world is a bad place."

Bodhi: "In my experience, the world is a bad place."

Amber is using all-speak—sweeping, generalized, unqualified language. She is essentially claiming that her own personal set of beliefs is universal; in other words, she is basically speaking for all people for all time in a godlike fashion. That's a problem. First, that statement slams a huge set of assumptions onto the ears of everyone who hears it. After such a huge and sweeping statement, what sorts of follow-up questions can people around her even ask? The conversation might go into a philosophical, super-abstract direction or just fall off awkwardly. It's hard to engage her words meaningfully. Second, all-speak whitewashes nuance and tends to close space on other people's experience and voices. It doesn't let people in; it just announces a closed judgment.

Third, all-speak is usually easy to disprove. By mentioning a few exceptions, someone can poke holes in all-speak: "The world is a bad place, Amber? Then what about puppies? Puppies are objectively wonderful. How can something wonderful come from an inherently bad place? Booyah."

Bodhi is using I-speak. He's not claiming to speak for anyone but himself. He is referring to his own unique context and experience. By grounding his opinions and beliefs in personal, accountable language, Bodhi is making it much easier for people around him to interact and ask questions; listeners are invited into the stories and memories that support his perspective. I-speak opens up dialogue. It focuses on personal story and voice while at the same time leaving space for other people's story and voice. Finally, using I-speak is much harder to disprove. No one can say with any kind of validity, "Bodhi, your experiences of the world are wrong." Someone's experience is their experience, and their individual take on the world is largely authoritative as far as they filter and interpret things as a person.

Using I-speak in the ways we communicate is more solid, more effective, more collaborative, and more full-bodied.

The Verbal Shortcuts of Modern Language

Modern language is packed with what I call verbal shortcuts. Gone are the days when we spend a paragraph to tell someone how hard we laughed at their joke, how it made us feel, how we held our gut and cried over the hilarity of their joke. Instead, we say, "I'm cracking up," or even just, "ROFL" (for Rolling On the Floor Laughing). We might use the emoji of the little face laughing with tears coming out. Emoji are a particularly fascinating form of communication shortcut—they bypass verbal language altogether! An emerging etiquette is developing, with subcultures across the globe negotiating how and how not to use those images "properly" in conversation.

Do we use shortcuts because we hate language? I don't think so. I think it's because the pace of our lives is fast; we don't have a lot of time or patience to explain things. I'm probably one of the worst offenders. My attention span is the size of a—brb, I smell cookies . . . j/k lol.[60]

When we talk about hard issues, buzzwords are a popular form of verbal shortcut. It's almost as if we hold an internal sense of pride when we get to use a new trendy word that holds cultural significance. YOLO, selfie, millennial, rightsizing, optics, snowflake—these words, these inventions, so to speak, come with a host of assumptions attached to them.

Verbal shortcuts are fun and often useful. But there is a downside to using them in difficult conversations: because of the host of assumptions attached to them, they will mean different things to different people. When we take these shortcuts into conversations with people from very different worlds than we're in, the chance that we start speaking past each other becomes high.

For example, I've talked about the word *privilege*.[61] This word has become popular in progressive conversations around inequality, for good reason. *Privilege* has become a highly complex verbal shortcut that invokes several layers of meaning:

- The history of racism, as well as other negative -isms, like sexism
- The social, cultural, economic, political, and legal systems that reify those -isms
- The personal experience of being granted more opportunity, trust, or respect if you were born a certain way
- A challenge to be aware of and cautious about inequality

Phew! That's a lot of stuff packed into one little word!

That single word has an entire story attached to it. When someone uses that word, it probably means they agree with a long list of foundational beliefs and assumptions about the way the world works. That's certainly not a bad thing. It's brilliant that we can do these things with language—truly amazing. However, in difficult conversations, how can you be sure that your conversation partner understands that word in the same way you do unless you take time to compare notes, unless you make sure you are one the same page?

When it comes to having a productive conversation with someone who is coming from a very different place than we are, we must establish

ALL-SPEAK VS. AXIOMS

All-speak is different from an *axiom,* or an axiomatic truth, which is a self-evident principle that is generally accepted as true. Examples are "The shortest distance between two points is a line," "Two wrongs don't make a right," "What goes up must come down," and "The early bird gets the worm." To use axioms, you need a consensus about their role as foundational *a priori* assumptions.

common meaning before we use verbal shortcuts. Even then, those verbal shortcuts can be distracting. Until we know the person we are speaking with agrees to use that verbal shortcut and has a similar sense of its meaning, it's likely our verbal shortcut is just going to come across as a "dog whistle" to that person.

A dog whistle is a buzzword that gets people particularly upset and calls them to action. Dog whistles are generally associated with types of rhetoric that are highly partisan. They are even viewed (by the opposition) as being related to groupthink, a kind of social brainwashing.

For example, if I don't know the full story of the word *privilege,* or if I'm not on board with parts of its assumptions, using that word around me might be fruitless or even create hostility.

If that were the case, you might continue to use the word *privilege* in an activist sense to make a point. You certainly can do that. But is it effective? That's a very good question.

In some contexts, it might be more effective to talk about the things *privilege* refers to, making sure there is common understanding, and then ask, "Do you mind if I use the word *privilege* to symbolize all of that?" They may say yes or no. This is a process of negotiation.

Here's another example of a famous verbal shortcut: swearing. Please don't think less of me, but I can enjoy swearing. It feels $*@!-ing cathartic. It helps me express and release emotion.

Obviously, not everyone likes swearing, and I can understand that. Some feel it's unfitting for discourse and disrespectful to the common spaces we share in society. Some think it's wrong and offensive on religious grounds. I can understand these views. When I swear around people who feel this way, all they probably hear is the swear words, not my message. That's incredibly significant if I want to be persuasive and winning. I don't wish to alienate the people with whom I most want to be in conversation.

So, personally, I choose not to swear in difficult conversations, but not for moral reasons. I choose not to swear because I view verbal shortcuts as a problem. Swear words, depending on context, can mean any number of things. They aren't clear. Even more importantly, swear words can be lazy, cop-outs for a better and more specific expression. Using swear words allows me to avoid actually naming my feelings, fully explaining difficult concepts, or fully expressing the nuance of my convictions. Swear words, like many verbal shortcuts, represent a missed opportunity to communicate well. So I don't use them in discourse or persuasion.

When we hold off using verbal shortcuts and instead take the time to explain ourselves, we open up the conversation to many more opportunities to talk about core beliefs and assumptions. We embody a kind of myth busting for those who oppose us, because we show we understand what we are talking about and aren't just throwing fancy words around to be trendy with our crew. These opportunities are missed when we rush.

Here is some advice for working with verbal shortcuts:

- Be aware when we are using a verbal shortcut.

- When using a verbal shortcut, figure out whether we have a relatively common understanding or a difference of understanding with our conversation partner.

- Based on the process of negotiation, gauge whether that shortcut may be better used in long form, so we can explore assumptions and beliefs.

- Acknowledge the gravity that the verbal shortcut carries; don't just lob it around carelessly or turn it into a weapon. All the meaning we pack into that word deserves our respect.

- If someone uses a verbal shortcut and we are not 100 percent sure what they mean, pause the conversation and ask them, "What do you mean when you say ＿＿＿?"

I know it is more challenging to make a case without using all of our favorite words. I am not trying to constrict anyone. I hope to bring into awareness the possibilities of truly persuasive speech and the choices we make in the process of creating effective, responsible arguments. I hope to persuade you to be more persuasive.

Persuasion: The Art and Challenge

Think back to a time when you changed your mind about something. Hold that memory in your mind. Does that memory involve someone screaming at you?

For most of us, the answer is no. There is a scientific reason for this.

When we experience a state of stress, a chemical in our bodies called cortisol spikes. Cortisol is a major fight-or-flight chemical. People with high levels of cortisol have decreased abilities to think and learn.[62] Feeling dominated or overwhelmed stresses us out, and being stressed literally makes us less able to engage difficult ideas. What is more, anxiety and panic can cause people to start disconnecting from reality (a set of phenomena called dissociation, derealization, and depersonalization). It can cause people to feel like reality isn't connected, have an out-of-body experience, or feel like they are in a dreamlike state.[63] Disconnecting is something our bodies do to protect us when we sense danger and are extremely stressed or triggered.

What this means for difficult conversations is that when tensions rise and things get heated, it causes us—sometimes literally—to feel and act less like ourselves. Not only are we inhibited from learning and engaging new ideas, we are sometimes feeling, thinking, and acting in unfamiliar ways. The results include conversations that run in circles, conversations where people talk past each other,

THREE TYPES OF RHETORIC[67]

Rhetoric, or language used for a desired effect, falls into three categories:

- Forensic—accusing or defending

  "You took my socks!"

  "I did not! The dog ate them!"

- Deliberative—deciding whether something is good or bad, helpful or harmful

  "Nickelback is the greatest band to ever live. Here are all the reasons."

  "Bro, really?"

- Ceremonial—praising or criticizing (usually used in formal settings)

  "Mrs. Alvarez's constant vigilance and ability to inspire each and every student are why we are naming her Teacher of the Year."

Remembering these terms is less important than understanding that all of types of rhetoric involve tools of persuasion. Persuasion is not necessarily related to winning, like in a debate. Neither is it manipulative, like tricking someone into agreeing. When it's done well, persuasion is focused on *being winning*—that is, making a strong case for something, to the best of our ability.

conversations where people say things they wouldn't normally say, and conversations where people hyperfocus on taking sides. Rising tensions often push people in the exact opposite direction we want them to consider going.

For not only moral but also biological rea-
sons, persuasion should never involve domina-
tion or force of any kind. Domination doesn't care
if its ideas stink; it doesn't want to be challenged or called
to a higher level. It doesn't want to improve. It refuses to
acknowledge when its opponent makes a good point or has
a valid case. It doesn't care if it has to resort to manipulation.
It just wants to win.

Persuasion is the polar opposite of screaming at, forcing, or controlling
someone. Persuasion is an art; it is the art of getting people to see our view
as valid. They don't need to agree, but they will at least (hopefully) see us as
credible people with ideas that hold water.

True persuasion is loud and strong, confident and eloquent, but it also
encourages mutual respect and dignity. It shows leadership in a way that can
jump-start relationships stuck in harmful cycles of conflict. Persuasion is *being
winning*, not winning for the sake of winning.

Learning to be persuasive is a necessary part of living in a diverse world.
Wanting to be seen is good and right. In being seen, persuasion takes responsibility for the ways we are coming across. It takes responsibility for the short-
and long-term effects we are having on the rest of the world—especially the
effects we are having on those who disagree with us.

Persuasion in Contexts of Harm

What if you are trying to persuade someone, trying truly to convince them,
that their actions are hurting you? What if you are trying to persuade them
to give up a destructive behavior, and it will cost them to do so?

Sometimes the truths we need to tell are not appealing.

There is an old saying, "Don't burn down my house. Build me a better
one." This idea is my biggest guiding light in difficult conversations. Instead
of just pointing to the problem, we also should seek to use our creative
energy and suggest a better alternative.

Let's say I approach my neighbor and say, "Nelson, your house is a hazard. This is a dangerous house for you and for me, totally unsafe. It's causing massive problems in the neighborhood. Get out now."

Nelson might say, "I don't see any issues," but what he might mean is "I have nowhere else to go." So I rally my neighborhood, and I raise money, and I build Nelson a better house. Then Nelson gladly moves, because the new house is better and safer for him and for everyone in the community.

Persuasion works in a similar way. Persuasion doesn't just burn things down. It doesn't just deconstruct. Burning down the house just makes everyone miserable and risks the whole neighborhood catching on fire. Burning down structures puts us closer to chaos and anomie.

We have to construct something else. We have to build something better.

Persuasion says, "We have a tough reality, but here is a better and more productive way to look at it. Here is how to deal with the problem and move forward."

The Persuasion-without-Domination Paradox

Sometimes even when people do their best to be persuasive and winning, justice is still withheld. Sometimes people trying to make a change cannot convince those hurting them to stop or even to recognize there is a problem. Sometimes people hide behind the masks of domination.

Three years after Rev. Dr. Martin Luther King Jr.'s famous "I have a dream" speech, Dr. King said, "A riot is the language of the unheard."[64]

How did he go from a positive and hopeful message to talking about riots?

At the beginning of the civil rights movement, people of all races and backgrounds were peacefully organizing. The civil rights leaders were adamant that the movement should be as positive and winning as possible in their sharing of hard truths—that segregation and racism were killing Black America, figuratively and literally.

The organizers chose to use a technique called non-violent resistance. Civil rights workers peacefully demonstrated for years, staging sit-ins and marches and rallies. They sacrificed limited time, energy, and precious resources to convince white domination culture that segregation and discrimination were unacceptable. They didn't have an assurance of success.

It's easy to think of the civil rights movement as a quaint thing of the past, as if a few months of picketing resulted in a cross-cultural celebration in the Oval Office, where happy leaders signed a pretty new law that ended all our nation's problems. The reality, however, is raw: the movement lasted from 1954 to 1968. That's fourteen years! Can you imagine fighting like that for fourteen years? Imagine sacrificing immense time, energy, resources, and safety for fourteen years, following decades and decades of working to change legislation and cultural beliefs that Black and African American people were not fully human or fully citizens. Can you imagine persisting in weariness without the guarantee of any kind of change?

What an exhausting ultramarathon of a struggle.

Fourteen years—when I think about this, I can begin to understand why Dr. King's tone went from winning and hopeful to talking about riots. Playing by the arbitrary rules of civility was going nowhere.

At the beginning of the fight, Dr. King was trying to build a better house. He had a dream to see little white and black children playing together, going to school together, and worshipping together. He had a beautiful dream of Community. In response, he and other freedom fighters were beat down, imprisoned, slandered, demonized, and even killed over and over and over and over. While he was alive, Dr. King was not the well-beloved figure he is now. His face was not painted in murals. He did not have a monument in DC. He was hated. He was on an FBI watch list.[65]

Sometimes we try to build a better, safer, healthier house, and people still won't move out of their old dangerous house. And they will hate us for trying to help.

The civil rights movement was eventually successful in a legislative sense —the Civil Rights Act eventually passed, and schools were desegregated— but America still struggles with racism and systemic racial inequality. In some ways, the movement was tragically unsuccessful; it didn't end racism. Domination still lingers, bitter and emboldened, by its loss of power.

Here is the ultimate question in the art of persuasion. How do we fight for justice to overcome domination, without using domination? How do we convince people to hear us and come willingly to our side, without using violence, force, or manipulation?

How do we build a better house and get people to move in?

The paradox of working to make the world a better place is that we can't force someone to move into the new house; we can't use domination to end domination. But we can engage imaginations and use rhetoric that invites rather than shames. We can suspend the drive to "fix" and instead engage the secrets of impasse: making time to see, making time to build a resilient relationship.

True Persuasion Says, "I Can't Know until I Ask"

Today, in the public arena, I see some social-justice warriors screaming, "Everyone who doesn't move into the new house is a Nazi racist jerk who deserves to be punched in the face!"

Even though I am proud to stand for social justice, every time I see this kind of rhetoric, I feel sick. I see the cracks in our Community get a little wider.

First of all, a lot of people who just heard those words are now diving into their Fear Bunker and refusing to engage in any meaningful conversation. The social-justice warrior who spoke those words just burned down the old house, and the new house, and the whole neighborhood.

Second, without doing the work of understanding why people don't want to move into the new house, how can social-justice people speak to these issues effectively? We will never find the root of motivation or understand what anti-social-justice people truly care about, what is truly in their hearts...unless we actually engage them and get to know them.

Yes, a small percentage of people don't want to move into the new house because they *want* to openly embrace domination like racism, sexism, and so on. However, the vast majority of people don't want to be oppressive. Most people have an innate sense that domination is destructive. Most people value freedom and equality. They might not understand or acknowledge their complicity in structures of domination, but most people want to be good people.

What are their working assumptions? They might believe that moving to the new house will cost them a price they can't pay. They might believe that to embrace social justice means they will have to be ashamed of their old house, as well as everything they are as a person. They may believe they have to compete for scarce resources when they are barely eking out a living as it is. They may believe social-justice warriors don't let people be beginners, but demand immediate and full ideological conformity, and they see that as dangerous. They may think social-justice warriors secretly hate or resent them. They may think if they become a social-justice advocate, the needs of their people will get ignored. They may think their friends or political party will reject them for being social-justice warriors.

There could be a hundred different reasons.

We don't know the risks or costs of someone's journey until we take the time to ask. Before making our case, we have to learn what's at stake for our conversation partner. We have to show love, courage, and leadership that surpasses ideological conformity; we can't control the other person.

Showing this kind of hospitality and collaboration, we hope our conversation partner will take the time to understand what's at stake for us. We create opportunities for everyone involved to empathize and humanize. Even if they don't reciprocate our persuasion and respect, we still will have done everything in our power to have a meaningful and effective conversation. At the very least, in engaging difficult conversations, we will have gained new and important information that allows us to speak more effectively to the heart of the matter. And we will have built a bridge instead of a bonfire.

Arguing Versus Advocating

Once we clearly and deeply understand the stakes of the issues at hand for our conversation partner, we can start making our case.

Persuasion boils down to the art of making solid arguments. For many people, arguing means something quite negative. It involves wounds and insults:

A STORY OF ENGAGING IMPASSE:
THE HANDS ACROSS THE HILLS PROJECT

After the 2016 election, as the United States experienced a wildly polarized political landscape, a solidly Democratic group from Massachusetts decided they wanted to build a great big bridge in Trump country. They contacted a civic group in a small coal-mining region of Eastern Kentucky and asked if they could develop a relationship.

When the Kentuckians were first contacted by the liberals, they recall being taken aback. They thought the Massachusetts group was intent on educating or changing them. But the Kentucky community was relieved to understand the East Coasters didn't want to change them, but to see them. They embraced the goal, stated on their website, of "meeting face to face with others who voted differently than us, eliminating the voices of politicians and the media, who seek to divide us, to see us as enemies, red versus blue."

The groups began to make spaces for discussing different economic, environmental, social, and political concerns. Again quoting the website, "The heart of each gathering was structured dialogue, in which feelings could be expressed honestly and deeply, creating trust and care for each other. In addition to these face to face sessions, we experienced each other's community and family life through potlucks, music, excursions and home stays."

Overcoming many odds, the participants of the Hands Across the Hills Project have built a remarkable bond. These two communities have chosen to model innovative ways to engage impasse and transform conflict. After doing the hard work of creating resilient relationships, they have gained the momentum to collaborate on common issues in meaningful ways:

> The bonds between us pushed political differences into the background. We came to be friends. Now, as friends, we are working on a range of common projects, including reaching out together with our dialogue process to another region of the country, collaborating on agriculture, working on gun control issues we agree on. Hands Across the Hills has melted away stereotypes so that we can see each other's human face.[68]

To learn more, you can listen to the remarkable story of this initiative that aired on National Public Radio: Robin Young, "Conservatives In Kentucky, Liberals In Massachusetts Try to Bridge Political Divide," *Here and Now*, WBUR, November 28, 2018, www.wbur.org/hereandnow/2018/11/28/conservatives-kentucky-liberals-massachusetts-politics. You can also visit handsacrossthehills.org.

"You barf bucket! Your mother was a hamster, and your father smelled of elderberries." However, in the realm of persuasion, arguments are not something we need to be afraid of. Making a persuasive argument means giving someone a set of reasons, in an orderly way, to explain why your opinions make sense. In effect, persuasion is the opposite of fighting: it is learning to advocate for something we believe, in a way that is reasonable, legitimate, and ultimately convincing.

When two conversation partners make their case well, it creates space for deep discussion of the pros and cons of each other's ideas. Each holds the goal that the other person will recognize that their argument is valid, even if they don't agree with each other. When we can establish validity, we can find common ground and common assumptions. We can interpret each other's meaning better.

A *valid* argument is a case that makes sense. It has a consistent kind of logic or basis in experience. Saying an argument is valid doesn't mean we agree with it. It means we recognize that the argument is somewhat reasonable; there aren't gaping holes in it.

For example, you might believe Monopoly is the best game ever and tell me your reasons why. You cite the number of games sold, the long life it has had, the way it brings families together. I might despise Monopoly because it takes way too long and I am an impatient person. However, since you make a reasonable argument that is well articulated and supported by evidence, I would say, "Your points are valid."

An *invalid* argument is an argument that has holes. It's not reasonable. Arguing that my hair is purple and therefore everyone in the entire world thinks it's ugly, when in reality my hair is actually blond (and objectively adorable) is not valid because that argument is based on false facts and draws inconsistent conclusions through shaky logic.

What is shaky logic? "Shaky logic" is a fancy term for not making sense because we missed something important, we are being too hasty, or we are being unfair.

Ancient Tools of Persuasion

Remember that rhetoric is any kind of persuasive speech or language. Fortunately, we don't have to invent the wheel when it comes to understanding right and wrong ways to persuade. We have three tools at our disposal that come from the world of Greek rhetorical philosophy: logos, ethos, and pathos.[66] In general, *logos* is an appeal to logic and is a way of persuading an audience by reason. *Ethos* is an appeal to ethics and is a means of convincing someone of the credibility of the persuader. *Pathos* is an appeal to emotion; it involves the emotional response of the listener. To bring these ideas into modern times, let's call them Head, Cred, and Thread.

Head

Head (logos) represents the logic and reasoning of an argument. It gauges whether or not the speaker's case is sound (free of logical fallacies) and valid (internally consistent; the whole argument makes sense and does not contract itself). In persuasion, Head deals with the words that the speaker is saying, the logical flow of how they get from point A to point Z, the examples and reasons they use to persuade, and the conclusions they reach.

A Head argument would be Jimmy's mother saying, "Jimmy, please clean your room. You will be able to find things and relax when your room is clean." She is using logic to try to convince him.

Cred

Cred (ethos) represents credibility—in other words, the character and reputation of the speaker. In order to be credible, the speaker needs to use reliable and trustworthy sources of information. Cred also deals with the relationship between the speaker and the listener, including how the speaker wields power as they try to persuade. Cred means wielding power ethically and with authority but not seeking to be controlling or use domination.

A Cred argument would be Jimmy's mother saying, "Jimmy, you should clean your room because I'm your mother, and you should listen to me." She is evoking the authority of her position to try to convince him.

Thread

Thread (pathos) represents the thread of emotion and individual perspective that is always woven through any argument. It's right and good to speak from experience when forming an argument, so long as it's in the form of accountable language—speaking from one's own perspective and bias, not trying to speak for everyone. Thread reminds us that we all have a perspective and a set of experiences; no speaker is totally impartial. It's also right and good to share feelings, so long as it's done in healthy ways. The use of emotion can lead to manipulation if we're not careful. A sob story is usually

HEAD: LOGIC AND REASONING

- Reasoning is sound
- Assumptions are valid
- Conclusions are reasonable
- Consequences are accounted for

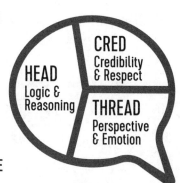

CRED: CREDIBILITY AND RESPECT

- Sources of information are factual and verifiable
- Calls to action are ethical
- Opponents are shown respect
- Speaker has a good track record and reputation

THREAD: PERSPECTIVE AND EMOTION

- Language is accountable (arguments are contextualized in the speaker's own social location and experiences)
- Speaker shares from their heart and passion
- Emotional elements humanize and do not manipulate
- Biases and blind spots are named

Thread rhetoric unbridled. In persuasion, no speaker is beyond the responsibility of using emotion carefully.

An argument using only Thread would be Jimmy's mom saying, "Jimmy, when you don't clean your room, it breaks my heart." She is using heavy emotional language to try to convince him (language that could be seen as manipulative).

Making Full-Bodied Arguments

Full-bodied arguments are arguments that use all three rhetorical tools together in perfect harmony. This is where the art of persuasion goes full-throttle.

Leaning on only one type of argument is problematic. For example, using only Head arguments can feel dry and lacking in emotion. Using only Cred is too authoritative, focusing too much on the title or status of the speaker and not the listeners' ability to make reasonable choices for themselves. As mentioned, an argument based only in Thread can be manipulative.

Using two tools without the third is also ineffective. Without the Head, arguments don't make logical sense. Without the Cred, arguments aren't reliable or believable. Without the Thread, arguments lack personality and emotional connection.

AVOIDING SHAKY LOGIC: TEN PERSUASION PITFALLS

While we all have different backgrounds and experiences, and we each express our opinions through many different communication styles, it's important to remember there is a difference between solid logic and shaky logic. How do we tell the difference? Fortunately, there are basic ground rules for argumentation that we can follow. If we don't follow these rules, our arguments become easy to disprove, and we make our persuasion ineffective. If we do follow the rules, we will be more persuasive and credible to people who disagree with us.

Traditionally, shaky logic is use of a "logical fallacy" to argue one's case. Many logical fallacies are still referred to in the original Latin. For the sake of contemporary audiences, let's modernize them and call them "persuasion pitfalls." Here are ten all-too-common persuasion pitfalls to avoid when you practice making effective arguments:[69]

1. **MY NEIGHBOR CATHY.** This pitfall involves taking a single instance and using it to represent a global rule or norm. It is a form of jumping to conclusions.

    One time my neighbor Cathy gave me cookies, and now I believe and expect that all of my neighbors will always give me cookies.

    My conservative coworker yelled at me; therefore, all conservatives yell.

HOW TO FIX: Collect more evidence and examples. Explore examples that might oppose the claim. Explore the idea that the example you are using might be an outlier (something unusual instead of normal). Yes, Cathy gave me cookies, but that might just be Cathy having a good day and wanting to do a nice thing. What are the other neighbors doing? What have my neighbors done in the past?

2. **2 + 2 = PICKLES.** This pitfall is another form of jumping to conclusions that takes pieces of evidence and claims a conclusion that the evidence doesn't necessarily support.

    The sky was a funny color tonight, and I heard a weird sound; therefore, aliens must be invading.

    HOW TO FIX: Consider other possible explanations. It could be aliens, or it could be a meteor shower.

3. **PICKLES = 2 + 2.** Instead of jumping to conclusions, "pickles = 2 + 2" means taking a conclusion and assuming causes that aren't necessarily true.

    Neil has brown eyes; therefore, both of his parents must have brown eyes.

    HOW TO FIX: Consider a wide range of other possible causes. It's also possible that Neil's mom has brown eyes and his dad green eyes, or Neil is wearing colored contacts, or the viewer is color-blind.

4. **OH, LOOK, THERE'S A CHICKEN!** This pitfall involves bringing up something that doesn't relate to the argument at hand but pretending it does.

    We should implement universal free breakfast in schools because animals get "free" food in the wild.

HOW TO FIX: Focus on staying on topic, select fewer central arguments, and stick to them more closely.

Here are all the reasons why universal free breakfast would be good for our country: full kids can concentrate much better than hungry kids. Studies show free school breakfast makes teaching more effective, raises test scores, and increases future economic success. We owe it to our children to improve educational outcomes.

5. **FAULTY FLASHLIGHT.** A faulty-flashlight argument shines light only on evidence that supports my argument and ignores other important facts or ideas.

One hundred percent of people value clean oxygen; therefore, all chemicals should be banned forever.

HOW TO FIX: This argument ignores the fact that nearly 100 percent of people rely on products that require chemicals to make. Take a good hard look at all the factors, data, and needs at stake. It's true that we need chemicals to produce most of the products we all use every day, but we have to find a way to reduce airborne emissions that are making us sick.

6. **STICK FIGURE.** A stick figure is representing your conversation partner's argument in a simplified, extreme, or untrue way, so it's easier to beat, much as a drawing of a stick figure is way more simplified and less nuanced than a photograph.

"The mayor thinks the drinking age should be 31."

"I never said I think the drinking age should be 31. I said our town should regulate alcohol better to encourage responsibility and reduce accidents."

HOW TO FIX: Delve into the complexity and nuance of the other side until you really understand, and represent the "other side" generously. While the mayor wants to spend tax dollars legislating alcohol, that would encroach on individual freedom, and there are other ways to combat alcohol abuse that don't require using government resources or oversight.

7. **BLACK HOLE.** The black-hole pitfall is saying something must be true because it has never been proven or disproven.

> We don't have evidence of the Lizard People; therefore, they definitely exist and are really good at hiding.

HOW TO FIX: Leave more room for ambiguity and paradox; don't force a conclusion that can't be made. The Lizard People *could* exist—we can't prove they do or don't—but let's look at all the arguments.

8. **EITHER/OR GLASSES.** This pitfall involves claiming something has to be one way or the other, ignoring other options.

> You're either pro-football, or you're anti-fun.

HOW TO FIX: Explore alternative choices. You could be anti-football and anti-fun. You could be anti-football but pro-baseball and pro-fun.

9. **IMAGINARY DOMINOES.** The imaginary-dominoes pitfall is claiming that if one thing happens, a whole bunch of bad things will definitely happen.

> If we go bowling tonight, someone will drop a bowling ball on their foot, and we will end up in the emergency

room, and we will get into a fight, and someone will punch a doctor, and then we will all land in jail, and is that really what you want?

HOW TO FIX: Consider ways the string of events in question wouldn't necessarily have to happen.

10. BIG MEANY HEAD. This pitfall involves resorting to name calling, labels, or personal attacks instead of sticking to the issues.

You lewd, crude, rude bag of prechewed food dude.

HOW TO FIX: Work on emotional regulation and humanizing your conversation partner. If you feel you can't continue the conversation without making things personal, take a break.

It's important to identify what kind of tool we are using at any given time. In this way, we can start to learn blend all three into perfect harmony.

For example, the best way to get Jimmy to clean his room would be to say, "Jimmy, I'm your mother, and I love you (Cred and Thread). I want you to go clean your room now. Doesn't it feel great to have a clean room? (Head and Thread). You can find things easily; you can relax when everything is in order (Head and Thread). When you clean your room, you get happier, and that makes me happy (Head, Cred, and Thread). Can you go do that for me now, please? (Cred and Thread)."

Using full-bodied arguments is the most effective way to make your case.

Of course, in the real world, Jimmy might still yell "No!" and then his mom would have to put him in time-out. At that point, argumentation and persuasion would cease, and Jimmy's mom would have to resort to using reasonable force granted to her by her responsibility as a mother.

Reasonable force is only used in parenting and the legal system. Most of the time, persuasion is pretty much all we have.

SUMMARY: True Persuasion Shares Power

Being passionate is a wonderful way to be. It's good and right to argue artic-ulately, to argue cleverly, and to argue to the best of our ability. We should be confident in sharing our ideas. We should not back down from a challenge if we feel up to the task. When we learn to meld our zeal with being intentional with our words, we become more effective communicators. When we learn to use the tools of rhetoric effectively, we can become highly persuasive people.

But watch out for domination.

The better we get at persuading, the more power we wield. As Voltaire—and Uncle Ben in *Spider Man*—said, "With great power comes great responsi-bility." While there are times to speak up, there will be times that we need to be quiet and focus on listening. There will be times we need to actively encourage others to speak confidently.

Full-bodied arguments encourage power sharing. Why? Because the combination of all three tools—Head, Cred, and Thread—protects us from leaning into styles of arguing that are overly manipulative, overly academic, or overly authoritative. True persuasion is not a monologue. It is a dialogue, a negotiation, and a collaboration.

In a larger sense, using full-bodied arguments shows leadership to people around us. When we take responsibility for the consequences of our words, we model respect and invite cooperation.

We build Community.

1. Did reading this chapter make you think about language differently? Why or why not?

2. Share your personal communication style, and compare it with someone else's style. How are your styles similar or different? How does knowing this information change the ways you might interact with each other?

3. What are your favorite verbal shortcuts? What is your opinion of using harsh language or swearing in public spaces?

4. How do you feel about arguing? After you read this chapter, did the way you think about arguing shift?

5. Do you agree with Dr. King that a "riot is the language of the unheard"? Or do you have a different take? In your opinion, what does it look like to advocate with confidence and conviction without using domination?

6. Share a time when you heard someone arguing a not-so-great cause but doing it really well. What did they do that made it so compelling? Is that something you would want to emulate or not? Why?

7. Share a time when you heard someone arguing a great cause but missing opportunities to do it well. What could they have done differently? Did they use any persuasion pitfalls?

8. When you make a case for your beliefs and opinions, do you lean on one rhetorical style (head, cread, or thread) more than the others?

CHAPTER 9

Creating Resilient Relationships

How Do We Live the Dream?

There once was a woman named Ruth, who was appointed to the same job as Antonin. Ruth was a champion of liberal feminist ideals; Antonin was a champion of conservative traditionalism. Ruth was Jewish; Antonin was Catholic. They disagreed fiercely and were at an impasse on nearly every issue under the sun.

A recipe for disaster, right?

"We were best buddies," Ruth Bader Ginsburg remarked after the death of fellow Supreme Court justice Antonin Scalia.[70] While on the bench in the Supreme Court, these two polar opposites went head-to-head on countless crucial disagreements. They wrote scathing dissenting opinions of each other's work. Outside the job, however, Ruth and Antonin were lifelong friends. They traveled together, ate meals together, and shopped together. Their families hung out on holidays, they went to shows together, and they shared joys and losses. From engaging each other articulately inside the courtroom to supporting each other loyally outside the courtroom, these powerful and highly opinionated people—who were literally paid to argue with each other for years over high-stakes issues with immense consequences—managed to build a resilient relationship.[71]

How in the world did they do it? *Why* in the world did they do it?

When asked why she maintained a friendship with Antonin, Ruth explained that her ultimate goal was to protect and strengthen the institution of the Court, and such a friendship made their work of arguing important matters stronger and more sustainable.

According to Antonin, "If you can't disagree ardently with your colleagues about some issues of law and yet personally still be friends, get another job, for Pete's sake."[72]

After Antonin died, the press asked Ruth for a statement. One can imagine opponents of Antonin licking their lips in anticipation of the greatest takedown of all time—something to the effect of "good riddance." Instead, Ruth responded with one of the most profound testaments to friendship and democracy: she said the Supreme Court would be a "paler place"[73] without him. Without Antonin's constant opposition to her ideas? Without his scathing dissents? Without him making her life utterly difficult? Yes.

Without the contrast of impasse, she knew something vitally important was lost: the Court would be less colorful, less vibrant, less sharp. That's an incredible statement from someone like Ruth, who holds passionately strong convictions about the way the world ought to work.

It would be a mistake to think that in order to be friends, these two brilliant minds were checking their ideals at the door or compromising their beliefs when they left the courtroom. This couldn't be further from the truth: both of these people dedicated their lives to fight for what they believed was right and good. Looking at their friendship, it's apparent that Ruth and Antonin understood a profound reality: resilient relationships are created through impasse, not in spite of it.

Let this be a lesson to us, in our present moment. If we don't actively create healthy and loving ways of relating to each other within the presence of impasse, here is what happens: impasse becomes corrosive, fracturing our connections and compromising our broader work in the world. When our relationships become brittle, those ties are less and less able to hold the weight of conflict. We hunker down in our Fear Bunkers, avoid each other, and even go to war with each other. Our crew becomes more important than love, more important than the well-being of our neighbors. Without healthy criticism and feedback, our ideas get inflated and even distorted. Fragile channels of communication compromise important processes of disagreement that families, communities, and societies need in order to be healthy.

Once we lose the will to work together, once we stop making an effort to see and be seen, we turn our society into a hopeless, toxic gridlock. In a state of gridlock, we can't get anything done; our families, communities, governments, and social systems start to break down.

For us to have a healthy society, we need resilient relationships. To have resilient relationships, we need to engage impasse.

What did people around Ruth and Antonin have to say about their friendship? According to Antonin's son Eugene, "Their ability to engage on ideas and yet respect one another's abilities and maintain a friendship is an instructive lesson. And I think they would both heartily agree that we want to have people on two sides of an issue to explain what the right answer is." [74] Did you catch that? He said we actually want "two sides of an issue to explain what the right answer is." Ruth and Antonin believed we need to negotiate many sides of truth, many angles, to get to what is right. Even though they completely disagreed, and furiously fought for their perspective on the law, they respected each other's vital role processes of collectively figuring out how to enact justice in the world.

The biggest lesson of Ruth and Antonin's friendship is that resilient relationships are not optional. They are necessary for our health and well-being, for the health of our ideas, and the health of our society.

It all comes down to this: if Ruth and Antonin can learn to forge a resilient relationship in such a high-pressure context, so can the rest of us.

Five Practices of Resilient Relationships

People who build resilient relationships know that such relationships don't happen by accident, and they don't happen overnight. Resilient relationships may look different across the board, but they all have commonalities at their core. While there are many positive ways of treating each other that make relationships healthy, resilience requires that five distinct practices be in place. These are practical, tangible behaviors we can work on if we want to create bonds with each other that can withstand the strain of conflict: (1) showing up for each other, (2) seeing and being seen, (3) sharing power, (4) disagreeing well, and (5) taking a break. If some or all of these practices are absent, the relationship will erode over time. All five are needed to build resilience in the presence of impasse. These guidelines don't have to be practiced perfectly, but they do need to be practiced.

The Five Practices of Resilient Relationships

1. Showing Up
2. Seeing & Being Seen
3. Sharing Power
4. Disagreeing Well
5. Taking A Break

1. Showing Up for Each Other

It might sound straightforward, but we can't have resilient relationships, or relationships at all, if we don't show up.

In today's media-driven, high-convenience world, it is easier than ever to avoid people and to interact only with people we agree with. There are many reasons people choose to do this, but here are a few:

- Relationships outside our crew, our "people," can feel like a minefield of awkwardness. It may seem better to invest in relationships within our own crew because we anticipate a higher level of comfort.

- In the past, we've been hurt and don't know who or how to trust. People like us—our crew—are less likely to hurt us, because they understand our needs and can provide us with safe space.

- It can feel cathartic to reject people before they (might) reject us. Avoiding the risk of rejection is a strong motivator for staying in our crew and not opening up.

- Our crew is less work. The people who think the way we think and believe what we believe don't need us to explain ourselves; they don't need us to constantly negotiate differences in communication or language.

While there is certainly nothing wrong with hanging out with people like us, it's really easy to fall into the trap of what I like to call "crewism." Crewism can be defined as a kind of loyalty to our own group at the expense of those outside.[75]

For example, I recently saw a social media post that went viral. It was talking to liberals and said something like "Hey, liberals, don't be so arrogant and classist by expecting people to sound educated like you. It's stupid and makes people resent us. Oh, but also, I hate so-and-so [conservative leader] and wish I could throw them into in a fiery volcano and watch them die. But don't be classist!" This writer was trying to call out crewism while perpetuating crewism. It's unclear whether they didn't realize they were using domination and violence or they realized it and didn't care. I'm not sure which is worse.

This kind of rhetoric isn't helpful. Bridges can't be built and burned at the same time.

Crewism means investing only in people who are like us. That might not sound so bad on the surface, but in crewism, it's mandatory to conform; only a small amount of difference is tolerated. This means that crewism relationships rely on similarity. When friendship is contingent on similarity (and not on something greater, like basic human dignity or unconditional love), it opens the door to the very real possibility that our crew might reject us if we exhibit too much difference. Once someone in the crew wants to explore options or when their beliefs or ideas start to change, they risk being attacked or even losing their community.

That's a pretty gross way of relating to each other.

Here are some other flaws of crewism:

- A tendency toward ideological flimsiness, because processes of disagreement are seen as threatening instead of teaching and learning opportunities

- A lethal lack of diversity that creates stagnation and lack of growth

- A preoccupation with "virtue signaling"—only shouting out to our own crew instead of actually trying to persuade effectively

- A failure of empathy, because crewism nurtures the us-versus-them thinking of war

Virtue signaling is saying things that show we belong to the crew, using insider language, lacking care for the consequences. While anger and outrage certainly play an important role in healthy dialogue, crewism often boils down to a big competition to see who can be the angriest, the most extreme, and the most loyal to the crew. Author Ryan Holiday describes the rampant crewism in our public spaces in terms of signaling:

> As we've become more polarized and more algorithmically sorted, we care a lot less about the people who think differently than us and put little effort into persuading them. That's because persuasion is no longer the goal—it's signaling. And with signaling, it's vehemence that matters, not quality. The constraints of social media also reduce the space for any nuance or qualification you might be inclined to offer; 140 characters or even 240 does not leave much room for humility or kindness. And the desire for viral sharing heightens the need for aggressive, simplistic arguments. This

callous, call-out culture has completely infected both sides of the political aisle, corrupting normal people and pundits with equal viciousness. [76]

Crewism doesn't work toward the common good; it smashes it. Therefore, crewism is both limiting and dangerous.

How do we get away from this way of thinking and acting in the world, without compromising the strength of our convictions? We work toward resilience. We work to invest in people outside our tribe. We work to build friendships that can hold the weight of impasse.

Resilient relationships believe the foundation of friendship is friendship, not sameness. These relationships resist the temptation to punish people who disagree, and instead they welcome the helpful role of disagreement and conflict in our lives. Resilient relationships believe people are more important than ideas. The table on the next page summarizes the differences between a crewism mind-set and a resilience mind-set.

So what exactly is a resilient relationship? Let's start with resilience. Resilience is hope in action. This means that resilient relationships are relationships that refuse to break because both people act on the hope that they are building something meaningful, despite the awkwardness or hardship they have to overcome to get there.

In other words, relationships are resilient when they can bounce back after conflict instead of fracturing.

Because engaging impasse taps into so much we hold dear, resilient relationships have to include trust, closeness, and boundaries. Most of us aren't comfortable with pouring out our hearts to a stranger at the grocery store. We need to know that the listener can hold our story and that there is some kind of commitment to be in our lives. Only then is it really healthy and appropriate to open up and discuss our deepest beliefs, fears, and values—especially across difference.

Therefore, the first practice of resilient relationships serves the interest of building trust: simply showing up. When people show up for each other and keep showing up for each other, they build history and prove their commitment and mutuality. Showing up means being intentional and making

CREWISM	RESILIENCE
The difference between us is more important than the relationship.	The relationship is more important than the difference between us.
Beliefs and ideas can justify me throwing dignity and empathy to the curb.	Beliefs and ideas are important, but they do not cause me to undermine human dignity or empathy.
Respect is circumstantial. You have to earn my respect. If I don't respect you, I will definitely show it. I don't care if that burns a bridge.	Respect is a choice. Even if I don't respect you, and even if you don't respect me, I will choose to show you respect, because that's who I want to be in the world. I choose to leave the door open to building trust.
I don't care if I misunderstand, flatten, or misrepresent your beliefs or ideas, because my goal is to make my crew look better than yours, no matter what.	I will believe the best about you and listen for the nuance of your arguments, so I can give credit where it's due and try to understand where you are coming from. Your experiences are valid.
I signal my virtue and loyalty to my crew by punishing you because you aren't in my crew.	I don't need to signal my virtue and belonging, because I know I have those things. I am interested in engaging you meaningfully, not punishing you.
I might have biases, but they aren't important. What's important is promoting the agenda of the crew and making sure everyone keeps agreeing.	I recognize my biases and leave room for the fact that I may be wrong or have incomplete information.
I invest only in people like me, because other people aren't worth it.	I invest in people from many walks of life, because relationships of difference, even hard difference, make me and my ideas stronger.
My identity and our relationship are based on being in the same crew. If you and I don't agree, friendship over.	My identity and this relationship are based on our shared humanity, not based on whether we agree or disagree. Our friendship relies on friendship.

an effort. It's a kind of perseverance—perseverance through awkwardness, through conflict and impasse, through difficult conversations, and even through dry times when relating to each other is a struggle. All of this culminates in a sense of trust.

But it can take a long time. Even if two people have an interpersonal spark, getting to know people well requires patience. Sometimes we treat relationships like instant coffee: if the raw ingredients like shared interests are there, just add a little small talk and—alakazam!—we have a new friend. I fondly remember the days of high school or college when I could strike up a conversation in the pizza line at lunch, and within five minutes I made a new bestie. For many of us as adults, building friendships has become astronomically harder. Especially if, like me, you have lived in many different places, it can be tough to stay in people's lives and feel the presence of strong roots.

Not only does it take an effort to meet people and get to know them, but pursuing potential friends can make us feel downright desperate, especially if they are outside our crew and not necessarily folks we would run into on a regular basis.

So how do we do it? How do we build resilient relationships with people that go beyond talking about the weather? How do we get close enough so that the relationship can start to take the weight of disagreement?

2. Seeing and Being Seen

A weird little cultural dance used to drive me up the wall when I was growing up in California. I don't know if it's a West Coast thing in particular, but I experienced it all the time. It went something like this:

"Oh, hey, [person I rarely see], great to see you!"

"Yeah, Mel, great to see you, too! We should hang out sometime."

"That would be awesome! When are you free?"

[awkward pause, then in a super-fake tone] "Yeah, we should definitely hang out. Have a great day!"

I've had this exact conversation dozens of times. Though I have good reason to believe I'm downright delightful, this kind of interaction makes

A RECIPE FOR SHOWING UP FOR EACH OTHER

The ingredients of a close, resilient relationship are the times we hang out together. The steps of this recipe sound simple but may challenge you: they boil down to showing up, again and again.

- **Hangout 1.** A stranger becomes a casual acquaintance. Learn each other's name, where they are from, how they spend their days, light common interests, etc.

- **Hangouts 2–5.** A casual acquaintance becomes a familiar acquaintance. Share information about values, family, hobbies; break the ice. This process requires a level of intentionality: it's not enough to just be accidentally in the same room. Intentionality means actively working to get to know each other.

  What to do: Start showing up—help them move, send a card, call when they get sick. Ask them to do things. Be there. Invite and accept their help in return.

- **Hangouts 6–10 (approximate).** A familiar acquaintance becomes a friend. Now that you feel comfortable with this person, you begin to share hopes and dreams, pains and joys. Share things close to your hearts that require trust to share. You can start disagreeing well and open the door to talking about difference. You can invite them to sharpen you and push against things you say.

  What do do: Keep showing up: call for no reason, watch their dog, tell them they matter. Let yourself be vulnerable and ask for things too.

- **Hangouts 10+.** A friend becomes Community. Now that you really have a solid understanding of each other, you can start to depend on each other when times are tough. You can begin to think of them as family. You can be vulnerable, asking for comfort in your weaknesses and celebrating your triumphs together. Silences become comfortable. You don't need to impress each other. This is when the relationship starts feeling like a favorite pair of shoes that provide support and comfort. This is when the relationship can start taking the full weight of conflict and impasse and will not break.

What do do: Show up again. Do life together. Argue well. Spread the love. Be there. Repeat.

Resilient relationships are not built in a day. They are built through logging hours, logging intentional hours. They are built by two people who rely on each other and who make themselves reliable in return. They are built by establishing depth, through mutuality and trust, over a long period of time. They are built by showing up, over and over and over. They are built with people because they are good friends to us, not necessarily because they are the same as us.

As long as people keep showing up for each other, the relationship can keep being resilient.

me feel small and worthless—or like maybe I smell bad and no one told me. I grew up feeling there was some mystery I wasn't allowed to solve, some kind of secret club where everyone else was out having fun and I was never invited.

Feelings like this can lead to social anxiety. My generation, Millennials, and younger generations are especially susceptible to social anxiety, which is a distinct fear of being judged or rejected in social situations. It can cause complete avoidance of interacting with others. While social anxiety can be a full-blown diagnosed disorder that affects a somewhat small percentage of the population, a high percentage of people in our society experience social fear on a regular basis—such as holidays with family, difficult conversations, parties, making new friends, making small talk, or even speaking on the phone. Evidence suggests that people today are increasingly anxious when it comes to relational dynamics (or at least experts are more aware of social anxiety and measuring it more often).[77] While social anxiety is still being studied, it may be caused by a rapidly changing world where it is easier than ever to connect and disconnect across great distance.

These days, it's incredibly easy to see relationships as consumables: easy to make, break, and toss away, like plastic bottles. Technology itself may play a role. Those of us who have grown up with technology sometimes develop weaker coping skills to navigate relational complexities. In a highly digital world where more and more of our interactions happen through a screen, we simply get less practice relating to others in person. During even the most basic of interpersonal exchanges, we sometimes just don't know how to do it. We fear being intrusive or making mistakes.

Then there are cultural factors. In highly individualistic societies, it's often considered awkward to express to other people how much we care about them. We want to appear strong, impassive, and cool, not burdensome, overly emotional, or needy. So we act on a silent assumption that vulnerability is weakness. When we are less vulnerable, we are less prone to affirm to the people around us how much they matter.

Consider the phenomenon known as ghosting, which is an acute example of failing to tell someone they matter. Ghosting in dating is when someone is too cowardly to tell the other person they don't want to be with them anymore. Instead of giving their partner the gift of closure and dignity, they just disappear. It's one of the most dehumanizing and emotionally crushing things people can do to each other.[78] From a grief perspective, ghosting can significantly prolong or contaminate someone's grieving process when the relationship ends.

Instead of a clean break for a seasonal relationship, people are left to wonder whether they ever mattered or whether anything they felt was real.

Flakiness, impassivity, and ghosting are cultural phenomena suggesting that many people in our society view interpersonal attachment, care, appreciation, and even communication as liabilities. They justify relating to each other in dehumanizing ways that lack empathy. No wonder many of us are left in a perpetual state of anxiety!

When did it become a virtue to send signals to other people that they don't matter? When did it become cool not to *see* each other?

We may find ourselves in a culture where it's "normal" to treat other people as if they don't matter, but we don't have to follow suit. We can rebel.

My friend Cindy is a high-powered corporate attorney. Her nickname at work is the Honey Badger, and no, I would not want to get into a fight with her. Once Cindy and I were hanging out running errands, and I noticed a curious thing about how she interacted with people. When she encountered service people—people bagging groceries or working the checkout counter—she would look them in the eye with a smile, ask them how their day was going, and then look them in the eye and wait for a response. Almost every time, the person she interacted with would sort of wake up. It was like putting water on a wilted plant: suddenly, people's faces would just flood with life. It seemed like every person she spoke to could tell, in an instant, that they were talking to someone who actually cared about them. Though they might have been treated like they were all but invisible all day, this interaction was somehow different. The service people would share things with her—little tidbits about their real life. "My daughter was sick last night, so I'm tired," one would say with a weary smile. Others said, "I'm taking classes at the community college, and I'm nervous about my test tomorrow," or, "My day is actually really good—thank you for asking!" Though these exchanges only usually lasted about three minutes, each person would walk away with a new bounce in their step.

After I watched this happen five or six times, I realized it felt weird to me to watch people interact this way; it made my heart ache. I didn't realize I had been missing human connection, and even these small moments felt profoundly meaningful.

I finally asked Cindy what had inspired her to do this. She started to say that before law school, she had worked for many years in retail, so she empathized with how hard the work was. But then she stopped herself. "You know, actually, I do it because it's rewarding for me to connect with people. I don't need anything from them. I just like the idea that taking a couple of minutes to care about someone can turn their whole day around. It helps me, too."

I came away from this feeling like the Honey Badger was a countercultural hero.

Cindy's goal was so simple that anyone can do it. Why did it seem so strange to me? And what exactly was the magic? What was it about the way she interacted with people that felt so special?

Cindy wasn't just saying, "People matter to me." She was showing that she actually believed it. She was putting the hope of meaningful connection into action. She didn't get preoccupied waiting for people to show her she mattered before she would respond. She was willing to be the first one. In short, Cindy took the time to see each of these people. They knew immediately that she was seeing them, and they let themselves be seen. It was gorgeous.

Resilient relationships are based on this simple act of taking the time to see each other and letting ourselves be seen.

Resilient relationships happen when we show and tell people they matter.

It's important to both show and tell, but showing is most important. True, the words "You matter to me" hold a special weight. But for people to understand on a deep level that they matter, actions and words need to align. Resilient relationships use a combination of words and actions to proclaim, "Hey, you—yes, *you*—you matter to me. I'm so thankful for you. I want you to know that you can be your full, human, awkward self, and I will celebrate you. You can make mistakes, and I will be generous with you. You can say some wrong things, and I may disagree, but I will give you the benefit of the doubt. We can talk about hard or awkward things, and I won't punish you. You can ask me to make adjustments in the way I work for you, and I will try to do it.

You can name the tension of our impasse, and I won't walk away. You can be boring and unimpressive, and I will still accept you. You can let your guard down, and I will hold your soul like it's my own. I have no interest in judging you, hurting you, forcing you to conform, or taking anything from you. I just want to be in community with you. Be my people; though we may not agree, I will be yours."

3. Sharing Power

Resilient relationships must balance love with justice. Without love, justice is harsh and authoritarian, sacrificing people on the altar of "the cause." Without justice, love has no backbone; it is subject to every slight breeze that pushes it to be silent, every gust of wind that asks it to compromise on important values.

Balancing love and justice can be summarized as sharing power. Saying true things without love for the person or concern for the relationship is *not* the true spirit of sharing power. If being "right" and feeling morally superior in the moment are more important than long-term consequences to the person, we are not building resilient relationships. That is domination in its most toxic form. Enforcing our view on someone regardless of the impact not only is harmful, but also is often utterly ineffective, pushing people in the entirely opposite direction from where we wish they would go. In failing to share power, we destroy our credibility and trust. Sharing power means inspiring, not controlling, and persuading, not punishing. Remember, "Don't burn down my house. Build me a better one."

Conversely, if we care so much about tranquility that we shy away from the courage of sharing hard truths or we shy away from confronting domination, we are also not building resilient relationships. There are times and places to create "safe space," but resilient relationships do not weaponize safety and use it to silence people. If we let our fears of disagreement overrule our ability to see and truly understand the person, we are embracing cheap peace. Resilient relationships are not passive or conciliatory; they are not eggshells. Resilient relationships are stronger and more meaningful. They can handle the awkwardness of challenge, honesty, and paradox.

Power sharing starts with self-regulation—controlling our own internal and external circumstances while refraining from controlling others. Self-regulation comes in many forms:

- *Self-regulation of power* is knowing what power you wield, when, and why. It means watching out for ways you might use domination (even accidentally) and watching for when your exercise of power or rights might prevent others from exercising their power or rights. Self-regulating power means that when you realize you are using domination, you pull back, reassess, and use the full spectrum of your imagination to re-create better ways of sharing (see chapter 3).

- *Self-regulation of emotion* is being aware of the baggage you are walking in the door with and dealing with it before, during, and after with the best tools you can access. It means understanding that no one can "make" you feel a certain way; you are responsible for your own feelings (see chapter 6).

- *Self-regulation of ideas* is being aware of your structure of meaning and assumptions, knowing what values and beliefs are most significant to you. In this way, you recognize that no one can "make" you think or believe a certain way; you are fully in control of your ideas and beliefs, and you refrain from trying to control or enforce the ideas or beliefs of others (see chapter 7).

- *Self-regulation of rhetoric* means taking responsibility for the language you use, the logic you use, and persuasion you use. It means presenting your case to the very best of your ability, using full-bodied arguments, paying keen attention to nuance. It also means protecting your credibility: when you use sources, facts, references, examples, and stories, you use these things responsibly and get them from trustworthy places so they are as close to the truth as possible (see chapter 8).

BOUNDARIES: WHEN TO SHOW UP AND WHEN TO DRAW THE LINE

What do we do if we make every effort to see and be seen, to tell people they matter, but they don't reciprocate the care we are giving? Boundaries are absolutely important. For the most part (possibly excepting the case of parents), it's not right to give and give and give ourselves into the dust for people who don't or can't appreciate it.

When someone does not treat us like we are treating them, we have some options. Here are four stages of response, from gentle to severe, depending on the situation:

1. **Maintain.** We can keep seeing, being seen; we can keep telling people they matter, because that's just the type of person we want to be in the world. Doing so models healthy ways of relating for other people and is simply good for our own well-being. We can be teachers and caregivers to people who can't really give back to us in return. Therefore, keeping at these practices is inherently good, regardless of whether care is reflected back to us. So long as we are not putting ourselves in a compromising or harmful position, sometimes it's okay to simply keep giving. We might understand in this case it's not healthy for us to bare our soul to this person and trust them with the deepest parts of ourselves, but we can still exercise plenty of love.

2. **Engage.** If, after some time, care still isn't reciprocated but we really want to be or need to be in the person's life (as in the case of a family member), we might invite them into a conversation around the kind of relationship we want and the ways we would like to treat and be treated. Make sure it's not a confrontation;

it's a dialogue, a two-way negotiation, about what you both need and hope for. Ask open questions, and be gentle, understanding that there are probably forces at work in that person's life that you don't know about.

3. **Release.** If it becomes a heavy burden to have a one-sided relationship and if the person we are trying to invest in won't or can't return the investment and care, it may be time to let that relationship go dormant for a while. We don't have to sever ties, but we also shouldn't force a resilient relationship when the other person clearly doesn't want to build one. Instead, we might around look for find other people to invest in. Resilient relationships do not make one person always be the caretaker. Each of us deserves to build roots with people who will both receive and give care. Importantly, we shouldn't waste time trying to be close to splashy, impressive people who won't really be there for us. The people worth investing in are the people who will make an effort and commitment to us in return.

4. **Protect.** In the rare instance when we realize our goodwill is opening us to the harm or manipulation of a person with bad or unhealthy intentions, it's perfectly right to sever ties firmly and without guilt. This is often a horrible choice, but the healthiest choice we can make to protect ourselves or others from abuse. Helping professionals are a wonderful resource in assisting us to deal with any repercussions and move on.

In addition to self-regulation, sharing power sometimes includes naming domination and holding it to account. Some people refuse to self-regulate, and their actions cause harm. In this case, they have to be confronted. It's vitally important to confront domination strategically and consider the long-term consequences of this work. Once we confront domination, we can begin to set up boundaries to contain the damage and protect anyone who is vulnerable. This often means gently taking someone out of a position of leadership, getting them help, and calling for them to make things right. Domination doesn't like to be demoted, healed, or made to reconcile, so it will fight against those efforts with all its strength. In our work of calling domination to account, we need to be sure we are not using domination to overcome domination. Resilient relationships share power so effectively that they don't make space for domination.

What is the primary, most active, most effective way to share power? Let's return briefly to the example of Ruth and Antonin. Both of these justices disagreed fiercely, all the time, but they did it in such a way that showed each other tremendous respect. Ruth recalled that even when Antonin would talk about an issue in a way that "ruined" Ruth's weekend because she disagreed with him so strongly, she was moved by the fact that he would always turn in his work with plenty of time for her to review it and respond.[79] In working this way, Antonin wasn't just saying he respected Ruth, he was showing it. He was not backing her into a corner; he was not trying to dominate her just to win. While exercising his power, he made sure to give her time and space to exercise her own power. He showed that he valued her as an equal through collaborating with her. He facilitated her ability to thrive and do her job well.

The respect these two people chose to show one another, in the ways they worked and communicated, over a long period of time, built up an amazing reserve of trust and even friendship. This is a perfect picture of power sharing.

4. Disagreeing Well

Relationships are resilient when they can hold the weight of conflict and impasse. Instead of running away from disagreement, we can learn to disagree well. What is disagreeing well? It means, after seeing and being seen and after sharing power, learning to effectively and intentionally engage each other on tough issues in ways that make us stronger. Disagreeing well includes the following behaviors:

- **Suspending the desire to resolve.** Pretend every conflict is an impasse. It's okay to sit with the awkwardness and discomfort. Paradox is okay; it's part of life, not necessarily a bad thing. There can be forms of truth on many sides of an argument. Learn to focus on the relationship beneath the conflict or impasse. The goal is to understand, not to fix (see chapter 1).

- **Banishing shame.** When we let ourselves make mistakes and change our minds without shame, we further reduce anxiety and animosity. No one likes to operate in a *gotcha!* environment; no one likes to be policed or hear "I told you so." Snarkiness and cynicism are deadly; don't let them in. Learn to be gentle with yourself and others. The payoff in building trust and resilience is immense (see chapters 1 and 8).

- **Understanding the real fears.** We need to understand the fears that motivate us and be empathic to the real fears that motivate others. Give each other the benefit of the doubt (see chapter 2).

- **Inviting opposition to our "side."** This means not only inviting in conversation partners who challenge us and sharpen us, but also expressing true thankfulness for them because they make us better (see chapter 4).

- **Learning the art of asking great questions.** When we learn this art, we can engage and understand more deeply, which is a crucial process in making the world more just (see chapter 5).

- **Representing our ideas, beliefs, and values well.** We should represent these passionately and to the best of our ability, and we should invite people to engage us with nuance, as we have engaged their ideas fairly (see chapter 8).

Those of us who don't have substantial ways to practice skills of conflict might feel lost when we try to disagree, because it feels like being thrown into the ring without any training. For this reason, it's helpful to create sandboxes where people can practice and play out conflict and difficult conversations. That way, when conflict happens (because it will!), we feel more prepared and can see it as an opportunity for growth.

Planning for conflict might sound strange, but it's utterly practical. When we set up in advance systems that allow people to address issues, we let people release tension slowly and in healthy ways before situations become explosive.

HOW TO PLAN FOR CONFLICT

1. **Make a resilience commitment.** It's a powerful thing for two people to say to each other, "I accept the fact that we may not agree. Unless you are trying to hurt me, I won't walk away. You matter to me, and conflict with you doesn't scare me. I invite you to disagree with me. Let's throw away the eggshells and be real with each other." Committing like this means that when conflict happens, we don't have to panic, because we know we will still be accepted at the end of the day. We know we matter. This kind of commitment is usually reserved for marriage vows, but we have every reason to make platonic commitments to each other in friendships and working relationships.

2. **Establish ground rules before conflict starts.** If both parties co-create rules of how they want to treat each other before conflict happens, it creates healthy boundaries. It's important from a power-sharing perspective that everyone involved gets a direct say in these rules, so everyone has ownership.

3. **Set up practice spaces.** Preparing for conflict before it starts means setting up low-risk and structured environments to build important skills. Practice spaces give people opportunities to

try on different communication styles and rhetorical approaches without the fear of negative repercussions.

4. **Create channels of communication to process conflict.** Regular check-ins, surveys, and open-ended invitations go a long way. When people know they will have regular opportunities to air grievances, it reduces anxiety and animosity. These are what we call a meta-conversation—a conversation about conversations. Questions might include these: Do you feel good about the ways we communicate, or could we improve? Do we have any tension that needs to be named? Are there any conflicts or issues we should plan to address? Make sure these check-ins are welcoming, not punishing, and focus on I-speak language instead of all-speak (see chapter 8).

5. **Make time and space for disagreement.** When it comes to resilient relationships, don't rush past points of disagreement that can make ties and ideas stronger. Communicate that healthy, respectful disagreement is a gift we give each other. It's something we make space for, something that is welcome in our friendship, family, or group (see chapter 4).

6. **Draw on helping professionals.** Therapists, psychologists, clergy, chaplains, and mediators are trained to help people navigate conflict and impasse. If you are in over your head, ask for help.

Making space for conflict and impasse in our lives plays a strong role in building resilient relationships; this is where the rubber hits the road. As people flex for each other and work together on a regular basis, relationships become less brittle and more pliable. Through planning, conflict and impasse are able to take a rightful place in everyday life and make us stronger.

5. Taking a Break

Dealing with conflict and impasse requires a lot of resources. We expend time, energy, emotions, and even money to navigate tough situations. This work can be exhausting, especially if it is prolonged.

If we go too long without taking a break, it might start to seem like we spend all our time talking about the relationship instead of having one. It might seem like the only thing that keeps us in Community is our disagreement. How do we replenish our resources—especially when we've spent a lot of time driving each other up the wall?

As a rubber band snaps back after being stretched, resilient relationships must also bounce back. At a point, we need to take a break from conflict—at the very least, we need to take a break from talking about the conflict. The relationship just needs to *be* a relationship.

However, taking a break can be difficult. Sometimes after intense conflict, the relationship has to find a new normal. This can be ambiguous, awkward, and confusing. How do we go back to enjoying each other's company? How do we stay together in Community, after we just shared hard truths?

* * *

When I was young, my good-natured father used to walk into a room where the rest of the family was having a conversation and yell in a very dad-like fashion, "Hey, everybody! Who wants to make a memory? Let's go on an adventure!" We liked to tease him about this, because we were perfectly content to sit around and talk, but Dad understood something we did not.

Dad understood something about the vital role of memory in relationships.

The way communities exist and create identity is through one principal function: memory.[80] Why are memories so important? According to Joshua Foer, a memory expert, who we are essentially boils down to the cultivation of our memories, both as individuals and as groups:

> How we perceive the world and how we act in it are products
> of how and what we remember. . . . No lasting joke, invention,

insight, or work of art was ever produced by an external memory. . . . Our ability to find humor in the world, to make connections between previously unconnected notions, to create new ideas, to share in a common culture: All these essentially human acts depend on memory. Now more than ever, as the role of memory in our culture erodes at a faster pace than ever before, we need to cultivate our ability to remember. Our memories make us who we are. They are the seat of our values and source of our character.[81]

Making memories together reminds us that we are more than the sum of our opinions. It gives us concrete stories to tell, mental pictures of being together that we can hang onto when times get tough. Making memories, even having fun together, reminds us of our shared humanity. We are people who need to love, to laugh, to eat, to adventure, to build, create, and connect. Memories solidify the deep understanding that we are accepted and worthy just as we are. Memories humanize us and help us humanize each other.

When we create positive memories together, our intentional moments—our reasons for abundant living—get to be suspended in time within our hearts. They get to be separated from the cataclysms of the world and the knowledge of global forces that are too big for our shoulders. Though we are finite, our ability to make memories permits us to help shape reality; we get to choose what to celebrate and uplift and share. This is an act of creation.

Making memories together involves actively telling the story of ourselves. In celebrating the good, we are casting vision for the future—deciding who we want to be in the world, modeling for those to come what it means to live a good life. We are reminding ourselves what makes the struggle with conflict worth it. We are reminding ourselves why we work to have relationships, especially for relationships that take a lot of work.

To make memories with people we are in conflict with, we have to learn the important skill of compartmentalizing. We have to put conflict in the storage room of our brain for a while and not look at it. If Antonin and Ruth could take a break from arguing in the Court and go to opera performances together, we can learn to take a break too. Taking a break keeps things in perspective and reminds us that conflict is part of life, not all of life.

Compartmentalizing can be really hard, especially when it feels like the stakes are high. Here are some tools that can help us compartmentalize, keep things in perspective, and maintain a relationship outside conflict and impasse:

- **Laughter.** Laughter is more than frivolity or a break from heavy problems. It releases tension, plays an important role in reminding us of the limitations of our humanity, and helps us find our way back to each other after we have existed in opposition. Back when Corey and I were newlyweds, we had been quietly frustrated with each other all day over some dumb thing or another. The atmosphere was tense. Corey made hamburgers for dinner and asked me how I wanted mine prepared. I told him I was going to skip the bun and eat it over a "nice bed of kale." He looked at me with wide eyes and yelled, "YOU DO SAD THINGS!" We stared each other down in total silence for several seconds, and then we both erupted into laughter. After sharing such a good belly laugh, we felt as if we had opened a big window that let fresh air into our relationship. With the tension dispersed, the disagreements of the day became easy to resolve. It's fair to say that resilient relationships need laughter to stay resilient. To incorporate laughter into difficult situations, we've got to learn to take ourselves less seriously. Remember that our basic dignity resides in simply being human; we don't have to earn it by acting a certain important or serious way. Sometimes people laugh when they're uncomfortable, but even that can be an important release. It turns out that science is starting to back up the idea that laughter is medicine. According the Mayo Clinic, laugher is a stress reliever, immune-system booster, and mental-health stimulator.[82] So please exercise tact, but don't be afraid to let laughter play a part in difficult conversations.

- **Gratitude.** Gratitude also is being studied by researchers for its health benefits. The Greater Good Science Center at the University of California, Berkeley, reports that in addition to gratitude being healthy for relationships and psychological well-being, findings suggest "grateful people may have better sleep, healthier hearts, and fewer aches and pains."[83] Gratitude plays a central role in resilience; it reminds us of the good things when it's so tempting to be overwhelmed by the bad. In this way, gratitude keeps situations in perspective and brings us back to the big picture: we are alive, we are loved, and things are going to be okay. Naming things we are grateful for might feel incredibly trite, but this practice can go a long way in boosting our outlook and sense of hopefulness. Gratitude also helps us remember to tell people they matter. When is the last time you went out of your way to tell someone you have conflict with that you are thankful for them? Making sure to not only feel grateful but also express gratitude helps reduce our social anxieties and lets us feel more accepted and less antagonistic toward each other, which in turn makes conversations more fruitful and nuanced. Gratitude is a crucial part of resilience.

- **Meaning making.** In times of deep grief, pain, or loss or when people's real fears are kicking into high gear, it's incredibly harmful to start making jokes or talking about what we are thankful for. Our response needs to exhibit a level of empathy appropriate for the pain people are expressing. In these times and in all times, a helpful tool is to talk about the why. Why are we in relationship? What does it mean for us to show up for each other? What has this relationship added to our experience on earth? Why is wider community significant? Why do we keep going? Reminding ourselves of the why, of the meaning, helps us keep things in perspective and summon our strength. It's a great exercise to not only do this internally but also process meaning with people with whom we disagree. We might learn some important information about the way they see the world, which helps us build bridges.

- **Celebration.** Let's be real: the world can be a crappy place. We are all riding on this wild train together. Celebrating is a much-needed practice. Resilient relationships celebrate progress together. "Hey, remember when we could only talk about politics for five minutes, and now we can talk about it for twenty minutes? That's cool! We're getting better at this!" Noting progress and growth is a wonderful thing to do together. Resilient relationships also celebrate just because the relationship exists. Throw a party just because, just to do life together. After a good drag-out argument, why not host a barbecue? After a difficult conversation, how about you take everyone bowling or play Frisbee? It's okay to compartmentalize and invite joy and fun back in. In fact, resilient relationships depend on this bounce-back ability. So consider taking a break from a heavy heart and be lighthearted together for a while.

In all, resilient relationships hold a profound and important sense of wisdom at their core: engaging conflict and impasse must involve rest and play, or relationships will be overtaken by the hardship of constant and unceasing disagreement. Taking a break means actively remembering that we truly value people over issues; we seek to balance our justice with love. When we remember to spend time just having a relationship, we are living out the belief that the basis of friendship is friendship, and the basis of human connection is shared humanity—not similarity, not conflict, not anything else that comes with a list of contingencies. Humans deserve care and love and kindness simply because. We don't have to act a certain way to deserve those things.

When times get toughest, remembering to have a relationship outside of conflict is the glue that holds us together.

SUMMARY: Resilience and the Dream of Community

As humans sharing a planet with other humans, what obligations do we have toward each other? Surprisingly, very few. We can choose to live a decent life in a decent little bubble, avoiding all conflict. We can choose the catharsis of hunkering down with our crew and surrounding ourselves only with people who agree with us.

It is true that each of us has the freedom to live the life we wish.

If we choose the bubble life, we may find some measure of contentment. But we may never know the deep satisfaction of resilient relationships—relationships that get stronger with impasse, relationships that bounce back after conflict, relationships that stick with us. For those of us who have experienced truly resilient relationships, the sense of security they bring is what makes life worth living.

Community—the dream of resilient families, neighborhoods, and societies—has a special power to take our lost and broken selves and root us into health and significance. Deep and genuine connection, unconditional and founded on a shared humanity, is what grounds us and teaches us that we matter. It's what inspires us together to build a more just and loving world.

Learning to approach difficult relationships with resilience and conflict transformation has helped me reconnect with people I love. It has given me a sense of stability that I've lacked during times of my life when I've embraced fear and domination, times when I've been wrapped up in my crew and my own little bubble. In such a state, I believed I couldn't be close to people from different walks of life, because of the vastness of our disagreement. But once I learned how to transform conflict, once I learned to see and be seen instead of trying to resolve the unresolvable, I became happier and more thankful for the people around me. I gained opportunities to grow and mature, and I began to see the world in a more nuanced way. I learned the art of brave talk.

Practicing courageous dialogue has enhanced my ability to empathize and humanize, my ability to stretch and be uncomfortable, and my ability to understand challenging and paradoxical ideas. Learning how to interact with people so unlike me, people who believe very differently than I do, has expanded my capacity to love and be loved.

I didn't find a new way of being by forcing myself to like conflict. I found it by changing my relationship with conflict. When I began to understand the value of disagreement, appreciate the role of conflict, and engage impasse, my imagination began to wake up to new possibilities of being effective in the world.

This is not easy work. But it's full of meaning. And that's the difference.

In Conclusion: May Your Impasse Be Blessed

Thank you for thinking deeply with me about impasse, disagreement, and resilience. I hope you have developed a better relationship with conflict as a result of this book. I hope you feel encouraged and inspired to engage others across difference in new and better ways.

I believe in your ability to do this work against great odds, and I am cheering you on.

Here is my blessing for you:

> May the impasse you find be fruitful;
> May the disagreements you engage be rich with meaning;
>
> May you know the strength and ability of your voice to speak
> hard truth;
> May you understand the capacity of your soul to see and be seen;
>
> May your imagination be stretched to share power;
> May you lead the way in balancing justice with love;
>
> And may you experience the depth, refreshment, and wonder
> of building resilient relationships in the face of conflict.

1. What's your experience with resilient relationships—relationships that can handle the weight of conflict and difference?

2. Do you experience social anxiety? If so, when is it most strong, and when is it is least strong? What puts you at ease?

3. When is the last time someone told you that you matter? When is the last time you told someone else that they matter? How did it feel?

4. Share a time when you felt supported and held by a relationship, when someone showed up for you. What did that feel like?

5. Share a time when a relationship broke down or let you down. What did that feel like?

6. What current relationships do you have that give you life? What current relationships don't give you life? Which of the Five Practices of Resilient Relationships is missing in these relationships? Is there anything you can do to change the situation?

7. If you could build a resilient relationship, your dream relationship, what would it look like? How would you and the other person interact with each other?

8. What's your biggest takeaway from this book?

Epilogue
Epic Impasse Pep Talk

I used to be so bad at difficult conversations. Truly bad. I would get flustered, feel sick, and forget how to talk. I would develop a stutter and do everything in my power to run away.

If I can learn to do this, you can learn to do this.

Here are some things to remember:

- **It's not just about you.** It's about the relationship you have with that person. It's about showing them love and kindness and understanding to a ferocious degree.

- **This is work.** You are doing work. It might feel like just a conversation, but it's work. It's work full of meaning. It's work you get to practice getting good at. You have lots of time to get good at it.

- **You should advocate for things you believe in with all the articulate, passionate energy you can muster.** But when you do, do it in a way that meets other people where they are and that invites rather than dominates. When you extend an open hand instead of a fist, it doesn't mean you have to forget that you have strong convictions. It means you are taking responsibility for the long-term consequences of your words. That takes strength and wisdom.

- **Things will sometimes get awkward or uncomfortable.** If that happens, give yourself a high five, because you are doing something awesome that most people are afraid to even try.

- **Sometimes this work will even be painful.** You will hear stories that will hurt your heart. As your muscles of empathy get stronger, you will see more of the fears and loneliness below the surface of anger and hatred. You will feel more. That's okay. These experiences will broaden you as a person.

- **Things will sometimes be funny.** Sharing a smile goes a long way in difficult conversations. Laughter reminds us that we are all human. Laugh in respect and reverence. Laugh with the core of your being. Laugh at the absurdity and beauty of life. Laugh when you feel joy. It's okay to not take things so seriously sometimes.

- **Courage means sharing your heart, understanding the risks of opening yourself up.** Courage does not wait for others to open. Courage leads, even without hope of reciprocation. Even if you get nowhere, you have modeled a better way of being in the world. That is significant.

Impasse is hard. Difficult conversations are hard. Conflict is hard. These are some of the hardest things we face in life. But with the challenge comes tremendous opportunity for growth and connection. That's why difficult conversations are so important. Resilient relationships can't be built without them. Community doesn't happen without them.

You can do this. I believe in you.

Appendices

TOOLS FOR THE REAL WORLD

Appendix A

Brave Talk Base Camp

A Group Exercise for
Practicing Courageous Dialogue

Brave Talk Base Camp is an interactive experience that helps groups of two or more people practice difficult conversations and build skills of courageous dialogue. The following is a preview of the opening lines:

Imagine that you are a Traveler, standing at the base of a mountain.

The mountain represents an issue you feel strongly about.

On the other side of the mountain is a fellow traveler. They see the mountain from a totally different perspective.

Here is your challenge: Make it to the top of the mountain and have a productive conversation where you suspend the desire to change each other, but instead, gain a deeper understanding of the other person's world. Are you ready?

Get the *Brave Talk* companion book, including the full text of the Brave Talk Base Camp and many other helpful tools and resources, at bravetalkproject.com.

Appendix B
Top Ten Conversation Hazards

Here is a go-to reference for behaviors to avoid during difficult conversations. These are called "hazards" because they can totally derail productive discourse. Can you think of any to add to this list?

1. **Trolling.** The internet term for provoking someone in order to knock them off balance is *trolling*. Some people do it unintentionally. When you're tempted to troll, consider your motives in the moment. Are you trying to win or create drama? Are you unearthing strong feelings in yourself or others that you don't want to deal with, so you're trying to create a distraction? Or are you truly trying to understand?

2. **Wearing the crown.** This means being condescending or acting superior. Avoid this at all costs; it fosters resentment and power grabbing. You may be an awesome, well informed, or educated person, but that doesn't erase your need for human equality, for seeing and being seen. Let yourself be a human.

3. **Pontificating.** Avoid using big words and ideas that no one else can speak to or giving long-winded speeches that don't allow for engagement. If you find yourself talking *at* other people, try using words of one or two syllables for a while. Try using shorter sentences and asking more questions. For the sake of the conversation, challenge yourself to dial it back and share space.

4. **Bigfooting.** Don't engage in "bigfooting," or spreading conspiracy theories that are unproductive. Yes, conspiracy theories are fun, but they are fundamentally unprovable. Stick to what you know that you know and what is reasonable to discuss with your conversation partner.

5. **Bunny trailing.** Veering the conversation away from the heart of the matter—bunny trailing—may be intentional or unintentional. Either way, it causes missed opportunities by spending time on things that aren't relevant.

6. **All-speak.** Another hazard is all-speak, or using grand, sweeping statements that can neither be proven nor refuted or trying to speak for everyone or an entire group of people. Stick to your social location, your experiences, your sources, your feelings, your convictions. These are enough. You don't have to be an expert.

7. **"My neighbor Cathy."** As we saw in chapter 8's examples of shaky logic, "my neighbor Cathy" is the fallacy of wrongly assuming an isolated instance is the norm. It's like that one time your neighbor Cathy gave you cookies, and now you assume all your neighbors will always give you cookies.

8. **Downstreaming.** Another mistake to avoid is downstreaming—getting stuck looking at the results without seeking to unpack causes. If you're studying the problem of a polluted lake, it would be a mistake not to look at the rivers that feed the lake. Instead of downstreaming, ask questions: What are the causes? What causes those causes? Who benefits from them?

9. **2 + 2 = pickles.** In chapter 8, we called jumping to conclusions "2 + 2 = pickles." Often people do this out of a frantic, insecure

desire for resolution. You don't have to rush. Take your time, and don't be afraid to explore many options, even options you aren't likely to agree with. You don't need to decide everything or try to read someone's mind. No one can force you to believe anything you don't want to believe, so you don't have to be in a hurry deciding. You are in control.

10. **Shutting down.** A final situation to avoid is one where you get to a state of no longer being able to engage, whether because someone feels emotionally unsafe or because someone has reached their limit of the conversation. If you feel yourself shutting down, first of all, acknowledge yourself for a good job of being self-aware. Consider sharing how you feel with the group; sometimes this can make your experience much easier for you and others to deal with because it's simply reality. Once you are aware of it, you can either work through it together or take a break. Both of these options are good. The only way you can fail is by shutting down but pretending you're fine.

None of us are perfect at avoiding these hazards all the time, but the only way we can fail is to give up. As long as you keep trying, there is hope for growth. Good luck as you practice.

Appendix C

Difficult Conversations on Social Media

Social-media conversations can be a veritable land mine of communication issues. The fundamental question to ask in the digital age—*Should I post this?*—haunts many a good soul. Here is a handy flowchart for deciding when it's appropriate to post something on social media.

SHOULD I POST THIS ON SOCIAL MEDIA?
—A FLOWCHART—

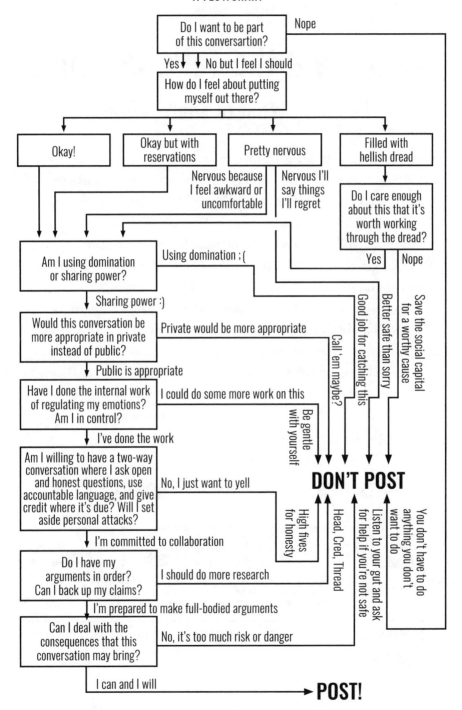

Appendix D
All Aboard the Talking Train
Deciding What to Share, When

It can be confusing to figure out what to share in which situation and with which people. Sharing our story, feelings, experiences, or even opinions is unfamiliar territory for some of us. If we aren't used to sharing, we might have a difficult time feeling out what's appropriate. Especially when strong emotions are present, it can feel like a geyser is unleashed as words come tumbling out. The Talking Train is a tool that breaks down the decision process, helping us figure out what's okay to share and when it's okay to share it.

The Talking Train is a flowchart that starts with the engine: The engine is where we first take time to gauge our emotions to make sure we are in a good personal place to share something difficult. Next, we move to the box cars, where we reflect on the context clues that help us decide what's appropriate to share, given the situation and relationship: we have with our conversation partner. Finally, we end with the caboose: a consideration of the consequences and timing of what we plan to share.

THE TALKING TRAIN: DECIDING WHAT TO SHARE, WHEN

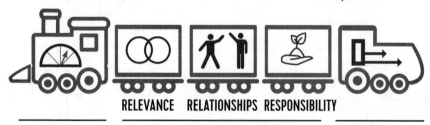

RELEVANCE   RELATIONSHIPS RESPONSIBILITY

EMOTIONAL
ENGINE

CONTEXT CARRRS

CONSEQUENCE
CABOOSE

1. WHAT ARE MY EMOTIONS DOING IN THIS CONVERSATION?

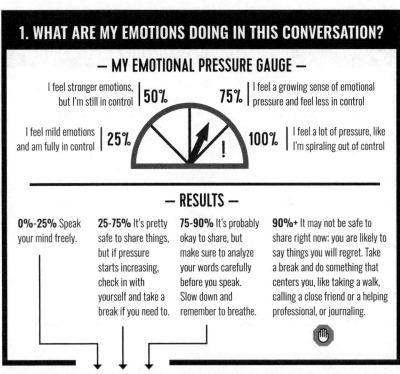

— MY EMOTIONAL PRESSURE GAUGE —

I feel stronger emotions, but I'm still in control | **50%**

75% | I feel a growing sense of emotional pressure and feel less in control

I feel mild emotions and am fully in control | **25%**

100% | I feel a lot of pressure, like I'm spiraling out of control

— RESULTS —

0%-25% Speak your mind freely.

25-75% It's pretty safe to share things, but if pressure starts increasing, check in with yourself and take a break if you need to.

75-90% It's probably okay to share, but make sure to analyze your words carefully before you speak. Slow down and remember to breathe.

90%+ It may not be safe to share right now; you are likely to say things you will regret. Take a break and do something that centers you, like taking a walk, calling a close friend or a helping professional, or journaling.

2. WHAT IS THE CONTEXT OF THIS CONVERSATION?

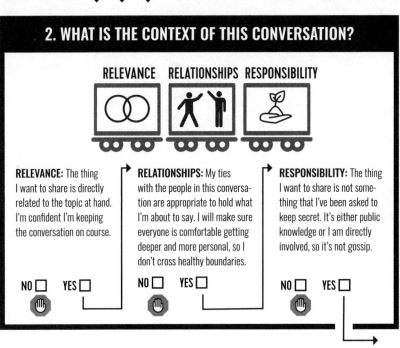

RELEVANCE   RELATIONSHIPS   RESPONSIBILITY

RELEVANCE: The thing I want to share is directly related to the topic at hand. I'm confident I'm keeping the conversation on course.

RELATIONSHIPS: My ties with the people in this conversation are appropriate to hold what I'm about to say. I will make sure everyone is comfortable getting deeper and more personal, so I don't cross healthy boundaries.

RESPONSIBILITY: The thing I want to share is not something that I've been asked to keep secret. It's either public knowledge or I am directly involved, so it's not gossip.

NO ☐   YES ☐

NO ☐   YES ☐

NO ☐   YES ☐

3. WHAT ARE THE CONSEQUENCES OF THIS CONVERSATION?

SHORT-TERM CONSEQUENCES

What will saying this COST me in the short term?

What will saying this GET me in the short term?

LONG-TERM CONSEQUENCES

What will saying this COST me in the long term?

What will saying this GET me in the long term?

ASSESSMENT
Can I live with ALL of these consequences?

NO☐ YES☐

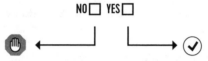

Appendix E
Glossary of Awesome Words

accountable language: Using I-speak instead of all-speak; speaking for ourselves, from our own perspective, instead of trying to talk for others. Accountable language keeps itself in check and doesn't make grand claims that can't be backed up. *See* chapter 8.

all-speak: Trying to speak for everyone, versus using I-speak. *See* I-speak; social location.

analysis: A thorough, detailed exploration of a set of information, usually for the purposes of discussion. It tries to take many sides of an issue into account before making judgment.

anxiety: The physiological, psychological, and emotional experience of being on edge or on high alert that something negative might happen. In many cases, anxiety is a natural and self-protective reflex, so it's not completely avoidable. But it can be managed with the right tools and skills. *See* chapter 6.

argument: Making a case for your point of view. In rhetoric and dialogue, making an argument is different from "having an argument," which usually has a negative connotation. *Persuasive argumentation* has a positive connotation, as in advocating for something we believe. *See* chapter 8.

assumption: A belief, idea, or fact we take as given without needing to prove it. Sometimes the assumptions we hold are solid, and sometimes they are faulty. Assumptions are built on our experiences and beliefs and the facts we understand to be true. They inform our values and opinions. *See* chapter 7.

Awesome If: The technique of imagining, to the best of our ability, what it would be like to have the experiences of our conversation partner. By humanizing, contextualizing, and empathizing with them, we might gain a deeper understanding of their truth and their structure of meaning, even if we strongly disagree with their views. We can't fully know what things were like for someone else, but we can try. In this way, we show our purpose is to care and connect, not to judge or win. *See* chapter 7.

boundaries: In interpersonal relationships, the rules created to protect appropriate levels of intimacy and emotionally healthy interactions. Boundaries differ in different settings and in different relationships. For example, boundaries with a coworker will differ from boundaries with a spouse physically, psychologically, spiritually, and emotionally. In healthy relationships, boundaries are negotiated and mutually agreed on; they represent an informal social contract. If boundaries are violated, people may experience difficult emotions like anger, fear, or disgust, even if they don't consciously recognize that boundaries have been violated.

brave space: A co-created space where people cease policing or dominating each other and instead collaborate across difference to try to understand each other more deeply and share power. It is the result of creating encounters where people from different perspectives practice holding the paradox, ambiguity, and discomfort of difference, using measures of emotional safety and healthy boundaries in shared spaces.

civil discourse: Respectful, kind sharing of ideas or debate. The term has been used to describe an ideal for difficult conversations—specifically, that the participants keep a calm tone and "right" behavior. An alternative that is less likely to enable domination is to focus instead on courageous dialogue. *See* courageous dialogue.

civility: A historically fraught term that has been weaponized in many ways throughout the world. For some, this is a positive word with good connotations; for others, this is a painful word. *See* chapter 4.

cognitive dissonance: The experience of an internal conflict or inconsistency in our structure of meaning—specifically between our beliefs, assumptions, values, opinions, experiences, and actions. *See* chapter 7.

common sense: Knowledge of what everyone "ought" to know; assumptions derived from an appeal to natural law. Examples include "Look both ways before crossing the street"; "All people should be free and happy"; "The earth is valuable and deserves to be treated with respect."

community/Community: When spelled with a lowercase *c*, a group of people who choose to associate with each other and do life together. When spelled with an uppercase C in this book, an ideal or dream of families, friends, neighborhoods, societies, and cultures who build resilient relationships. *See* resilient relationships.

conflict transformation: In engaging conflict and impasse, focusing on relationships instead of resolution. This book recommends that transforming conflict starts with pretending the conflict is unresolvable until everyone has had time and space to see each other and let themselves be seen. *See* chapter 1.

courageous dialogue: The respectful sharing of hard truths. Courageous dialogue focuses on seeing and being seen, emotional honesty, and conflict transformation. *See* chapter 1.

credibility: The reliability of a source, speaker, or argument. Credibility is usually marked by having a track record and reputation for telling the truth, not exaggerating or sensationalizing, being measured and fair, and keeping biases accountable. *See* sensational.

crewism: Loyalty to a group at the exclusion or expense of others. Crewism includes othering and us-versus-them thinking that shuts down Community. *See* chapter 9.

critical thinking: The skill of weighing arguments and opinions fairly and in depth.

debate: A formal kind of discourse where two people with opposite views compete to see who can argue their view better. It is usually done in a public setting.

deductive: Term for the type of reasoning that starts with a hypothesis and tests several examples of evidence to weigh its truthfulness. Example: "Dave has a very particular sense of fashion. On Monday, he wore a gray shirt, and on Tuesday, he also wore a gray shirt. If he continues to wear gray shirts over a period of time, the pattern I observe might support my hypothesis that he loves gray shirts so much that he only wears gray shirts. But I will also leave possibilities open, such as the possibility that Dave wears gray shirts selected by his wife out of a deep sense of love, even though he hates them, and it is his wife who is the true champion of gray shirts." Reasoning may be deductive or inductive. *See* inductive.

demonization: Regarding someone or a group of people as inherently bad, nonhuman, less than human, or unworthy of basic human rights. *See* chapter 4.

discourse: Respectful communication intended to weigh heavy topics. It is written or spoken.

dog whistle: A buzzword that gets people particularly upset and calls them to action. Dog whistles are generally associated with types of rhetoric that are strongly partisan or even related to groupthink. *See* chapter 8.

domination: An unhealthy or abusive use of power that seeks to control or force others to do its will. Domination can be carried out by individuals or larger structures and is characterized by power hoarding, unmitigated privilege, and a failure of empathy. In its wake, domination leads to many forms of violence, including psychological violences of inequality, economic violences of poverty, legal violences of injustice, political violences of undemocratic systems, ecological violences of resource or environmental abuse, and social violences of discrimination. *See* chapter 3.

Head, Cred, Thread: Terms used in this book to refer to the types of argumentation known as *logos* (Head), *ethos* (Cred), and *pathos* (Thread). *See* logos, ethos, pathos. *See* chapter 8.

hegemony: The oppression or domination of one person, social group, or country over others.

I-speak: Speaking from one's own social location and from one's own experiences and perspective, versus using all-speak. *See* all-speak; social location. *See* chapter 8.

impasse: The state of being unable to resolve conflict because of different experiences, interests, beliefs, or convictions.

inductive: A form of reasoning that takes a small example and makes a broad, unsubstantiated claim from it. Example: "I saw Dave wearing two gray shirts. Therefore, Dave only wears the color gray." The other major form of reasoning is deductive. *See* deductive.

injustice: A state of social, legal, political, psychological, economic, or ecological unhealth where someone's ability to thrive has been compromised. *See* justice.

intersectional: A description of situations in which forms of oppression overlap and happen at the same time, making it unhelpful to try to isolate one form of oppression or privilege while neglecting the bigger picture. For example, it's not helpful to talk about gender oppression unless we take into account concurrent economic oppression, political oppression, historical oppression, racial/ethnic oppression, geographic oppression (rural vs. urban), and so forth.

invalid or valid: Ways to describe the nature of an argument and its underlying logic without necessarily agreeing or disagreeing with it. An invalid argument is an argument that has been shakily made. Something in its head, cred, or thread is faulty. The argument might claim a conclusion that seems true, but the way the speaker got there was suspect, so the argument can be said to be invalid. A valid argument is an argument that is well made; its logic, ethics, and emotional appeals are solid. An argument can be described as valid and even respectable regardless of whether the person describing it agrees with it. *See* head, cred, thread.

justice: Social, legal, political, psychological, economic, or ecological health where the ability of all to thrive and have basic rights is protected and respected. *See* injustice.

lens: In dialogue, a point of view from which a person chooses to see something, using a guiding critical analysis or field of study. For example, I might use a sociological lens, a racial lens, a religious lens, or the lens of a particular author or thinker's framework to look at an issue in a certain light. We all use lenses all the time; sometimes we are more aware of it than others. As we can with eyeglasses, we can to a considerable degree learn to take lenses on and off to see different angles of a given topic. It is impossible to see something from a completely unbiased or lens-free view. Though we can adapt and learn to see things from other perspectives, we all come from a specific social location that will always inform our perspective. *See* social location.

logos, ethos, pathos: The three types of argumentation as defined in ancient Greek rhetorical philosophy. *Logos* refers to logic and reasoning. *Ethos* refers to credibility and ethics. *Pathos* refers to the personal or emotional aspects of an argument. In this book, these types of argumentation are referred to as Head, Cred, and Thread, respectively. *See* chapter 8.

normativity: In a sociological sense, the determination of what is considered "normal" and who gets to decide what is normal. Normativity tends to result in othering anyone who doesn't observe its norms or fall into its categories; it draws a line between normal/accepted and abnormal/unaccepted. Making an argument based on normativity differs from making an argument about morality or justice. For example, an argument that "women who have beards are not natural" fails to take into account that women who have beards are still women; they aren't doing anything wrong or unjust by having beards. It's simply a function of their bodies and is therefore quite literally natural. Excluding women with beards from the definition of normativity implicitly labels them "abnormal" and thereby impermissible or undesirable. Questioning who gets to establish normativity around gender expectations for something like facial or body hair ultimately means asking deeper questions of who is in power, who gets to belong, and who is considered fully and acceptably human. Challenging normativity is often an effective way to critique power structures. *See* othering.

othering: The act of considering someone or a group of people to be alien, inherently different, and impossible to relate to, empathize with, or understand (therefore implying that their humanity is less than). *See* chapter 4.

power: The ability to make any kind of change in the world. *See* chapter 3.

power sharing: Actively looking for imbalances of power and seeking creative and innovative ways to equalize power so everyone has the ability to make positive political, economic, social, or ecological change. The process of power sharing must involve calling domination to account and addressing systems that harbor domination. *See* domination.

privilege: A helpful lens for understanding why some people in the world are historically, economically, socially, legally, or politically granted more power than others by society. The implication is that those without privilege ought to have the same allowances as those who are privileged, but they don't because of structures of injustice. Application of the term *privilege* is meant to be a critique against domination, to teach the understanding that some people may experience a greater sense of power but as part of a larger context into which they were born, and they may indeed have that power at the cost of someone else. *Brave Talk* discusses privilege as an important step in learning to understand systematic oppression but suggests that awareness is not the end goal. The end goal is to use awareness to call domination to account and build a world that better shares power. *See* chapter 3.

real fear: A fear that resides at the center of who we are and informs our view of the world. For example, avoidance of violence or starvation or chaos may be driven by real fears of ceasing to exist. It is important to understand and honor the real fears that guide our own actions and beliefs, as well as the actions and beliefs of those with whom we disagree. Another term for real fear is core fear. *See* chapter 2.

resilient relationships: Relationships that can handle the weight of conflict and not break, but instead get stronger as a result of disagreement, conflict, and impasse. *See* chapter 9.

rhetoric: The art of persuasion, through speaking, writing, or using media. Rhetoric can be healthy, positive, passionate argumentation (using *ethos*, *pathos*, and *logos* together in harmony), or it can be manipulative and harmful as a result of omitting *ethos*, *pathos*, or *logos*. *See* chapter 8.

safe space: An intentionally-created atmosphere where people can share how they really feel about sensitive subjects without the presence of opposition. While this is a laudable ideal, it can sometimes be problematic when needs for safe space contradict. For example, someone who is gay may seek a safe space to express their pride in being gay, and this vision may go against the idea of safe space for someone who has religious objections to being gay and wants a place to be able to express their beliefs. If these two people were in the same room, they would likely try to silence each other in the goal of creating a space that is "safe" for each of them personally. While safe spaces are crucially important for many communities, *Brave Talk* is not focused on safe spaces. Instead, it seeks to teach readers how to create brave space. *See* brave space.

sensational: Description of an extreme or far-fetched version of reality in a way that is often intended to provoke or mislead. Sensationalism is a form of invalid argumentation, even if the intention is to motivate people toward positive action. Being sensational erodes credibility.

sharing power: *See* power sharing.

social location: Someone's perspective from their place in history, geographic region, race/ethnicity, gender, economic resources, sexual orientation, political power, and social place. Speaking from one's social location is a way to contextualize truth as coming from a particular place, time, and conditioning experiences.

source: The place from which a fact, evidence, or piece of supporting information originated. Some sources are more credible than others. *See* credibility.

structure of meaning: The web of beliefs, assumptions, values, experiences, opinions, and actions that make up the core of who we are and how we see the world. *See* chapter 7.

subtext: Thoughts expressed between the lines or left unspoken. Unspoken beliefs and assumptions beneath an argument are part of the subtext.

tenable or untenable: Options for describing something as justifiable or acceptable. A tenable argument or belief system is acceptable and can be supported or defended. An untenable argument or belief system can't be justified and therefore is not acceptable.

transformative: Causing a significant change. Something is transformative when it has a strong impact. For example, someone might change their mind on an issue after going through a transformative event or hearing a transformative story.

trauma: In a psychological sense, the experience of something so disturbing or horrific that it changes the way we function, whether on an emotional level, a neurological level, a physical level, or all of these levels. Post-traumatic stress disorder (PTSD) is a diagnosis of a long-term psychological condition that has an adverse impact on a person's day-to-day life. *See* chapters 2 and 6.

untenable: *See* tenable.

valid: *See* invalid.

Recommended Reading

Benjamin, Ben, and Amy Yeager. *Conversation Transformation: Recognize and Overcome the Six Most Destructive Communication Patterns.* New York: McGraw Hill, 2012.

Bretherton, Luke. *Resurrecting Democracy: Faith, Citizenship, and the Politics of a Common Life.* New York: Cambridge University Press, 2015.

Hicks, Donna. *Dignity: Its Essential Role in Resolving Conflict.* New Haven, CT: Yale University Press, 2011.

Kraybill, Ronald S., R. Evans, and A. Frazer Evans. *Peace Skills: Manual for Community Mediators.* San Francisco: Jossey-Bass, 2001.

Lederach, John Paul. *Preparing for Peace: Conflict Transformation across Cultures.* Syracuse, NY: Syracuse University Press, 1995.

———. *The Little Book of Conflict Transformation.* Intercourse, PA: Good Books, 2003.

Porter, Thomas J. *The Spirit and the Art of Conflict Transformation: Creating a Culture of Justpeace.* Nashville:, TN Upper Room, 2010.

Pranis, Kay. *The Little Book of Circle Processes: A New/Old Approach to Peacemaking.* Intercourse, PA: Good Books, 2005.

Ross, Rupert. *Returning to the Teachings: Exploring Aboriginal Justice.* Toronto: Penguin Canada, 2006.

Stone, Douglas, Bruce Patton, and Sheila Heen. *Difficult Conversations: How to Discuss What Matters Most.* New York: Penguin, 1999.

Zehr, Howard. *The Little Book of Restorative Justice.* New York: Good Books, 2014.

Bibliography

Alcock, James. *Belief: What It Means to Believe and Why Our Convictions Are So Compelling.* Amherst, NY: Prometheus, 2018.

American Psychological Association, Working Group on Stress and Health Disparities. "Stress and Health Disparities: Contexts, Mechanisms, and Interventions among Racial/Ethnic Minority and Low-Socioeconomic Status Populations." Accessed December 12, 2018. https://tinyurl.com/yxhbl2a8.

———. "APA Stress in America˜ Survey: US at 'Lowest Point We Can Remember'; Future of Nation Most Commonly Reported Source of Stress." News release, November 1, 2017. https://tinyurl.com/y3599x56.

Augsburger, David. *Conflict Mediation Across Cultures: Pathways and Patterns.* Louisville, KY: Westminster/John Knox Press, 1992.

Bakke, Dennis. *Joy at Work: A Revolutionary Approach to Fun on the Job.* Seattle: Pear Press: 2005.

Bates, Karen Grigsby. "When Civility Is Used as a Cudgel against People of Color." *All Things Considered,* National Public Radio, March 14, 2019. https://tinyurl.com/y55hey7k.

Bedeau, Hugo Adam, ed. *Civil Disobedience: Theory and Practice.* New York: Pegasus, 1969.

Benjamin, Ben, and Amy Yeager. *Conversation Transformation: Recognize and Overcome the Six Most Destructive Communication Patterns.* New York: McGraw-Hill, 2012.

Bejan, Teresa. "On Civility." Harvard University Press blog, June 27, 2018. https://tinyurl.com/y2gm5qm8.

Benson, Herbert, and Miriam Z. Klipper. *The Relaxation Response.* New York: Harper Torch, 1975.

Booth, W. James. "Communities of Memory: On Identity, Memory, and Debt." *American Political Science Review* 93, no. 2 (June 1999): 249–63. https://tinyurl.com/y3ceq5fq.

Bremner, J. Douglas "Traumatic Stress: Effect on the Brain." *Dialogues in Clinical Neuroscience* 8, no. 4 (December 2006): 445–461, available at https://tinyurl.com/yeb3bbr8.

Bretherton, Luke. *Resurrecting Democracy: Faith, Citizenship, and the Politics of a Common Life.* New York: Cambridge University Press, 2015.

Cavanaugh, Jillian R. "Performativity." In *Oxford Bibliographies,* March 10, 2015. https://tinyurl.com/yxtnqelk.

Davetian, Benet. *Civility: A Cultural History.* Toronto: University of Toronto Press, 2009. https://tinyurl.com/y4xwf4yd.

Delmas, Candice. *A Duty to Resist: When Disobedience Should Be Uncivil.* New York: Oxford University Press, 2018.

Farber, Sharon K. "Chronic Pain Syndrome and Other Psychosomatic Illness." *Psychology Today,* June 13, 2013. https://tinyurl.com/y3zqzmmo.

Ferrer, David. "Fifteen Logical Fallacies You Should Know before Getting into a Debate." The *Quad,* last updated August 1, 2019. https://tinyurl.com/yy2by8vf.

Foer, Joshua. *Moonwalking with Einstein: The Art and Science of Remembering Everything.* New York: Penguin, 2012.

Franklin, Benjamin. *The Autobiography of Benjamin Franklin*. New York: P. F. Collier & Son, 1909.

Freire, Paulo. *Pedagogy of the Oppressed*. New York: Bloomsbury, 2000.

Harvard Medical School. "Anxiety and Physical Illness." *Staying Healthy* (Harvard Health Publishing blog), updated May 9, 2018. https://tinyurl.com/yyrz7d9q.

———. "Understanding the Stress Response." *Staying Healthy* (Harvard Health Publishing blog), updated May 1, 2018. https://tinyurl.com/y2wlhp7t.

Heid, Markham. "You Asked: Is Reading the News Bad for You?" *Time*, January 31, 2018. https://tinyurl.com/yxurlqn6.

Herman, Judith. *Trauma and Recovery: The Aftermath of Violence—from Domestic Abuse to Political Terror*. New York: Basic Books, 1997.

Hicks, Donna. *Dignity: Its Essential Role in Resolving Conflict*. New Haven, CT: Yale University Press, 2011.

Holiday, Ryan. "It's Not Enough to Be Right—You Also Have to Be Kind." *Medium*, March 26, 2019. https://tinyurl.com/yyr5dahs.

Hsa, Hua. "The Civility Wars." *New Yorker*, December 1, 2014. https://tinyurl.com/y2y2h9gm.

International Society for the Study of Trauma and Dissociation. "Dissociation Frequently Asked Questions." Accessed January 25, 2019. https://tinyurl.com/y5gla548.

JustPeace Center for Mediation and Conflict Transformation. "The Circle Process." Accessed December 17, 2018. https://tinyurl.com/y2okgkyz.

Kolb, Bryan, and Ian Q. Whishaw. *The Fundamentals of Human Neurosychology*, 6th ed. New York: Worth, 2009.

Kraybill, Ronald S., R. Evans, and A. Frazer Evans. *Peace Skills: Manual for Community Mediators*. San Francisco, CA: Jossey-Bass, 2001.

Lang, Beral. "Civil Disobedience and Nonviolence: A Distinction with a Difference." *Ethics* 80, no. 2 (January 1970): 156–59. https://tinyurl.com/yjggkh8l.

LeBaron, Michelle, and Venashri Pillay. *Conflict across Cultures: A Unique Experience of Bridging Differences*. Boston: Intercultural Press, 2006.

Lederach, John Paul. *The Little Book of Conflict Transformation*. Intercourse, PA: Good Books, 2003.

———. *The Moral Imagination: The Art and Soul of Building Peace*. New York: Oxford University Press, 2005.

———. *Preparing for Peace: Conflict Transformation across Cultures.* Syracuse, NY: Syracuse University Press, 1995.

Lieberman, Matthew D. "The Mind-Body Illusion: Why There Is No Escaping It." *Psychology Today*, May 17, 2012. https://tinyurl.com/ycjq9tk8.

Living Justice Press. "About the Circle Process." Accessed December 17, 2018. https://tinyurl.com/yxvkvscb.

Mathew, Sarah, and Charles Perreault. "Behavioural Variation in 172 Small-Scale Societies Indicates that Social Learning Is the Main Mode of Human Adaptation." *Proceedings of the Royal Society B: Biological Sciences* 282, no. 1810 (July 7, 2015). https://tinyurl.com/y289jgsj.

Mazo, Adam, and Ben Pender-Cudlip, dirs. *Dawnland.* Upstander Project, June 2018, 86 min. Available at https://upstanderproject.org/dawnland.

McIntosh, Peggy. "White Privilege: Unpacking the Invisible Knapsack." *Independent School*, Winter 1990. Reprint accessed at https://tinyurl.com/y5nxvs77.

Merton, Robert K. "Social Structure and Anomie." *American Sociological Review* 3, no. 5 (October 1938): 672–82.

Meyer, Erin. *The Culture Map: Breaking through the Invisible Boundaries of Global Business.* New York: Perseus, 2014.

National Institute of Mental Health. "Anxiety Disorders." Mental Health Information: Health Topics, last revised July 2018. https://tinyurl.com/y3ngzwho.

Neimeyer, R. A. *Meaning Reconstruction and the Experience of Loss.* Washington, DC: American Psychological Association, 2001.

Nevid, Jeffrey S. "Thinking through Anxiety." *Psychology Today*, April 30, 2017. https://tinyurl.com/y2tncqre.

Nordquist, Richard. "How the Three Branches of Rhetoric Differ." *ThoughtCo*, April 20, 2018. https://tinyurl.com/y3ovakyc.

Pavlic, Ed. "The Forgotten Economic Vision of Martin Luther King." *Institute for New Economic Thinking* blog, April 4, 2018. https://tinyurl.com/yywf4ll7.

Pew Research Center. "The Changing Global Religious Landscape." April 5, 2017. https://tinyurl.com/y5sv8j9y.

———. "U.S. Religious Landscape Survey: Religious Beliefs and Practices." Chapter 1 of *U.S. Religious Landscape Survey.* June 1, 2008. https://tinyurl.com/yfx3r66s.

Porter, Thomas J. *The Spirit and the Art of Conflict Transformation: Creating a Culture of Justpeace.* Nashville: Upper Room, 2010.

Pranis, Kay. *The Little Book of Circle Processes: A New/Old Approach to Peacemaking.* Intercourse, PA: Good Books, 2005.

Rapp, Christof. "Aristotle's Rhetoric." In *Stanford Encyclopedia of Philosophy*, ed. Edward N. Zalta. Revised February 1, 2010. https://tinyurl.com/yxvufdzq.

Rearick, Lauren. "Eight Stats That Prove Social Anxiety Needs to Be Taken Seriously." *Huffington Post*, April 17, 2018. https://tinyurl.com/y49jb4k2.

Robinson, Howard. "Dualism." In *Stanford Encyclopedia of Philosophy*. Revised February 29, 2016. https://tinyurl.com/y2xa722e.

Rogers, Mary Beth. *Cold Anger: A Story of Faith and Power Politics*. Dallas: North Texas Press, 1990.

Ross, Rupert. *Returning to the Teachings: Exploring Aboriginal Justice.* Toronto: Penguin Canada, 2006.

Sarkis, Stephanie. "Emotions Overruling Logic: How Belief Bias Alters Your Decisions." *Forbes*, May 26, 2019. https://tinyurl.com/ygobqke6.

Schneiderman, Neil, Gail Ironson, and Scott D. Siegel. "Stress and Health: Psychological, Behavioral, and Biological Determinants." *Annual Review of Clinical Psychology* 1 (2005): 607–628. https://tinyurl.com/y8m8blba.

Schwitzgebel, Eric. "Belief." In *Stanford Encyclopedia of Philosophy*. Accessed November 2, 2019. https://tinyurl.com/yzusgg63.

Sit, Ryan. "Here's What the FBI Had on Martin Luther King Jr." *Newsweek*, January 15, 2018. https://tinyurl.com/y44kp5sf.

Thurman, Robert A. F. *The Seven Deadly Sins: Anger*. New York: Oxford University Press, 2005.

Turner, Victor. *The Ritual Process: Structure and Anti-Structure*. New York: Taylor & Francis, 1969.

Vogel, Susanne, and Lars Schwabe. "Learning and Memory under Stress: Implications for the Classroom." *npj Science of Learning* 1, article 16011 (June 29, 2016). https://tinyurl.com/y9f6rdrw.

Zehr, Howard. *The Little Book of Restorative Justice*. New York: Good Books, 2014.

Endnotes

Chapter 1

1 Victor Turner, *The Ritual Process: Structure and Anti-Structure* (New York: Taylor & Francis, 1969).

2 Donna Hicks, *Dignity: Its Essential Role in Resolving Conflict* (New Haven, CT: Yale University Press, 2011).

3 As it stands, the global community of the United Nations has developed a widely acknowledged definition of human rights. See "Universal Declaration of Human Rights," accessed April 25, 2019, https://tinyurl.com/y6st4s5y.

4 For an excellent introduction to indigenous systems of justice, see Rupert Ross, *Returning to the Teachings: Exploring Aboriginal Justice* (Toronto: Penguin Canada, 2006).

Chapter 2

5 "Stress-related illness and injury are estimated to cost the United States more than $300 billion per year, including costs related to stress-related accidents, absenteeism, employee turnover, diminished productivity, and direct medical, legal, and insurance costs (American Institute of Stress, 2013)." American Psychological Association, Working Group on Stress and Health Disparities, "Stress and Health Disparities: Contexts, Mechanisms, and Interventions among Racial/Ethnic Minority and Low-Socioeconomic Status Populations," accessed December 12, 2018, https://tinyurl.com/yxhbl2a8.

6 "APA Stress in America˜ Survey: US at 'Lowest Point We Can Remember'; Future of Nation Most Commonly Reported Source of Stress," news release, American Psychological Association, November 1, 2017, https://tinyurl.com/y3599x56. See also Markham Heid, "You Asked: Is Reading the News Bad for You?," *Time*, January 31, 2018, https://tinyurl.com/yxurlqn6.

7 Robert A. F. Thurman, *The Seven Deadly Sins: Anger* (New York: Oxford University Press, 2005), 32.

8 Robert K. Merton, "Social Structure and Anomie," *American Sociological Review* 3, no. 5 (October 1938): 672–82.

9 "Anxiety and Physical Illness," Staying Healthy (Harvard Health Publishing blog), Harvard Medical School, updated May 9, 2018, https://tinyurl.com/yyrz7d9q. See also Sharon K. Farber, "Chronic Pain Syndrome and Other Psychosomatic Illness," *Psychology Today*, June 13, 2013, https://tinyurl.com/y3zqzmmo.

10 Neil Schneiderman, Gail Ironson, Scott D. Siegel, "Stress and Health: Psychological, Behavioral, and Biological Determinants," *Annual Review of Clinical Psychology* 1 (2005): 607–28, https://tinyurl.com/y8m8blba.

11 Judith Herman, *Trauma and Recovery: The Aftermath of Violence—from Domestic Abuse to Political Terror* (New York: Basic Books, 1997), 35.

12 "What Is a Trigger?," University of Alberta, Sexual Assault Centre, October 8, 2018, https://tinyurl.com/y383u54g.

13 Herman, *Trauma and Recovery*, 39.

14 "Anxiety Disorders," Mental Health Information: Health Topics, National Institute of Mental Health, last revised July 2018, https://tinyurl.com/y3ngzwho.

15 That said, these structures can fail us. We can dive into our fear bunkers preemptively. The trauma fence can signal someone or something is unsafe when it actually isn't dangerous. Some people use the word *trigger* when they mean that they are offended, not that they are actually receiving a shock from their trauma fence. "Crying trauma wolf" has disastrous consequences for people living with real PTSD. It's the responsibility of the person using the language of trauma to decide whether the trauma fence is actually providing important safety information, or if it's misfiring. It's also that person's job to determine how those experiences might actually shape reality.

16 Sarah Mathew and Charles Perreault, "Behavioural Variation in 172 Small-Scale Societies Indicates that Social Learning Is the Main Mode of Human Adaptation," Proceedings of the Royal Society B: *Biological Sciences* 282, no. 1810 (July 7, 2015), https://tinyurl.com/y289jgsj.

17 "The Changing Global Religious Landscape," Pew Research Center, April 5, 2017, https://tinyurl.com/y5sv8j9y.

Chapter 3

18 Ed Pavlic, "The Forgotten Economic Vision of Martin Luther King," Institute for New Economic Thinking blog, April 4, 2018, https://tinyurl.com/yywf4ll7.

19 The anti-domination framework in this book is inspired by many sources, but most notably the work of Paulo Friere in *Pedagogy of the Oppressed* (New York: Bloomsbury, 2000).

20 Peggy McIntosh, "White Privilege: Unpacking the Invisible Knapsack," *Independent School*, Winter 1990, reprint accessed at https://tinyurl.com/y5nxvs77.

21 Sasha Ingber and Vanessa Romo, "Captain Who Rescued Migrants at Sea Refuses Paris Medal, Calling It Hypocritical," NPR, August 21, 2019, https://tinyurl.com/yj4aaews.

22 Beral Lang, "Civil Disobedience and Nonviolence: A Distinction with a Difference," *Ethics* 80, no. 2 (January 1970): 156–59. Accessed at https://tinyurl.com/yjggkh8l.

23 Henry David Thoreau, "On the Duty of Civil Disobedience," in *Civil Disobedience* (New York: Harper Collins, 2013).

24 Candice Delmas, *A Duty to Resist: When Disobedience Should Be Uncivil* (New York: Oxford University Press, 2018), 47ff.

25 Dennis Bakke, *Joy at Work: A Revolutionary Approach to Fun on the Job* (Seattle: Pear, 2005).

Chapter 4

26 Bill Finch, "The True Story of Kudzu, the Vine That Never Truly Ate the South," *Smithsonian Magazine*, September 2015, https://tinyurl.com/yxo73ast.

27 For further reading, see Benet Davetian, *Civility: A Cultural History* (Toronto: University of Toronto Press, 2009), https://tinyurl.com/y4xwf4yd.

28 Teresa Bejan, "On Civility," Harvard University Press blog, June 27, 2018, https://tinyurl.com/y2gm5qm8.

29 Karen Grigbsy Bates, "When Civility Is Used as a Cudgel against People of Color," *All Things Considered*, National Public Radio, March 14 2019, https://tinyurl.com/y55hey7k.

30 The two parties chose to use a methodology called a truth and reconciliation commission, a model of restorative justice created to restore relationships in the wake of apartheid South Africa. For more information on this film, see www.dawnland.org.

31 Hua Hsa, "The Civility Wars," *New Yorker*, December 1, 2014, https://tinyurl.com/y2y2h9gm.

32 Nor did we win for the next several decades, as that song is one of the worst earworms to ever be composed. If anyone can find a recording of this song, please do *not* share it with me. I will not forgive you.

33 "Performativity" is a philosophical concept made famous by feminist scholar Judith Butler to argue that some presumably natural expressions of humanity, like gender, are socially constructed. The word coined by philosopher John L. Austin has a wider meaning that describes language that has a transformational effect on action and realities. For a great overview of this concept, see Jillian R. Cavanaugh, "Performativity," in *Oxford Bibliographies*, March 10, 2015, https://tinyurl.com/yxtnqelk.

34 Unless you have done or said anything to make me believe your intentions are malicious or dangerous to my physical safety. If this happens, establish boundaries.

35 Special thanks to my shrewd copy editor and mother, Rev. Amy Hunt, for helping me with this beautiful acronym.

Chapter 6

36 Dualism has many forms. One historically influential form is "Platonic dualism," where the soul is seen as trapped in the body, and the body is of a "lower" order needing to be mastered by the "higher" soul. Another historically influential form is "Cartesian dualism," where a person has a mind in the spiritual world and a body in the physical world. In this form of dualism, mind and body are seen as very separate things, and generally the mind is seen as more important. *Stanford Encyclopedia of Philosophy*, s.v. "Dualism," August 19, 2003, https://tinyurl.com/y2xa722e.

37 Matthew D. Lieberman, "The Mind-Body Illusion: Why There Is No Escaping It," *Psychology Today*, May 17, 2012, https://tinyurl.com/ycjq9tk8.

38 Bryan Kolb and Ian Q. Whishaw, *The Fundamentals of Human Neuropsychology*, 6th ed. (New York: Worth, 2009), 111ff.

39 R. A. Neimeyer, ed., *Meaning Reconstruction and the Experience of Loss* (Washington, DC: American Psychological Association, 2001).

40 "Understanding the Stress Response," *Staying Healthy* (Harvard Health Publishing blog), updated May 1, 2018, https://tinyurl.com/y2wlhp7t.

41 Jim Phelps, "Three Brains in One," Psycheducation.org, December 2014, https://tinyurl.com/y6jjwuyq.

42 Herbert Benson and Miriam Z. Klipper, *The Relaxation Response* (New York: HarperTorch, 1975). See also Carrie Elizabeth Lin, "'Everything's Going to Be Okay': How Good Are You at Self-Soothing?," Addiction.com blog, June 1, 2015, https://tinyurl.com/yxdypq9r.

43 Kolb and Whishaw, *The Fundamentals of Human Neuropsychology*, 193ff.

44 For a helpful article on anxiety management techniques, see Jeffrey S. Nevid, "Thinking through Anxiety," *Psychology Today*, April 30, 2017 https://tinyurl.com/y2tncqre.

45 Mary Beth Rogers, *Cold Anger: A Story of Faith and Power Politics* (Dallas: North Texas Press, 1990).

46 Years after Elisabeth Kübler-Ross and David Kessler's seminal book *On Grief and Grieving*, Kessler named a sixth stage of grief: meaning making. David Kessler, *Finding Meaning: The Sixth Stage of Grief* (New York: Scribner, 2019).

47 This is a tool I learned at my grief support group. Origins unknown.

48 J. Douglas Bremner, "Traumatic Stress: Effect on the Brain," *Dialogues in Clinical Neuroscience* 8, no. 4 (December 2006): 445–461, available at https://tinyurl.com/yeb3bbr8. For a reader-friendly discussion of trauma and the brain, see Arielle Schwartz, "The Neurobiology of Trauma," blog of Arielle Schwartz, PhD, October 27, 2016, https://tinyurl.com/ye6hjfrj.

49 "Understand the Facts: Symptoms of PTSD," Anxiety and Depression Association of America, accessed November 4, 2019, https://tinyurl.com/yep53a7l.

50 Ben Martin, "In Depth: Cognitive Behavioral Therapy," PsychCentral, last updated June 19, 2019, https://tinyurl.com/yz4t59kx.

Chapter 7

51 Ann O'Leary, "Teaching Tip Sheet: Cognitive Dissonance," American Psychological Association, accessed August 3, 2019, https://tinyurl.com/y5zvxhn7.

52 Eric Schwitzgebel, "Belief," in *Stanford Encyclopedia of Philosophy*, accessed November 2, 2019, https://tinyurl.com/yzusgg63.

53 Stephanie Sarkis, "Emotions Overruling Logic: How Belief Bias Alters Your Decisions," *Forbes*, May 26, 2019, https://tinyurl.com/ygobqke6.

54 "U.S. Religious Landscape Survey: Religious Beliefs and Practices," chap. 1 of *U.S. Religious Landscape Survey*, Pew Research Center, June 1, 2008, https://tinyurl.com/yfx3r66s.

55 For the record, I didn't realize that banana peels carry pesticides. I killed every one of those worms. The guilt haunts me to this day.

56 Jason S. Baehr, "A Priori and A Posteriori," in *Internet Encyclopedia of Philosophy*, accessed September 18, 2018, https://tinyurl.com/y5f2lyru.For the record, I didn't realize that banana peels carry pesticides. I killed every one of those worms. The guilt haunts me to this day.

Chapter 8

57 One of the most helpful frameworks I could find is outlined by Erin Meyer in *The Culture Map*. Meyer outlines eight sliding scales of communication. These scales have been simplified and adapted in *Brave Talk*, with the addition of two dynamics that account for abstraction and expression preferences. See Erin Meyer, *The Culture Map: Breaking through the Invisible Boundaries of Global Business* (New York: Perseus, 2014), 16.

58 For the sake of creating a do-it-yourself tool, the sun/moon/dawn/dusk model I have developed in this book is largely simplified from more complex communications theory. Specifically the "What's Your Communication Style" inventory is adapted from Erin Meyer, *The Culture Map*. For in-depth reading on culture-based communications theory, see Michelle LeBaron and Venashri Pillay, *Conflict across Cultures: A Unique Experience of Bridging Differences* (Boston: Intercultural Press, 2006), 32–55.

59 Benjamin Franklin, *The Autobiography of Benjamin Franklin* (New York: P. F. Collier & Son, 1909), 18.

60 These abbreviations made popular by texting have the following meanings: brb means be right back; j/k means just kidding, and lol means laughing out loud.

61 Peggy McIntosh, "White Privilege: Unpacking the Invisible Knapsack," *Independent School*, Winter 1990, reprint accessed at https://tinyurl.com/y5nxvs77.

62 Susanne Vogel and Lars Schwabe, "Learning and Memory under Stress: Implications for the Classroom," *npj Science of Learning* 1, article 16011 (June 29, 2016), https://tinyurl.com/y9f6rdrw.

63 "MLK: A Riot is the Language of the Unheard," CBSNews, August 25, 2013, https://www.cbsnews.com/news/mlk-a-riot-is-the-language-of-the-unheard.

64 "Dissociation Frequently Asked Questions," International Society for the Study of Trauma and Dissociation, accessed January 25, 2019, https://tinyurl.com/y5gla548.

65 Ryan Sit, "Here's What the FBI Had on Martin Luther King Jr.," *Newsweek*, January 15, 2018, https://tinyurl.com/y44kp5sf.

66 Christof Rapp, "Aristotle's Rhetoric," in *The Stanford Encyclopedia of Philosophy*, ed. Edward N. Zalta, revised February 1, 2010, https://tinyurl.com/yxvufdzq.

67 Richard Nordquist, "How the Three Branches of Rhetoric Differ," ThoughtCo, April 20, 2018, https://tinyurl.com/y3ovakyc.

68 "About Us," Hands Across the Hills Project, accessed November 1, 2019, https://tinyurl.com/yhze9kdq.

69 These persuasion pitfalls can be loosely mapped to classical terms for logical fallacies as follows: my neighbor Cathy is flawed inductive reasoning; 2 + 2 = pickles is false conclusion; pickles = 2 + 2 is causal fallacy; oh, look, there's a chicken is a red herring or *ignoratio elenchi*; faulty flashlight is confirmation bias; stick figure is a straw man or *reductio ad absurdum*; black hole is an appeal to ignorance or *argumentum ad ignorantiam*; either/or glasses corresponds to a false dilemma or false dichotomy; imaginary dominoes is a slippery slope; big meany head is a personal attack or *ad hominem*. See David Ferrer, "Fifteen Logical Fallacies You Should Know before Getting into a Debate," *The Quad*, last updated August 1, 2019, https://tinyurl.com/yy2by8vf.

Chapter 9

70 "Ginsburg and Scalia: 'Best Buddies,'" *All Things Considered*, National Public Radio, February 15, 2016, https://tinyurl.com/y287aog2.

71 Irin Carmon, "What Made the Friendship between Scalia and Ginsburg Work," *Washington Post*, February 13, 2016. https://tinyurl.com/y6tamfg3.

72 Carmon, "What Made the Friendship Work."

73 Tracy Schorn, "Justice Ginsburg Remembers Scalia: 'Court Is Paler Place without Him,'" DC Bar, September 23, 2016, https://tinyurl.com/yyojdzo2.

74 Sasha Zients, "Justice Scalia's Son: Washington Can Learn from Dad's 'Rich Friendship' with RBG," CNN, August 23, 2018, https://tinyurl.com/yk6aho8x.

75 With the term crewism I propose an alternative to the word *tribalism*. Native activists have raised awareness about the harm of associating tribes with negativity. Often, the word *tribalistic* is used as a synonym for mob mentality or groupthink, which is demeaning to the sociocultural reality of tribes. While it is true that the concept of "tribe" is ancient—tribes have existed around the world for millennia, so perhaps this word and idea don't belong to just one group of people—the word *tribe* evokes ethnic and familial bonds that should be treated with utmost respect. I prefer the word *crew* because it accounts for voluntary associations, wherein individuals choose to align to a "crew" because they adopt and identify shared values, beliefs, and aesthetics, not necessarily because they inherit shared traits in families or clans. In the age of mass media, sometimes crew allegiances represent great and global efforts to find like-minded others. Being part of a crew is not inherently negative; interpersonal loyalties are a natural part of life. It's when we cease to demonstrate empathy or cease trying to make meaningful connections outside our crews—when our crews become closed to the "other" —that Community is at risk of breaking down. Thus, when referred to as an -ism, "crewism" refers to unhealthy group-based abilities of exclusion and us-versus-them thinking that fails to appreciate intellectual difference, freedom of expression, or equality.

76 Ryan Holiday, "It's Not Enough to Be Right—You Also Have to Be Kind," *Medium*, March 26, 2019, https://tinyurl.com/yyr5dahs.

77 Lauren Rearick, "Eight Stats That Prove Social Anxiety Needs to Be Taken Seriously," *Huffington Post*, April 17, 2018, https://tinyurl.com/y49jb4k2.

78 Jennice Vilhauer, "This Is Why Ghosting Hurts So Much," *Psychology Today*, November 27, 2015, https://tinyurl.com/ya6vwmjr.

79 Carmon, "What Made the Friendship Work."

80 W. James Booth, "Communities of Memory: On Identity, Memory, and Debt," *American Political Science Review* 93, no. 2 (June 1999): 249–63, https://tinyurl.com/y3ceq5fq.

81 Joshua Foer, *Moonwalking with Einstein: The Art and Science of Remembering Everything* (New York: Penguin, 2012).

82 "Stress Relief from Laughter? It's No Joke," Mayo Clinic, April 21, 2016, https://tinyurl.com/y6kue9h5.

83 Summer Allen, "Is Gratitude Good for Your Health?" *Greater Good* (Greater Good Science Center, University of California, Berkeley), March 15, 2018, https://tinyurl.com/y3vr5ksj.